Ius Gentium: Comparative Perspectives on Law and Justice

Volume 110

Ius Gentium is a book series which discusses the central questions of law and justice from a comparative perspective. The books in this series collect the contrasting and overlapping perspectives of lawyers, judges, philosophers and scholars of law from the world's many different jurisdictions for the purposes of comparison, harmonisation, and the progressive development of law and legal institutions. Each volume makes a new comparative study of an important area of law. This book series continues the work of the well-known journal of the same name and provides the basis for a better understanding of all areas of legal science.

The *Ius Gentium* series provides a valuable resource for lawyers, judges, legislators, scholars, and both graduate students and researchers in globalisation, comparative law, legal theory and legal practice. The series has a special focus on the development of international legal standards and transnational legal cooperation.

Yifan Shang

A Historical and Legal Comparison between Tianxia Wei Gong and Quod Omnes Tangit

Springer

Yifan Shang
Passau, Germany

ISSN 1534-6781 ISSN 2214-9902 (electronic)
Ius Gentium: Comparative Perspectives on Law and Justice
ISBN 978-3-031-46466-9 ISBN 978-3-031-46467-6 (eBook)
https://doi.org/10.1007/978-3-031-46467-6

This dissertation is submitted for the degree of Doctor of Law at the University of Passau.
Supervisory Committee: Prof. Dr Ulrike Müßig and Prof. Dr Ulrich Manthe

This Springer imprint is published by the registered company Springer Nature Switzerland AG
The registered company address is: Gewerbestrasse 11, 6330 Cham, Switzerland

Acknowledgment

My dissertation accompanied me from my twenties to my thirties in Germany. I realized how my thoughts deepened and are reflected in my work over the course of these years.

For this growth, I am deeply indebted to my supervisor, Prof. Ulrike Müßig, for her support and nurturing over all these years. She lent me the greatest space for the freedom of research while also setting the strictest borderline for diligent academic work. I would also like to extend my deepest gratitude to an important member of my committee, Prof. Ulrike Manthe. It was he who provided me with printed excerpts from ancient Chinese literature relevant to my dissertation, which at once conferred the warmth of paper and a feeling of academic inheritance in our digital era. I am often in awe of his erudition in both Chinese and Roman law.

I am also grateful to Prof. Benjamin Pißler's insightful advice. I very much appreciate the forum Lucie Schultz and Sandra Röseler organized for my presentation. Many thanks to Bohan Xu, Haobo Liu, Yuqi Liu, Yizhou Liu, and Maike Schwiddessen, who offered valuable discussion and encouragement.

I sincerely thank my editor, Anja Trautmann. It was wonderful to be recognized during an academic conference by your editor and then be able to talk with each other face to face. I thank her for passion and professional attitude.

My gratitude also goes to the librarians of the University of Passau. They helped me not only by doing their work but also by telling me to take a rest for vacation. I am also thankful for all my friends in Germany and in China. It is only possible to name a few here: Silvia, Sarah, Laura, Ceylan, Ping Wang, Mengzhen Xie, and Ting Huang.

Words cannot express my gratitude to my parents, Hong Shang and Ying Hu, who are always there for me. I would also like to thank my parents-in-law and brothers-in-law, Josef, Ursula, Christian, and Michael. Since I lived with them in the later years of writing my dissertation, they have taken care of me as if I were their daughter and sister. My special thanks to my husband, Alexander Demmelhuber, for sharing responsibilities and being my soulmate.

Yifan Shang

Contents

Chapter 1
Introduction

Why are the Chinese so welcoming of surveillance and a nationwide credit scoring system? How is China taking the leading position in the development of internet technology? Apart from scientific factors, politics, tradition, society and culture also play a vital role in these development trends. This thesis aims to provide an answer to those questions from a legal and historical perspective.

Contemporary history has witnessed a profound integration of all fields of society through a boom in the sharing economy, with Airbnb and Uber being the typical examples and pioneers in their respective fields. These two entities focus on people's most basic concerns: accommodation and transport. It is notable that throughout human history, there have always been tensions between private and public spaces, with their respective demands waxing and waning. In primitive societies, people saw themselves forced to form communities due to the shortage of necessary daily commodities. However, in modern societies, we enjoy our own private space in cars or apartments. To cut costs, many forms of sharing have emerged, like mushrooms, because we have come to understand that sharing with others can be beneficial to our society.

This newly emerged phenomenon aligns with an old Chinese saying by Confucius, "Tianxia Wei Gong," one of the leading themes in this thesis. Its meaning will be explicitly analyzed in the following chapters.

At the same time, people are trying to implement mutual integration not only at the micro level but also at the macro level, as seen by different cooperation efforts between parties and nations. Take one of the most attention-catching trends as an example: with the cooperation among EU countries and their goal of establishing a united constitution, an old but not outdated principle comes to mind, *Quod Omnes Tangit*, which is the other main theme in this thesis. Even today, *Quod Omnes Tangit* is, according to the theory of Habermas, still adopted to interpret the representative

Y. Shang, *A Historical and Legal Comparison between Tianxia Wei Gong and Quod Omnes Tangit*, Ius Gentium: Comparative Perspectives on Law and Justice 110,
https://doi.org/10.1007/978-3-031-46467-6_1

modern Western constitution.[1] Regarding the question of how to form consensus based on individual will, Europe has offered two models as possible answers.[2] The starting point was initially at Hobbes, who rejected the rational and correct will of the individual; thus, it was impossible to form a rational and correct consensus.[3] A society therefore needs either consensus, *Quod Omnes Tangit*, or a legitimated authority.[4] The other model, originating from the ideas of Locke and Kant, put confidence in rational consensus, to which every individual will contribute.[5] Both models were of the opinion that consensus, rather individual will, would support the method of legitimation to implement a functional society.[6]

Its origin, development and meaning will also be explored in the following chapters.

One might question why I am comparing these two principles. The answer is rather simple: I attended a seminar taught by my professor, in which the research on *Quod Omnes Tangit* was one of the themes discussed. After having chosen said subject, I was asked if the same principle occurs in Chinese legal history. I could not answer the question immediately because it is well known to all Chinese law students that Chinese legal history in its entirety is almost exclusively the history of criminal law. I was not sure if it was even feasible to find such a principle, but I was already intrigued. Then, I set off to formally hunt for this mysterious principle. Vertically on the timeline, I have read through all schools of ancient Chinese philosophers; horizontally, I have mentally traversed Chinese history for clues. At times, desperation got the better of me and told me it was ludicrous to assume that there are democracy-resembling principles in Chinese history. Tianxia Wei Gong is a common gospel in all those sayings from sages and slogans by politicians. It did not catch my attention when I came across it at first or even many times after. After learning that the Qing Emperor quoted it in his Abdication Edict,[7] however, I was astonished—after all, Edward I quoted *Quod Omnes Tangit* in the summoning of parliament,[8] whose meaning is also akin to Clauses 12 and 14 in the Magna Carta.[9] What a coincidence! Or is it? The more time I spent following this clue to compare Tianxia Wei Gong and *Quod Omnes Tangit*, the more I was astonished. Their resemblance is striking. At the same time, it is obvious that they are not one and the same, as they were born and grew in distinct backgrounds and underwent

[1] Habermas (1992), pp. 112–134.

[2] See also Stasavage (2016), p. 146.

[3] Hobbes (1998), ch. 13, pp. 83–86. See also Skinner (2002), pp. 304–307.

[4] Johnston (2010), pp. 31–33.

[5] Locke (1960), pp. 330, 331, ch. 8, para. 95, 96; Kant (2016), pp. 68–96; Johnston (2010), pp. 33–34.

[6] Johnston (2010), pp. 33–34.

[7] Shen (1967), p. 1251. See also Mühlemann (2006), p. 356.

[8] Stubbs (1913), p. 480. Cf. Marongiu (1980), p. 185; Congar (1980), p. 150–151; Prestwich (1997), p. 412.

[9] Holt et al. (2015), pp. 382–384.

differing development progresses. These similarities and distinctions are such that they may hint at the universality of certain principles on one hand, indicating that people are ultimately alike; on the other hand, they may help explain why East and West are different and to what degree they are different.

Thus, I will elaborate on the next question one might be inclined to ask:

A productive way of reproducing Western cultures is to project their pasts into the Chinese future. Chinese conversations about Western learning offer a rich and insightful source for theorizing engagements with foreign knowledge. In other reformed countries, such as Japan, Russia and Thailand, the projects were aggressive, rapid and successful. Sometimes their success is such that dissenters had fewer opportunities to explain their objections to such projects and defenders, in turn, felt less pressed to elaborate on their reasons for pursuing them. Consequently, Easterners committed to broader exploration of various facets when it came to the study of foreign cultures, as there were differing points of view on how to learn from the West. In Leigh Jenco's words, "[a]s a result, debates over Western Learning produced one of the most sustained, syncretic, wide-ranging, and theoretically rich conversations in human history".[10]

Hence, it is meaningful to compare not only the characteristics of these two principles but also their functions in certain historical backgrounds.

John Head, in his grand work *Great Legal Traditions*, compared the legal traditions of "civil law, common law, and Chinese law".[11] A possible best definition of the concept "legal tradition" comes from John Henry Merryman, who defined one of our keywords as follows:

"A legal tradition, as the term implies, is not a set of rules of law about contracts, corporations, and crimes, although such rules will almost always be in some sense a reflection of that tradition. Rather, it is a set of deeply rooted, historically conditioned attitudes about the nature of law, about the role of law in society and the polity, about the proper organization and operation of a legal system, and about the way law is or should be made, applied, studied, perfected, and taught. The legal tradition relates the legal system to the culture of which it is a partial expression. It puts the legal system into cultural perspective."[12]

Head emphasizes that the crux of this definition is "attitude,"[13]an aspect of which, Merryman asserted, constructed legal tradition when the attitude is about law.[14] In this way, legal principles or constitutional principles are then a gathering point, condensed form and intensive reflection of those attitudes. Referring to tradition, Head concluded that Glenn's idea of tradition could legitimize change by providing

[10]Jenco (2015), pp. 17–18.

[11]Head (2011), p. 7.

[12]Merryman and Pérez-Perdomo (2007), p. 2. See also Head (2011), p. 5.

[13]Head (2011), p. 6.

[14]In the footnote, Head reported another comparative scholar, Pierre Legrand, who had a similar opinion to Merryman. See Legrand (2010), pp. 45–46. See Head (2011), p. 6.

cohesion and facilitating change,[15] which is clearer, more concise, and more definite than the original text. Head emphasized the importance of history and tradition in a comparative study of law.[16]

Regarding the structure of such a study, Head provided six angles:

(i) "Legal Self-Awareness and Self-Identity
(ii) Law Reform
(iii) Sociological Understanding
(iv) A Tool of Construction
(v) Cross-Border Legal Practice
(vi) Contributing to a Harmonization of Law"[17]

One might be inclined to presume that Head used several standards to clarify his aims, e.g., self and other, theory and practice. However, his clarifications seemed to overlap each other. "Law Reform" and "A Tool of Construction," "Sociological Understanding" and "Cross-Border Legal Practice" appear to be separate but are virtually identical. In fact, adopting two classifications is the basis of fulfilling the task of explaining the aim of comparative law: self and other, similarity and distinction. Comparative law aims at recognizing or understanding, developing, or improving, and harmonizing or optimizing the similarities and distinctions between self and other legal traditions. Further questions will be discussed in the following chapter about methodology.

At the time of writing this thesis, comparative studies of *Quod Omnes Tangit* and Tianxia Wei Gong, two substantial principles in Chinese and Western cultures, remain nonexistent. Thus, the selection of these two principles and the realization of the comparative method applied to them might be treated as one of the author's contributions to academic research. Furthermore, the content of their similarities and differences found in the research process constitutes another contribution. Finally, it is necessary to emphasize the interpretation of Liang Qichao[18] because he is, thus far, the one and only figure who referred to both Tianxia Wei Gong and *Quod Omnes Tangit*.

Research on solely *Quod Omnes Tangit* has increased in the past few years to some degree, although it was mentioned on most occasions as a subordinate to another principle or one part of another theory. This is not surprising because *Quod Omnes Tangit* belongs to one of those principles, which is tightly tied to other principles, such as representation and consent. The canonists belong to the first, who studied and interpreted *Quod Omnes Tangit*. Their interpretation then became an indispensable part of the study of *Quod Omnes Tangit*.

[15] Glenn (2007), p. 24, cited in Head (2011), p. 8.

[16] Head (2011), p. 9.

[17] Head (2011), pp. 22–25, with changes of number form for differentiating from the title number of this thesis.

[18] For quoting *Quod Omnes Tangit*, see Liang (2014a, b), p. 44; Liang (2015), p. 181. Liang's work quoting *Quod Omnes Tangit* was first published in 1919, see Liang (2014a, b), p. 221.

Among different publications, the articles written by Yves Congar and Gaines Posts are the only ones focusing mainly on *Quod Omnes Tangit*.[19] These two scholars set the academic standard of research on *Quod Omnes Tangit*, dating back to 1943. Post's article still holds sway, as it was he who pointed out the meaning of the maxim to parliament for the first time.[20] Having said that, he believed that *Quod Omnes Tangit* took a back seat in comparison to another relevant maxim: *plena potestas*; hence, he focused primarily on *plena potestas*, with few discussions reserved for *Quod Omnes Tangit*, asserting that *plena potestas*, with *Quod Omnes Tangit* as an appendix, was adopted only in procedural law rather than substantial law.[21] However, he thought that these maxims played an even more important role in court law than in substantial law because on one hand, these principles led the whole process in court, while on the other hand, judges and lawyers interpreted law according to these principles.[22] In his book published in 1964, he elaborated on *Quod Omnes Tangit* explicitly after the research on *plena potestas*, studying Henry de Bracton's research on *Quod Omnes Tangit*.[23]

What can be considered the milestone of the ongoing research on the maxim is Congar's article from 1958, in which the author engaged with the questions as to where the maxim originated from, how it was adopted and what consequences it led to.[24] This article listed the most concrete examples of how *Quod Omnes Tangit* was quoted and applied. Referring to the question about the development of the maxim in the fourteenth century, Marongiu presented some proof of its existence and effect in his article published in 1962.[25]

Research solely on Tianxia Wei Gong is rare. Books bearing this name relate in most instances to moral education. Among them, two academics' works are exceptions and worth noting. Liang Zhiping explored the meaning of Tianxia and Wei Gong in history, providing abundant examples from Chinese classic works.[26] Zhao Tingyang envisaged a new global political system, the Tianxia System, analyzing the concept of Tianxia from a philosophic perspective.[27] Although Tianxia Wei Gong is often quoted, a deep and systematic study of this maxim lacks, among others, its political, legal and historical significance.

To gain a better understanding of these terms, it is necessary to trace back to the roots of their thinking and to systemize their development.

---

[19] Congar (1980), pp. 115–182; Post (1964), pp. 163–238.

[20] Post (1964), pp. 163–238.

[21] Post (1964), pp. 161–162.

[22] Post (1964), pp. 161–162.

[23] Post (1964), pp. 163–238.

[24] Congar (1980), pp. 115–182.

[25] Marongiu (1980), pp. 183–211.

[26] Liang (2014a, b), pp. 66–86; Liang (2016), pp. 5–31.

[27] Zhao (2011), pp. 23–107.

References

Congar Y (1980) Quod omnes tangit ab omnibus tractari et approbari debet. In: Heinz R (ed) Die geschichtlichen Grundlagen der modernen Volksvertretung. Wissenschaftliche Buchgesellschaft, Darmstadt, pp 115–182

Glenn HP (2007) Legal tradition of the world. Oxford University Press, Oxford

Habermas (1992) Faktizität und Geltung. Suhrkamp, Frankfurt am Main

Head JW (2011) Great legal traditions: civil law, common law, and Chinese law in historical and operational perspective. Carolina Academic Press, Durham

Hobbes T (1998) Leviathan. Oxford University Press, Oxford

Holt JC et al (eds) (2015) Magna Carta. Cambridge University Press, Cambridge

Jenco L (2015) Changing referents: learning across space and time in China and the west. Oxford University Press, New York

Johnston D (2010) A history of consent in Western thought. In: Miller FG, Wertheimer A (eds) The ethics of consent: theory and practice. Oxford Academic Press, Oxford, pp 25–54

Legrand P (2010) European legal systems are not converging. In: Merryman JH et al (eds) Comparative law: historical development of the civil law tradition in Europe, Latin America, and East Asia. LexisNexis, New Providence

Kant I (2016) Grundlegung zur Metaphysik der Sitten. Felix Meiner Verlag, Hamburg

Liang QC (2014a) The experience of travel in Europe. The Commercial Press, Beijing. (梁启超, 欧游心影录, 商务印书馆, 北京, 2014年)

Liang ZP (2014b) The concept of Wei gong. China Law Review 2:66–86. (梁治平, "为公"的理念, 中国法律评论, 2014年第2期, 第66-86页)

Liang QC (2015) Yin Bing Shi he Ji. Zhonghua Book Company, Beijing (梁启超, 饮冰室合集, 中华书局, 北京, 2015年)

Liang ZP (2016) The concept of Tianxia: from ancient to modern. Tsinghua University Law Journal 10:5–31. (梁治平, "天下"的观念:从古代到现代, 清华法学, 2016年第10期, 第5-31页)

Locke J (1960) Two treatises of government. Cambridge University Press, New York

Marongiu A (1980) Das Prinzip der Demokratie und der zustimmung (Quod omnes tangit, ab omnibus approbari debet) im 14.Jahrhundert. In: Rausch H (ed) Die geschichtlichen Grundlagen der modernen Volksvertretung, vol 1. Darmstadt, Wissenschaftliche Buchgesellschaft, pp 183–211

Merryman JH, Pérez-Perdomo R (2007) The civil law tradition. Stanford University Press, Stanford

Mühlemann G (2006) Chinas Experimente mit westlichen Staatsideen. Schulthess, Zürich

Post G (1964) Studies in medieval legal thought: public law and the state, 1100–1322. Princeton University Press, Princeton

Prestwich M (1997) Edward I. Yale University Press, New Haven and London

Shen YL (1967) Political documents of the years Xuantong. Taiwan Wen Hai Press Company, Taipei. (沈云龙主编, 宣统政纪, 台湾文海出版社, 台北, 1967年)

Skinner Q (2002) Conquest and consent: hobbes and the engagement controversy. In: Aylmer GE (ed) Visions of politics. Cambridge University Press, Cambridge, pp 287–307

Stasavage D (2016) Representation and consent: why they arose in Europe and not elsewhere. Annu Rev Polit Sci 19:145–162

Stubbs W (1913) Charters and excerpts illustrative of the reign of Edward I. In: Davis H (ed) Select charters and other illustrations of English constitutional history. Clarendon, Oxford, pp 417–506

Zhao T (2011) The Tianxai system. China Renmin University Press, Beijing. (赵汀阳, 天下体系, 中国人民大学出版社, 北京, 2011年)

Chapter 2
Methodology

Five methodological questions are discussed in this thesis. The first is the necessity of studying legal and political principles through history: legal and political principles are important. *Quod Omnes Tangit* and Tianxia Wei Gong are such principles. As Otto Hintze wrote, "[m]an does not live by bread alone; he wants to have a good conscience when he pursues his vital interests".[1] Legal and political principles can legitimate power, certifying a statesman's intention of good conscience.[2] History should facilitate the study of legal and political principles because "theories and facts [are] inextricably interwoven"[3] and these principles "were not engendered suddenly out of nowhere. . .they have a history".[4] As Joseph Chan put it, "Any form of political theorizing that lacks an ideal is like a ship embarking on a voyage without destination, and political theorizing that is insensitive to the constraints of reality is like a ship on rough seas without competent navigation."[5] Thus, it is necessary to examine *Quod Omnes Tangit* and Tianxia Wei Gong through history.

The second methodological question is the possibility of studying legal and political ideas through history, in other words, if such research is possible or reliable, touching upon the concept of a hermeneutic circle. Hermeneutic circles, which aim at pointing out some ideas that are worth noting during interpretation, have been altered through various interpretations from numerous disciplines.[6] There is a contemporary and an ancient idea of hermeneutic circle: the contemporary idea is that our understanding has presuppositions; the ancient idea is that when we understand a text, its whole and its part are working at the same time in our brain,

[1] Hintze and Gilbert (1975), p. 94.

[2] Tierney (1982), p. x.

[3] Tierney (1982), p. x.

[4] Tierney (1982), p. x.

[5] Chan (2014), p. 1.

[6] Grondin (2016), p. 299.

Y. Shang, *A Historical and Legal Comparison between Tianxia Wei Gong and Quod Omnes Tangit*, Ius Gentium: Comparative Perspectives on Law and Justice 110,
https://doi.org/10.1007/978-3-031-46467-6_2

and neither part can work alone.[7] This presupposition has been differently named: Heidegger's "anticipatory structure" (Vorstruktur), Gadamer's "prejudices," and other elements such as "culture, history, language and education."[8] For treating the hermeneutic circle, there is also a classical method and a contemporary method: the classical method views the hermeneutic circle as virtuous because it would lead to errors in understanding; the contemporary method treats the hermeneutic circle as unavoidable and rather favorable.[9] Heidegger thought we should clean up the false anticipations, thus interpreting the text in a correct manner.[10] Gadamer viewed anticipation as an ontological perspective of the hermeneutical circle, more or less building a variant of the classic method.[11] Ulrike Müßig adds and concludes that a hermeneutic circle exists not only in Gadamer's sense but also in the linguistic variation in diverse legal systems.[12] The author does not backtrack the history of this concept, the hermeneutic circle, but clarifies the standpoint that although the hermeneutic circle means that an interpreter's view is subjective, this circle is neither malicious nor fatal, which could adjudicate that all historians' research is meaningless; rather, it is constructive in two ways: first, the process of the hermeneutic circle can help us understand the past; second, it instructs the present.

Relating to hermeneutic circles, the author compares and comments on several scholars' opinions from legal and political perspectives. Tierney raised some methodological questions concerning historic research on constitutional ideas in his Wiles Lecture at the Queen's University: "[i]s it a legitimate undertaking for a historian to trace remote origins of modern ideas? Can he do this without falling into naïve anachronisms?"[13] Although he did not mention the term hermeneutical circle, the essence of this series of questions is the same. Tierney answered this question by quoting and revising Butterfield's opposing Whig approach.[14] Against Whig's approach, Butterfield thought the true historian should "study the past for the sake of the past" but "with the eyes of another century."[15] Tierney only partly agreed with Butterfield because he proposed that historians know more than people living earlier and thus can and should conceive, describe and explain the adaptations of tradition.[16]

---

[7] Grondin (2016), p. 299.

[8] Heidegger (1967), pp. 152, 153; Gadamer (1990), pp. 271, 273; Grondin (2016), p. 299.

[9] Grondin (2016), p. 299.

[10] Grondin (2016), pp. 299–300.

[11] Gadamer (1990), p. 271; see Grondin (2016), p. 300.

[12] Müßig (2016), p. 6.

[13] Tierney (1982), p. vii.

[14] Historians of Whig approach adopted present concept to explain the past, trying to find a root of modern time in the past and imagined the "heroes of the past were 'fighting to bring about our modern world'". Butterfield (1931), pp. 9–33; Tierney (1982), p. viii.

[15] Butterfield (1931), pp. 15, 24; Tierney (1982), p. viii.

[16] Tierney (1982), pp. viii-x.

Hwa-Yong Lee interpreted Richard Tuck's conclusion of the "old" approach as "investigating the classics in search for the values expressed in the texts"[17] and the new one as surveying "political and other ideas in the history of their actual circumstances."[18] The author finds this summary misleading. Lee's summary perfectly matched the old approach to the Whig attitude and the new approach to Tierney's statement. However, Tuck argued that the old approach focused on searching for universal value in the text, while the new approach added historical and political context to the text.[19] Both the old and the new approaches adopted modern concepts to examine history. Lee summarized these two approaches as reflecting the different methods of historical and political theorists: the first tended to determine when and how the idea started to sprout, while the latter concentrated on the relation of a given concept to that of the modern period.[20] This summary accorded with Tuck's argument, providing us with a method choice inside hermeneutic circles.

When considering hermeneutic circles, only two approaches are possible: first, retro, like Butterfield's approach, requires historians to pretend that they live in an earlier age and aims at understanding the past for the sake of the past; second, genuine, like Tierney's approach, allows historians to show what they know with the aim of explaining history. This thesis adopts the second approach, with the intention to avoid going to one extreme, the Whig approach. Thus, before diving into every single piece of important text, the author examines the historic background first, which could be checked in the skeleton and text.

The third methodological question is that concerning comparative research and whether similarities or differences should receive more attention. Tierney stressed similarities, the "certain recurring patterns of constitutional thought",[21] and "the problems a historian encounters in considering their origins and development."[22] He also suggested that the theme of a research study should decide how much weight a historian places on similarities and/or differences.[23] The author searches for similarities as the basis of comparison but emphasizes differences as understanding and explaining some discrepancy between the East and the West.

Regarding the functional equivalent, both the substance of the two maxims and their function will be compared. The ontological perspective presented in the content elucidates their meaning and origin. Regarding *tertium comparationis*, their function in historic legal codes, literature, documents and events serve as such. Both similarities and differences are discussed in two dimensions: in time, the continuity and either slight or essential change of the ideas; in space, the approach in China and the

[17] Lee (2008), p. 2; Tuck (2007), pp. 62–85.

[18] Lee (2008), p. 2.

[19] Tuck (2007), pp. 62–85; see also Tuck (2001), pp. 218–230.

[20] Lee (2008), p. 1.

[21] Tierney (1982), p. viii.

[22] Tierney (1982), p. viii.

[23] Tierney (1982), p. ix.

one in Europe. Both theoretical and practical reasons support this methodological choice. Practically, similarities did exist and can be found; history repeated itself to some degree in China in the nineteenth century, mimicking Europe in the seventeenth century. Theoretically, the logical premise of comparison is the existence of similarities in two objects. It only makes sense to conduct a comparison between similar objects. Similarities enable a comparison, after all. In practice, two identical objects are an exceedingly rare find, at least if they are complicated objects without any abstraction. Western constitutional ideas are complex on their own, not to mention when compared with Chinese ideas. This can be seen in the following section. Therefore, their differences must also be taken into consideration.

Conducting research on the differences between these two maxims and designing the skeleton of this thesis accordingly proved to be an unexpectedly arduous task. Common practice would dictate putting the reasons for the differences between the two maxims at the end of this thesis. While logically sound at first glance, this author decides against common wisdom for two reasons: (a) the multitude of reasons for the differences are such that, without proper clarification at the beginning of this thesis, they would spawn an almost endless cycle of questions raised by the reader, and (b) these maxims can only be properly presented and explained in a dynamic process, during which their differences and the reasoning behind them are clearly outlined. It is not as simple as "because of A, B exists." Bearing this in mind, the reasons for the differences between the two maxims are due to the differences in their historical development.

Serving as the context of the two maxims, several varieties of histories are essential to a full grasp of the comparison between our research objects, including but not limited to the history of Western political thought, the history of Western legal tradition, the history of the development of natural law, the history of parliament, the history of Confucianism and modern Chinese history. It is understood that these histories are not separable, separate, or isolated but indivisible, overlapped and interlinked.

One of the difficulties of this paper lies in the previous paragraph: all these histories piece together a kaleidoscope that displays the diversity of the world of thoughts in the past. Now there is a new angle and a fresh idea; if all the materials could be well-deployed, a novel scenery through which to see the world would appear. This is the mission of this paper and what the author resolves to do.

Diving deeper into the classification of disciplines, the fourth methodological question falls into comparative legal and political history. Konrad Zweigert and Hein Kötz commented on the relationship between legal history and comparative law as "surprisingly complex,"[24] which coexist at first sight in two dimensions: in space (horizontal) and in time (vertical).[25] Furthermore, the two are interconnected: on the one hand, all legal history adopts the comparative method, and "the legal historian cannot help bringing to the study of his chosen system, say Roman Law, the various

[24] Zweigert and Kötz (1998), p. 8.

[25] Head (2011), p. 29.

preconceptions of his own modern system"[26]; on the other hand, comparative law may include comparative legal history.[27]

Head listed some features in his book examining the comparative study of legal history, four of which will also be put forth in this thesis:

"Codes and other forms of written law"
"The 'packaging' of historical developments into eras or periods"
"Contemporaneousness of developments"
"The significance of individual and coincidences"[28]

The other two, "the development of courts" and "the geographical settings and coverage of the traditions,"[29] will be excluded due to the limitation of the main idea for this theme and the length of this thesis. Moreover, Head's standards for classification are anything but tight, resulting in him picking and choosing the elements he deemed worthy of studying, which makes it difficult for the reader to discern their context and importance. Among these four features, the second and third features, namely, the historical developments and contemporaneousness of developments, belong to the vertical timeline; the first and last features, namely, the codes and other forms of written law and individual and coincidences, are concrete research objects rather than standards of classification. While there is overlap between these two areas to some extent, they should be regarded as separate. Therefore, this thesis is primarily divided into two parts: similarity and difference. Each part contrasts the relatively static nature of objects and their dynamic development.

The organization of the chapters is partly chronological and partly thematic. This arrangement is made to better present the thought of the East and the West to facilitate a more focused analysis of the comparison between the different thoughts. These chapters concerning Tianxia Wei Gong and the comparison between Tianxia Wei Gong and *Quod Omnes Tangit* form the most ground-breaking part of the entire thesis, since no one has ever given this Chinese thought any clear and comprehensive analysis and no one has made such a comparison before.

The fifth, the methodological question, concerns the benefit of comparing European and Chinese legal and political cultures, with avoidance of the Eurocentric method, as well as the overall Chinese-origin method. Specifically, as Fred Dallmayr argued, there were at least three "goods"[30] in comparative political theory: "a

[26]Zweigert and Kötz (1998), pp. 7–8, cited in Head (2011), p. 29. Head slightly changed Zweigert and Kötz's words, which is more concise thus adopted here.

[27]Head (2011), p. 29.

[28]Head (2011), pp. 29–30.

[29]Head (2011), pp. 29–30.

[30]In Dallmayr's essay, he traced back to Aristotle to discuss "good" as a start point. He then explored some similarities to this good in Indian culture and in Confucian tradition. In the next chapters, he provided his own answer to this question: what it is good for comparative political inquiry. Dallmayr (2009), pp. 18–21.

'pragmatic-utilitarian' good,"[31] a "'moral-universal' good"[32] and "an 'ethical' or 'ethically transformative' good."[33] Studying other cultures and traditions enables us to be actively involved in global interaction and communication, to become more aware of the character of our own culture, its limitations, and prejudices, and to be better equipped to assess our own place in the world and our responsibilities toward others. The study of Chinese philosophy can provide a new perspective to academics researching issues of the Western tradition. Quoting Shogimen and Nederman, "[s]uch historical inquiries into the political thought of a 'non-Western' cultural, ethnic, or regional unit are capable of revealing unfamiliar intellectual worlds to Western audiences."[34]

Unsatisfactorily, considerable studies of the history of political thought have employed an Occident-centered approach,[35] yet recently, in comparative political studies,[36] academics have strived to explore a balanced and comprehensive method. What constitutes an Occident-centered approach? An Occident-centered approach adopts Western concepts, terminology, and systems to examine Oriental objects. The following two methods are not Occident-centered. First, if a study focuses on Western thought, it does not necessarily mean that this study falls into the category of the Occident-centered approach. In Oriental classrooms, much Oriental history is also being taught. It is natural that people are more interested in their own history than others', yet it would be advantageous that the history of others also arouses their interest. Second, if a study adopts Western concepts, terminology and systems to evaluate Oriental objects, it is not necessarily Occident-centered. It is natural to use familiar knowledge to recognize and learn new things. Hence, the key to judging whether a study is Occident-centered is that a study devalues Oriental objects.

At the same time, some scholars explored Oriental impact on Occidental history. John Hobson attempted to examine the ways in which Chinese ideas influenced the

[31] Referring to "a 'pragmatic-utilitarian' good," Dallmayr expressed that knowing better of others can bring oneself more self-interest, a case in point being economists and businesspeople. Dallmayr (2009), p. 18.

[32] Referring to a "'moral-universal' good," Dallmayr described such good as one for all, all for one, the "golden rule" of humanity, which is echoed by the Indian Classic Gita and Confucius' Analects. Dallmayr (2009), p. 19.

[33] Referring to "an 'ethical' or 'ethically transformative' good," Dallmayr evaluated such good as recognizing own limits and respecting others as they were. Dallmayr (2009), p. 19.

[34] Regarding "such historical inquiries," Shogimen and Nederman considered not only "Chinese" political thought but also other "non-Western" ones, such as "Islamic," "Indian," "Russian" and "Japanese." Shogimen and Nederman (2009), p. 2.

[35] Shogimen and Nederman explained "an Occident-centered approach" as "almost entirely confining itself to the Western intellectual traditions of Greco-Roman antiquity, medieval Latin Europe, modern Western Europe, and the New World." The author finds this definition inaccurate and discusses the concept of "an Occident-centered approach" in the text thereafter. Cf. Shogimen and Nederman (2009), p. 1.

[36] Shogimen and Nederman (2009), p. 2.

European Enlightenment[37] and the Chinese contribution to the British agricultural[38] and industrial revolutions.[39] He deemed that "Chinese ideas influenced European ideas on government, moral philosophy, artistic styles (e.g., rococo), clothes, furniture and wallpaper, gardens, political economy, tea-drinking and many other matters."[40] He provided us with an interesting point of view, a firm claim and enough argumentation. Nonetheless, Hobson's research focused on material aspects first and foremost. In this way, a study on the ideological aspect, rather than the material aspect, could to some degree be a beneficial supplement to the study of Hobson, although this thesis does not propose eastern origins of Western civilization as Hobson did but rather focuses on the parallel development of the two maxims and their possible intersection.

On the topic of romanization systems for the pronunciation of Chinese terms, the Wade-Giles system and the Pinyin system, this thesis adopts the Pinyin system because of its increasingly wide acknowledgment. However, Jeeloo Liu concluded that the West widely accepted Chinese philosophy works in the Wade-Giles system, for example, with "Tao" in the Wade-Giles system replacing "Dao" in the Pinyin system.[41] In addition, for names that had idiomatic usage, such as Sun Yat-sen (Cantonese) as opposed to Sun Yixian and Sun Zhongshan (mandarin Pinyin system), I adopted Cantonese. In conclusion, this thesis generally adopts the Mandarin Pinyin system, with some exceptions in the Wade-Giles system or in Cantonese.

The five methodological questions construct the foundation of the research method of this thesis. In Tierney's opinion, research on the history of ideas did not suffice to explain Western constitutional development, but this research is a necessary start.[42] Thus, partly in Tierney's words, while comparing the history of Western and Eastern ideas cannot explain the whole story of their constitutional development, but we will never begin to understand the whole story if we fully ignore such a comparison.

---

[37] Hobson notes that since 1687, with the translation of a Confucian work *Confucius Sinarum Philosophus* into English, Confucius started to influence Europe, where his impact climaxed in eighteenth century. Hobson also listed important thinkers who were influenced by Chinese ideas, "including Montaigne, Malebranche, Leibniz, Voltaire, Quesnay, Wolff, Hume and Adam Smith." (195) in Hobson (2004), pp. 194–201.

[38] For "[t]he Chinese origins of the British agricultural revolution," Hobson mainly discussed several farm implements such as "*The eighteenth-century iron moldboard plough (Rotherham plough),*" "*The rotary winnowing machine*" and "*Seed-drills and horse-hoeing husbandry.*" Hobson (2004), pp. 201–206.

[39] For "[t]he Chinese origins of the British industrial revolution," Hobson presented "*The steam engine*" and "*Iron and steel production.*" He also illustrated "The Chinese origins of British cotton manufacturing." Hobson (2004), pp. 207–218.

[40] Hobson (2004), p. 194.

[41] Liu (2006), p. x.

[42] Tierney (1982), p. ix.

References

Butterfield H (1931) The Whig interpretation of history. G. Bell And Sons, London
Chan J (2014) Confucian perfectionism: a political philosophy for modern times. Princeton University Press, Princeton
Dallmayr F (2009) Comparative political theory: what is it good for? In: Shogimen T, Nederman CJ (eds) Western political thought in dialogue with Asia. Lexington Books, Lanham, pp 13–24
Gadamer H-G (1990) Wahrheit und Methode. Mohr Siebeck, Tübingen
Grondin J (2016) The hermeneutical circle. In: Keane N, Lawn C (eds) The Blackwell companion to hermeneutics. Blackwell, Oxford, pp 299–305
Head JW (2011) Great legal traditions: civil law, common law, and Chinese law in historical and operational perspective. Carolina Academic Press, Durham
Heidegger M (1967) Sein und Zeit. Max Niemeyer Verlag, Tübingen
Hintze O, Gilbert F (eds) (1975) The history essays of Otto Hintze. Oxford University Press, New York
Hobson JM (2004) The eastern origins of Western civilisation. Cambridge University Press, Cambridge
Lee H-Y (2008) Political representation in the later middle ages: Marsilius in context. Peter Lang Publishing, New York
Liu J (2006) An introduction to Chinese philosophy. Blackwell Publishing, Malden
Müßig U (ed) (2016) Reconsidering constitutional formation I National Sovereignty. Springer, Cham
Shogimen T, Nederman CJ (2009) Western political thought in dialogue with Asia. Lexington Books, Lanham
Tierney B (1982) Religion, law and the growth of constitutional thought 1150–1650. Cambridge University Press, Cambridge
Tuck R (2001) History of political thought. In: Burke P (ed) New perspectives on historical writings. The Pennsylvania State University Press, Pennsylvania, pp 218–232
Tuck R (2007) History. In: Goodin RE et al (eds) Companion to contemporary political philosophy. Blackwell, Malden
Zweigert K, Kötz H (1998) An introduction to comparative law. Oxford University Press, Oxford

Chapter 3
Similarities

3.1 Origins of the Phrases

3.1.1 Tianxia Wei Gong

This phrase originated from a book called Li Gi, a part of Confucius' most significant series of works, known as the "Four Books" and "Five Classics."[1] Li Gi was one of the classics whose philosophy was deeply rooted in Chinese thought and culture. Li means rites, rituals, or customs; Gi indicates a record or document of something. The origin of the documentation of Li dates back to the Zhou 周 (1046-256 BC) and Qin 秦 (221-207 BC) Dynasties. However, its author and exact time of composition remain unknown.[2] In the reign of Xuandi 宣帝 (73-39 BC), Dai De 戴德 and Dai Sheng 戴圣, uncle and nephew, separately compiled Da Dai Li Gi, 85 chapters, and Xiao Dai Li Gi, 46 chapters.[3] With three more chapters added by Ma Rong 马融 (79-166) to Xiao Dai Li Gi, the version with 49 chapters became the most popular.[4]

Li 禮, with this character's left part 示meaning offering up a sacrifice to be blessed and its right part symbolizing a vessel containing two strings of jade shell as sacrifice, extended its meaning to ritual and rites.[5] Among all the possible translations of Li, ritual, rites, customs, etiquette, propriety, morals, rules of proper behavior and worship, Roger T. Ames preferred "observing ritual propriety," a "social grammar" passing on from generation to generation, including "all formal conduct, from table manners to patterns of greeting and leave-taking, to graduations,

[1]For more introduction of "Four Books" and "Five Classics," Schmidt-Glintzer (1990), pp. 106, 108; Feifel (1982), pp. 141–155.

[2]Feifel (1982), p. 147.

[3]Feifel (1982), p. 148.

[4]Feifel (1982), p. 148.

[5]Jiang (2011), p. 43; Xu S (1979), p. 7.

Y. Shang, *A Historical and Legal Comparison between Tianxia Wei Gong and Quod Omnes Tangit*, Ius Gentium: Comparative Perspectives on Law and Justice 110,
https://doi.org/10.1007/978-3-031-46467-6_3

weddings, funerals, from gestures of deference to ancestral sacrifices," which coordinated roles, relationships and institutions to provide guidance, to facilitate communication and to perpetuate values.[6] Joseph Chan defined Li as rites or rituals, the rhythm of society and the guidelines of religious and family life and categorized Li into three levels: Li Jiao 礼教, Li Yi 礼仪 and Li Zhi 礼治, corresponding to "ritual education," "ritual principles" and "ritual ruling." Chan clarified the meaning of these three concepts as Li Jiao 礼教 "help[s] moral cultivation by restraining unhealthy desires and refining feelings and attitudes," Li Yi 礼仪 "expresses the basic principles of human relationships and roles," and Li Zhi 礼治 "help[s] regulate society."[7] The author agrees in part with this categorization but also disagrees with it. Among the endings of these three concepts, Yi; the only noun, meaning ceremonies; is the content of Li Jiao 礼教 and Li Zhi 礼治; thus, Li Yi 礼仪 should come first; Jiao 教, meaning teaching or education, is much softer than Zhi 治, meaning ruling or punishing; thus, Jiao 教 should come second, and Zhi 治 should come third. Therefore, Li Yi 礼仪, Li Jiao 礼教 and Li Zhi 礼治make up the connotation of Li. Different theories exist in the literature regarding whether Li was only applied to the upper class.[8]

Seeing through these various perspectives from different academics, it can be concluded that Li, with a compound character touching upon the fields of legality, politics and ethics, falls under the scope of social regulation, which can exert immense psychological influence on the people living under the guidance of the moral standards therein.

Tianxia Wei Gong, sharing the same characteristics, was illustrated in detail in one chapter of Liji.[9] This chapter, named Liyun 礼运, discussed the implementation of the principles in customs and describes the utopian conceptions of Confucius, portraying great unity and a well-off society. Thus, this chapter would later also be called Liyun (Evolution of Rites) Datong (great unity).[10]

Regarding Tianxia Wei Gong, it may be necessary to examine it word by word at first.

Tian 天 the sky or the heaven
Xia 下 beneath
Wei 为, 爲 be (second tone); for the sake of (fourth tone)[11]
Gong 公 the public, commonwealth[12]

[6]Confucius (1998), p. 51.

[7]Chan (2014), p. 2.

[8]Ding (2020), pp. 92–99.

[9]Confucius (1994), p. 815, ch. 9. Strictly speaking, Liji is not written by Confucius alone but also includes the annotation of many of his students. Confucius (1885), pp. 364–367; Hsü (2000), pp. 365–366.

[10]Confucius (1994), p. 815, ch. 9; Confucius (1885), pp. 364–367; Hsü (2000), pp. 365–366. For a discussion of the translation of 大同, see Kang (1958), pp. 29–30.

[11]Wang (2009), pp. 460–462. The detailed use of Wei is complex. Unlike the transformation of the meaning of Gong, that of Wei did not bear so much cultural meaning; thus, I opted for the simplified use of Wei.

[12]See Sect. 4.2.1 of this book.

The whole phrase means "what is under the sky belongs to all." Tianxia is treated as one complete word according to linguistic convention. Since some Chinese characters have more than one lexical tone, the meaning of polyphonic characters usually varies with tone. Therefore, it is universally held by all Chinese that Wei has two tones, the second and the fourth tone. To acquire a proper comprehension of the whole phrase, it is essential to examine which tone of Wei should be adopted here. Thus, the whole chapter must be taken into consideration.

> When the Grand Course was pursued, a public and common spirit ruled all under the sky...men did not love their parents only, nor treat as children only their own sons. A competent provision was secured for the aged until their death, employment for the able-bodied, and the means of growing up to the young. They showed kindness and compassion to widows, orphans, childless men, and those who were disabled by disease so that they were all sufficiently maintained. Males had their proper work, and females had their homes. [They accumulated] articles [of value], disliking that they should be thrown away upon the ground, but not wishing to keep them for their own gratification. [They labored] with their strength, disliking that it should not be exerted, but not exerting it [only] with a view to their own advantage... This was [the period of] what we call the Grand Union [Universal Commonwealth].[13]

A conclusion could be drawn from the text that the second tone should be applied here, since it implies that people should take care of not only themselves but also others. However, historical backgrounds cannot be ignored. In the first sentence of this chapter, "When the Grand Course was pursued, a public and common spirit ruled all under the sky,"[14] Confucius referred to the golden times of the three Kings, Yao (2356-2355 BC), Shun (2255-2206 BC) and Yu (2205-2198 BC): in that epoch, succession to the throne was based on virtue and competence rather than bloodlines, a tradition known as the Shan-Rang System which regulated succession to the

[13]Confucius (1885), pp. 364–367, adopted the minor changes from Hsü (2000), pp. 365–366. Legge's translation is incomplete. See Couvreur (1950), pp. 497, 498: «Lorsque la grande voie de la vertu était fréquentée, le chef de l'empire ne considérait pas le pouvoir souverain comme un bien appartenant en propre à sa famille, (et le cédait volontiers à un étranger); il choisissait pour son successeur le plus digne et le plus capable, (c'est ce que firent Iao et Chouen). Il s'efforçait d'acquérir une vertu véritable et entretenait la concorde. Aussi les sujets ne bornaient pas leur affection à leurs parents, ni leur sollicitude paternelle à leurs propres enfants. Ils faisaient en sorte que les vieillards eussent le nécessaire jusqu'à la fin de leurs jours, que les personnes d'un âge mûr eussent ce qu'il leur fallait pour leur usage, que les enfants eussent ce dont ils avaient besoin pour se développer; que les hommes veufs, les femmes veuves, les orphelins, les vieillards sans enfants, les faibles et les malades eussent de quoi se sustenter; que les hommes eussent chacun un emploi ou un métier, et que les filles trouvassent des familles où elles pussent se marier. Ils auraient eu horreur de laisser perdre des biens (de récoltes) sur la terre; mais ils ne voulaient nullement les emmagasiner dans leurs greniers (et n'en rien donner à personne). Ils auraient eu horreur de ne pas dépenser leurs forces (dans un travail utile); mais ils ne voulaient nullement travailler uniquement pour eux-mêmes. Aussi les mauvais desseins étaient arrêtés et n'étaient pas exécutés. Il n'y avait ni fraude ni vol ni trouble ni brigandage. Les maisons avaient des portes à l'extérieur (contre le vent et la pluie), mais on ne les fermail pas (par crainte des voleurs). C'était vraiment ce qu'on peut appeler la grande union ou la fraternité universelle. »

[14]Confucius (1885), p. 364.

throne. Shun was not the son or any relative of Yao, but Shun took the throne after Yao because of Shun's virtue; it was the same when Yu took the throne after Shun.[15] Hence, everyone is entitled to the opportunity, and the world belongs veritably to everyone in those days. These are what the beginning of Liyun means: "大道之行也，天下为公。选贤与能……"[16] "选贤与能"[17] means "able and virtuous personage was selected, [to reign the world]."[18] Confucius commemorated the golden times so much that his utopia did exist as such in the real world. Tianxia Wei Gong could also be treated as his political ideals. Therefore, the second tone of Wei should be adopted here. The more appropriate comprehension of this sentence is that the world belongs to everyone.

The proper translation of classic Chinese is an intricate task, resulting in different interpretations.

According to James Legge:

> When the Grand course was pursued, a public and common opinion ruled all under the sky.[19]

According to Tsuchida Kyoson:

> When the Great Way is realized, the following will surely take place: all the world will be a common possession.[20]

According to Wu Kuo-cheng:

> When the great principle prevails, the whole world is bent upon the common good.[21]

According to Fung Yu-lan [Feng Youlan], as edited by Derk Bodde:

> When the great Tao was in practice, the world was common to all.[22]

The author:

> When the great Tao was in practice, Tianxia was for the common good and owned by all.

It is worthwhile to note that there is no exact counterpart in English for the Chinese phrase "Tianxia"; neither "the world" nor "the state" are exact counterparts. *Res Publica*, a Latin word describing a concept of metaphoric harmony for God's land surrounded by the sky and the earth,[23] is a more similar word in meaning to Tianxia. Tianxia, however, as a term oozing Chinese philosophical features, describes the world in a rather romantic or poetic way, a concept deeply rooted in Chinese

---

[15] Mathews (1931), pp. 844, 1090, 1142; Loewe and Shaughnessy (eds) (1999), p. 71.

[16] Confucius (1994), p. 815, ch. 9.

[17] Confucius (1994), p. 815, ch. 9.

[18] Confucius (1994), p. 815, ch. 9. The author translated.

[19] Confucius (1885), pp. 364–367.

[20] Kyoson (1927), pp. 194–195.

[21] Wu (1928), pp. 299–300, cited in Kang (1958) p. 28.

[22] Feng (1948), p. 202.

[23] Moos (2004), pp. 19–20.

mythology, the view toward the world and the universe. Bernardo Poetzelberger illustrated that during the Shang Dynasty, Chinese people perceived the whole world as a slow-walking tortoise, whose shell was regarded as the sky and its four limbs as the ground. Later, the "tortoise" gave way to the "vehicle," the form of the world consisting of a round sky and a square ground.[24] There are some synonyms in Chinese that can be helpful to understanding the word Tianxia, such as "Sifang," which is literally interpreted as "four directions," indicating the space on the ground in all directions. The number of directions accords with that of the tortoise's feet and that of the square's corners. The second synonym is Sihai, the Four Seas, which also shows that the Chinese tend to uncover some cosmopolitan truths when they talk about the whole world. As Confucius said, "then all within the four seas are his elder and younger brothers,"[25] a concept similar in meaning to Tianxia Wei Gong. These ancient cultural codes already contain the factors causing discrepancies compared with Western constitutional ideas, which will be further illustrated in the final chapter.

3.1.2 Quod Omnes Tangit

Quod Omnes Tangit[26] originated from Justinian's Codex: when more than one *tutor*[27] co-owns one individual *tutela*,[28] all of them must participate in the management and the nomination of *Tutoren*. The reason for the obligatory participation in the management is construed as follows: what touches all must be decided by all. Another example, invoked by both Ulpian and Papinian, was the concession of an aqueduct, showing how *Quod Omnes Tangit* was applied.[29] The agreement on an aqueduct by all people who were in some way connected with the water supply was needed. Another situation, which was often referred to, was before the court, under which circumstance all the plaintiffs and the defendants must participate in the

[24] Poetzelberger (1993), p. 102.

[25] Confucius (2010), p. 81. The original Chinese text is "四海之内，皆兄弟也。"(Within the four seas all men are brothers.) 论语·颜渊 (Lunyu, Yanyuan), ch. 12.5.

[26] Cod. Just. 5.59.5.2 (Justinian); Liber sextus 5.13.29 (Bonifaz VIII.); Can. 119 Nr. 3 Codex juris canonici. Richter (1939), p. 1122. Justinian (529-534) https://droitromain.univ-grenoble-alpes.fr/Corpus/digest.htm. Accesse 5 Dec 2022. Cf. Liebs (2007), p. 200. The most quoted articles are Post (1946), pp. 197–251; Post (1964), pp. 163–238; Congar (1980), pp. 115–182; Marongiu (1980), pp. 183–211. Constantin Fasolt noted the important authors for studying *Quod Omnes Tangit*: Congar, Post, Marongiu, McIlwain, Ullmann, Oakley und Tierney. Cf. Fasolt (2014), p. 226. For a detailed explanation of abbreviation in references to canon and civil law, see Brundage (2013), pp. 190–205.

[27] In the light of law history dictionary, *Tutor* means guardian. Köbler (2009), p. 947.

[28] *Tutela* means guardianship. Köbler (2009), p. 947.

[29] Ulpian, Dig. 39.3.8; Dig. 3.3.31.1; Papinian, Dig. 3.5.30.7; Cf. Congar (1980), p. 116; Cf. Fasolt (2014), p. 228.

process, with the decision of the judge binding all those who were present.[30] These are the basic meaning and execution of *Quod Omnes Tangit*.

3.1.3 A Comparison Between the Two Principles

Tianxia Wei Gong and *Quod Omnes Tangit* embrace a similar status in mainstream political thinking. The Grand Union 大同and the Small Tranquillity 小康[31] comprise an indispensable fragment of Confucian thought, reflecting Confucian understanding of ideal politics and society.[32] Confucian thinking has been promoted to mainstream political thinking since the Han Dynasty (206 BC–220 AD) in China. Confucianism has set the tone of Chinese philosophy.[33] *Quod Omnes Tangit* is closely related to democracy, which is and will remain a main theme in political discussion.[34] Thus, the two phrases enjoy a similar status in the background of their respective political cultural systems.

It is inspiring to launch a comparison between these two principles beginning with textual context from which they originated, the authors who created them and the ideological trend which they started. An attempt will be made to cover all coworking elements without comprising redundant content.

Both books, from which the two phrases originated, play an important role in history, forming the cornerstone in both cultures.

Richard Wilhelm believed that Li Gi, from different angles, could be compared with the Torah (The Five Books of Moses) in the Old Testament.[35] The author adds that Li Gi is also comparable with the Codex Civil of Justinian since Li might very well be regarded as the origin of law in Chinese law history. Since there was no private or administrative law but only criminal law in ancient times, Li functioned as a substitute. Gi shows that the book is a comment on Jing. Jing 经 originally meant the vertical line on a loom, as opposed to Wei 纬, the horizontal line, which extended later to the lines of street, river, blood vessel and transit line: Meridian, the longitude line, and Parallel, the altitude line.[36] As Meridian and Parallel constitute the skeleton

[30]Ulpian, D.3.3.31.1; Cf. Congar (1980), p. 116; Cf. Fasolt (2014), p. 228.

[31]Confucius (1994), p. 815, ch. 9. The Grand Union means a peaceful world in which everyone loves each other; the Small Tranquillity means a well-off society in which everyone loves his family member. The world of大同 is where Tianxia Wei Gong prevails. For a discussion of the translation of 大同, see Kang (1958), pp. 29–30.

[32]Chan (2014), p. 6; quoted from Joseph Chan with changes into simplified Chinese characters: Xiao (1998), pp. 68, 69; Kuang (1990), p. 247; Wang (2007), pp. 239–246.

[33]See also Encyclopaedia Britannica (2021a) https://www.britannica.com/topic/Confucianism/Confucian-learning-in-Jin-Yuan-and-Ming. Accessed Jun 29 2021.

[34]See also Lee (2008), p. 38.

[35]Wilhelm (1994), p. 16.

[36]The Codification Committee of the Great Compendium of Chinese Characters (1988), pp. 3402–3403.

of the world, Jing also acts as the guiding principle of Confucianists' spiritual world. The students of Confucius thus wrote comments on Jing. These interpretations formed another type of literature called Gi. Ding Ding identified that, in the beginning, Li Gi belonged to the category of Gi; however, with its influence increasing, it transformed into Jing in the Tang Dynasty.[37]

Another concept pertaining to Li is worth noting, namely, Fa. According to Xunzi (298–238 BC),[38] a Confucianist in the pre-Qin dynasty, Li is the starting point of the governance of a country, while Fa, the law, is the foundation of governance.[39] Li, the cadre of Fa, contains the principles of legislation. Unlike the predecessors of Xunzi; for example, Confucius; Xunzi paid equal attention to Li and Fa instead of solely focusing on Li. Recognizing the importance and irreplaceability of Fa, Xunzi made his contribution to the development of Confucianism and stimulated the thoughts of another school—the Legalists.[40] Li and Fa (law) have often been mentioned together.

Corpus Juris Civilis, whose name already existed in the High Middle Ages,[41] consists of four compilations: The Code, the Digest, the Institutes and the Novels.[42] "Corpus Juris Civilis is one of the greatest monuments of legal activity the world has known."[43] Mousourakis quoted this comment twice in his book, since he believed the importance of Corpus Juris Civilis can never be overstated, as it helps draw a picture of the evolution of Roman legal thinking over the course of eight centuries, from the first century B.C. to the sixth century A.D.; in addition, the civil law systems of most European countries, such as France and Germany, were based on the common ground supplied by Corpus Juris Civilis.[44] This common framework includes terminology, concepts and structure.[45]

In light of what has been discussed, it could be concluded that both works are the compilation of regulations, aiming at regulating social relationships and the allocation of interests. Nevertheless, the regulations in Corpus Juris Civilis possess the

---

[37] Ding (2014), p. 1.

[38] Xunzi, named also Xun Kuang, is one of the most important Confucianists of all time. He is famous for his proposal of evil human nature, in contrary to another significant Confucianist, Mengzi (372–289 BC). Xunzi stayed in States Qi, Chu, Zhao, and Qin, engaging as scholar and teacher. His students included Han Fei and Lisi, who "would become leading figures in the Legalist school and in the state of Qin, as well as several Confucian scholars who would assume an extremely influential role in the intellectual life of the ensuing Han dynasty." Bary and Bloom (1999), pp. 161–164; Feifel (1982), pp. 63–65.

[39] Shang et al. (2008), p. 76: "礼义者, 治之始也。" (Li and Yi is the start of governing.) (荀子·王制, Xunzi, Wangzhi) "法者, 治之端也。"(Law is the end of governing.) (荀子·君道, Xunzi, Jundao).

[40] Shang et al. (2008), p. 76.

[41] Manthe (2008), col. 901–907.

[42] Mousourakis (2003), p. 393.

[43] Mousourakis (2003), p. 395.

[44] Mousourakis (2003), p. 395; Mousourakis (2012), p. 82.

[45] Plessis (2015), p. 365.

character of practical guidance indicating which regulations should be obeyed and what should be done under which concrete circumstances. In comparison with these regulations similar to modern articles of law, the paragraphs and chapters in Li Gi are rather a declaration and philosophical contemplation. This difference not only appears here but also echoes the comparison between *Quod Omnes Tangit* and Tianxia Wei Gong.

Li Gi is to the school of Confucius what Corpus Juris Civilis is to Roman law. It is difficult to distinguish the influence of these great works from that of their background systems because they are an indispensable and integral part of these systems. The only difference lies in dimension – there are other works coworking in the whole system. Nevertheless, as Corpus Juris Civilis and Li Gi are such important works, they exercised the most profound influence. In this way, not only do their development processes but also their effects coincide with their background systems. Their significance was shown and stressed in the last chapter as proof of the value of this research. Thus, it is time to briefly introduce their development processes as the basis for a simultaneous comparison.

Roman law flourished two times: the first time was the compilation of Justinian, and the second time was the rediscovery in Italy at the end of the eleventh century, named the "first life" and the "second life" of Roman law by academics.[46] Within the first period, Roman law acted as *ius commune*, a law that effectively covered the territory of the Roman empire.[47] Even after the Roman Empire disintegrated, Roman law, thanks to the transformation and adaptation of Roman law by Italian and French jurists during the twelfth and thirteenth centuries, remained as a legacy and, together with canon law and local custom, became medieval learned law, which rose to *ius commune* in later medieval times, the second period.[48]

It might be astonishing to note that the flourishing of the Confucius school also experienced a "second life" – that is, the so-called "ousting [of] other doctrines and revering only Confucianism" 罢黜百家, 独尊儒术[49] in the Han Dynasty. I will take a closer look at this "second life" in the next chapter; the "first life" of the school of Confucius comes first.

[46]Head (2011), pp. 45, 72–86.

[47]Plessis (2015), p. 365.

[48]Plessis (2015), p. 365; Mayali (2015), pp. 375–376.

[49]Ban (1962), p. 212, "罢黜百家, 表章六经。" (Ousting the other schools and outstanding the six classics.); Ban (1962), p. 2525, "推明孔氏, 抑黜百家。" (Promoting Confucianism and repressing the other schools.).

3.2 Performance in the Historical Stage

There are two series of dramatic events and important documents in European and Chinese history that deserve examination outright before I begin to investigate the long history of the development of both phrases. However, there are some obstacles in the writing of this thesis because these events are integrated and consistent with the history of new interpretation. The addition of this background information at the beginning of each chapter might cause unnecessary repetition of historical materials; however, these problems gave way to the sharp contrast between the two series of events to avoid any possibility that similarity between the two phrases is overwhelmed by the tedious elaboration of their newly interpreted history. However, the background of the historic events in the following should not be separately considered; rather, they shall be read together with the background of the Renaissance of these two maxims because the background of the historic events and the background of the Renaissance happened in the same space-time and are substantially the same; the former is merely more specified.

3.2.1 Tianxia Wei Gong in the Abdicant Rescript of the Last Chinese Emperor

3.2.1.1 Xinhai Revolution

The Xinhai Revolution, which broke out in October,[10] 1911 (the year of Xinhai, according to the ancient Chinese Ganzhi[50]), could be regarded as the most qualified revolution in modern Chinese history compared with those that brought other developed countries, *inter alia*, England, France, and the United States, into the modern era. It is, affirmatively, of great value to lucubrate the similarities and differences among the Glorious Revolution, the French Revolution and the Xinhai Revolution. Nevertheless, as we are confined to the theme and the length of this paper, the aforementioned comparison will not go into detail, but the relevant aspects of the Xinhai Revolution will be scrutinized.

The Xinhai Revolution, led by Sun Yat-Sen, a crucial interpreter of Tianxia Wei Gong, resulted in the issuing of the Abdicant Rescript of the last Chinese Emperor on February 12, 1912, declaring the end of the Chinese feudal dynasty after a history of over 2000 years. However, the Abdicant Rescript did not lead to democracy but rather a dictatorship headed by Yuan Shikai, the most powerful commander in

[50]Ganzhi, a chronological system, adopts 10 Chinese characters as Tiangan, 甲乙丙丁戊己庚辛壬癸, and other 12 Chinese characters as Dizhi, 子丑寅卯辰巳午未申酉戌亥. Gan und Zhi have 60 combinations in total, thus this system is also called 60 Cycle. This method originated from Shang Dynasty and is still used today. For the general use of Ganzhi, see Chang and Wang (2019), pp. 15–23; for the origin of Ganzhi, see Feng (2001), pp. 146, 165, 166; for the western introduction of Ganzhi, see Xiao (2017), pp. 25–36; for the object assisting Ganzhi, see Li (2016), pp. 137–142.

Northern China, where the Qing Court was located.[51] In 1917, a short-lived restoration of the empire even occurred.[52] General Zhang Xun requested that Emperor Pu Yi regain his lost political power, which the latter agreed to. However, this restoration only lasted 12 days, demonstrating the great significance of the Xinhai Revolution in bringing imperial rule to an end. In addition, the rights of the other ethnicities were emancipated from the Man minority. From then on, state power was held by five ethnicities: Han, Manzhu, Mongolia, Muslim, and Tibetan.[53]

3.2.1.2 The Abdicant Rescript of the Qing Emperor

The Chinese text and its translation of the Abdicant Rescript[54] of the Qing Emperor should be quoted in full, despite its length, due to its significance:

> 奉旨朕钦奉隆裕皇太后懿旨:
>
> 前因民军起事,各省相应,九夏沸腾,生灵涂炭,特命袁世凯遣员与民军代表讨论大局,议开国会,公决政体。两月以来,尚无确当办法,南北暌隔,彼此相持,商辍於途,士露於野,徒以国体一日不决,故民生一日不安。今全国人民心理,多倾向共和,南中各省既倡议于前,北方诸将亦主张于后,人心所向,天命可知,予亦何忍因一姓之尊荣,拂兆民之好恶?是用外观大势,内审舆情,特率皇帝,将统治权公诸全国,定为共和立宪国体,近慰海内厌乱望治之心,远协古圣天下为公之义。袁世凯前经资政院选举为总理大臣,当兹新旧代谢之际,宜有南北统一之方,即由袁世凯以全权组织临时共和政府,与民军协商统一办法,总期人民安堵,海宇乂安,仍合满、汉、蒙、回、藏五族完全领土,为一大中华民国,予与皇帝得以退处宽闲,优游岁月,长受国民之优礼,亲见郅治之告成,岂不懿欤?钦此
>
> 宣统三年十二月二十五日。盖用御宝。.
>
> 内阁总理大臣、署外务大臣胡惟德、民政大臣赵秉钧、署度支大臣绍英假、学务大臣唐景崇假、陆军大臣王士珍假、署海军大臣谭学衡、司法大臣沈家本假、署农工商大臣熙彦、署邮传大臣梁士诒、理藩大臣達寿。.[55]

The next three paragraphs come a quoted version of the translation of the Abdicant Rescript of the Qing Emperor:

> We (the Emperor) have respectfully received the following Imperial Edict from Her Imperial Majesty the Empress Dowager Longyu:
>
> As a consequence of the uprising of the Republican Army, to which the different provinces immediately responded, the Empire seethed like a boiling cauldron, and the people were plunged into utter misery. Yuan Shikai was, therefore, specifically commanded some time ago to dispatch commissioners to confer with the representatives of the Republican Army on the general situation and to discuss matters pertaining to the convening of a

[51] Mühlemann (2006), p. 98.

[52] The following passage depends on Hsü (2000), pp. 475–483.

[53] Hsü (2000), pp. 475–483.

[54] The question, who is the author of the Abdicant Rescript of the Qing Emperor, is controversial. Some scholars believed that it was a work of collective wisdom: the ministers, especially Zhangjian, Yuan Shikai and the Empress Dowager Longyu all exerted influence on this text; an earlier view held that Zhangjian was the sole author. Song (2019), pp. 74–93, 166–167. For the situation of the Abdicant Rescript, see Hsü (2000), p. 561f.

[55] Shen (1967), p. 1251.

National Assembly for the decision of the suitable mode of settlement. Separated as the South and the North are by great distances, the unwillingness of either side to yield to the other can result only in the continued interruption of trade and the prolongation of hostilities, for, so long as the form of government is undecided, the nation can have no peace. It is now evident that the hearts of the majority of the people are in favor of a republican form of government: the provinces of the South were the first to espouse the cause, and the generals of the North have since pledged their support. Based on the preference of the people's hearts, the Will of Heaven can be discerned. How could We then bear to oppose the will of the millions for the glory of one Family! Therefore, observing the tendencies of the age on the one hand and studying the opinions of the people on the other, We and His Majesty the Emperor hereby cede sovereignty to the People and decide in favor of a republican form of constitutional government. Thus, we could gratify on the one hand the desires of the whole nation who, tired of anarchy, are desirous of peace, and on the other hand would follow in the footsteps of the Ancient Sages, who regarded the Throne as the sacred trust of the Nation.

Now, Yuan Shikai was elected by the provisional parliament [zi zheng yuan] to be the Premier. During this period of transference of government from the old to the new, there should be some means of uniting the South and the North. Let Yuan Shikai organize with full powers a provisional republican government and confer with the Republican Army as to the methods of union, thus assuring peace to the people and tranquility to the Empire, and forming to one Great Republic of China by the union as heretofore, of the five peoples, namely, Manchus, Chinese [Han], Mongols, Mohammedans [Hui], and Tibetans together with their territory in its integrity. We and His Majesty the Emperor, thus enabled to live in retirement, free from responsibilities, and cares and passing the time in ease and comfort, shall enjoy without interruption the courteous treatment of the Nation and see with Our own eyes the consummation of an illustrious government. Is not this highly advisable…

[February 12nd, 1912].[56]

Through this document, we may learn:

First, the Qing Dynasty lost the position of being representative of heaven. Therefore, they transferred the sovereignty of the emperor at that time to the nation as a whole to establish a constitutional republic state. Second, the regent, Dowager Longyu, expressed her hope that the five ethnic groups should be united in the Republic of China. Third, Yuan Shikai would be placed in a de facto position with the greatest political power, taking full authority to lead the establishment of a republican government. Fourth, there was a favored treatment for the royal family in the future after the abdication of the emperor.

This document holds heavy weight in history. The achievements of the Xinhai Revolution were confirmed in written form. In other words, the end of the Qing Dynasty could be marked by the Abdicant Rescript instead of the Xinhai Revolution. Until recently, academics could not agree with each other regarding the character of this document.[57] Some authors proposed reevaluating the Abdicant Rescript because it has not received the attention it deserves, deeming it a constitutional document; others questioned such an opinion and argued that although the Abdicant Rescript is important, its political and legal significance should not be overstated.[58] Whether the

[56]Cheng et al. (1999), pp. 211–213. Cf. Mühlemann (2006), pp. 356–358. The date was translated according to Hoang (1910), p. 346.

[57]For a general literature review, see Chen et al. (2012), pp. 104–12.

[58]Ling (2013), pp. 159, 160.

Abdicate Rescript bears a constitutional character or not or how essential it is are not points of further discussion in this thesis. What is more significant is to prove that it is at least feasible and meaningful to compare the Abdicant Rescript with the Magna Carta. In addition, Tianxia Wei Gong has played a cardinal role not only in this document but also in this historical event. In this aspect, both spectra of the discussion support the aforementioned argument. The researchers arguing for a constitutional characterization drew an analogy between the two historical events that occurred separately in 1912 in China and in 1689 in England and called the abdication the Chinese version of the Glorious Revolution.[59] They were aware that the Abdicant Rescript turned out to be a supplement of the constitution for the Republic of China.[60] This perspective supports the comparability between the Abdicant Rescript and the Magna Carta. The other school of thought, arguing against the constitutional character of the Abdicant Rescript, placed much stress on the principle of Tianxia Wei Gong. They viewed this principle rather than the admission of the emperor as the basis to establish a state. It is even emphasized that Tianxia Wei Gong should be considered the root of Chinese political tradition.[61] In this sense, Tianxia Wei Gong appeared in the Abdicant Rescript:

> 是用外观大势, 内审舆情, 特率皇帝, 将统治权公诸全国, 定为共和立宪国体, 近慰海内厌乱望治之心, 远协古圣天下为公之义。.[62]

> Therefore, observing the tendencies of the age on the one hand and studying the opinions of the people on the other, We and His Majesty the Emperor hereby bestow the sovereignty upon the People and decide in favor of a republican form of constitutional government. Thus, we can gratify on the one hand the desires of the whole nation who, tired of anarchy, are desirous of peace, and on the other hand will follow in the footsteps of the Ancient Sages, who regarded the Throne as the sacred trust of the Nation.[63]

3.2.2 Quod Omnes Tangit *in Comparison with the Magna Carta*

Edward I is related not only to *Quod Omnes Tangit* but also to the Magna Carta. It was through his confirmation of the Magna Carta in 1297 that the document exerted great influence on constitutional history.[64] The Magna Carta was first declared valid

[59]Gao (2011), pp. 83–104.

[60]Gao (2011), pp. 32–33.

[61]Ling (2013), p. 173.

[62]Shen (1967), p. 1251.

[63]Cheng et al. (1999), pp. 211–213. Cf. Mühlemann (2006), pp. 356–358. See original text in the appendix of this thesis.

[64]Breay (2002), p. 45.

in 1215 and then reissued in 1216, 1217, and 1225.[65] After experiencing these many ups and downs, it was finally and fully confirmed.

> In 1770, William Pitt the Elder called it 'the Bible of the English Constitution'. It remained on the Statute Book until the Law Reform Act of 1863 was passed. In 1956, the English judge, Lord Denning, described it as 'the greatest constitutional documents of all times – the foundation of the freedom of the individual against the arbitrary authority of the despot,'[66]

although its contents have also undergone some changes from time to time.

In Danziger and Gillingham's eyes, clauses 12 and 14 in the Magna Carta of 1215 bore "a kind of parliament in embryo."[67]

Clause 12 confirmed:

> No scutage or aid is to be imposed in our realm except by the common counsel of our realm, unless it is for the ransom of our body, the knighting of our eldest son or the first marriage of our eldest daughter; and for these only a reasonable aid is to be levied. Aids from the city of London are to be treated likewise.

Clause 14 asserted,

> And to obtain the common counsel of the realm for the assessment of an aid (except in the three cases aforesaid) or a scutage, we will have archbishops, bishops, abbots, earls and greater barons summoned individually by our letters, and we shall also have summoned generally through our sheriffs and bailiffs all those who hold of us in chief, for a fixed date, with at least forty days' notice, and at a fixed place; and in all letters of summons we will state the reason for the summons. In addition, when the summons have thus been made, the business is to go forward on the day arranged according to the counsel of those present, even if not all those summoned have come.[68]

"Aids" and "scutages" were two kinds of taxes. Clause 14 explained that the élite, the "archbishops, bishops, abbots, earls and greater barons," were the people who should be summoned to play their part in giving the king "the common counsel of the realm," and they received letters addressed to them individually when summoned. It also seems to be an embryo of *Quod Omnes Tangit* or, as the principle

---

[65] Holt et al. (eds) (2015), p. 33.

[66] Danziger and Gillingham (2004), pp. 277–278.

[67] Danziger and Gillingham (2004), p. 182.

[68] Holt et al. (eds) (2015), pp. 382–384.

Magna Carta, 12. "*Nullum scutagium vel auxilium ponatur in regno nostro, nisi per commune consilium regni nostri, nisi ad corpus nostrum redimendum, et primogenitum filium nostrum militem faciendum, et ad filiam nostram primogenitam semel maritandam, et ad hec non fiat nisi racionabile auxilium; simili modo fiat de auxiliis de civitate Londoniarum.*"

14. "*Et ad habendum commune consilium regni de auxilio assidendo aliter quam in tribus casibus predictis, vel de scutagio assidendo, summoneri faciemus archiepiscopos, episcopos, abbates, comites, et majores barones sigillatim per litteras nostras; et preterea faciemus summoneri in generali per vicecomites et ballivos nostros omnes illos qui de nobis tenent in capite ad certum diem, scilicet ad terminum quadraginta dierum ad minus, et ad certum locum; et in omnibus litteris illius summonicionis causam summonicionis exprimemus; et sic facta summonicione negocium ad diem assignatum procedat secundum consilium illorum qui presentes fuerint, quamvis non omnes summoniti venerint.*"

already existed, to put it more precisely, an echo of the developed meaning of *Quod Omnes Tangit*.

3.2.3 Comparison

Opinions on the role that *Quod Omnes Tangit* played in parliament history vary from person to person. Michael Prestwich found it inappropriate to base the conclusion on insufficient evidence, since *Quod Omnes Tangit* was cited by Edward I in only one writ in 1295,[69] summoning archbishop and clergy to parliament out of practical political reasons.[70] Yves Congar, on the contrary, held the opinion that *Quod Omnes Tangit* had developed into not only a practical custom of representative principle but also a systematic doctrine for constitutional affairs.[71] Through the comparison of the roles that *Quod Omnes Tangit* and Tianxia Wei Gong played, an answer to this question could be posed.

"Feudal Europe in the year 1100 resembled China during the Zhou Dynasty in many ways. There was a nominal monarch or ruling dynasty, but de facto power was split among a highly decentralized number of feudal lords who maintained their own military forces, kept order, administered justice, and were largely self-sufficient economically. As in China, certain dynastic houses distinguished themselves through greater organizational ability, ruthlessness, or luck, and began to consolidate territorial states over ever wider domains."[72] These two mentioned periods were also the time of Magna Carta and Tianxia Wei Gong.

Usually, the prediction about the occurrence of an epoch-making historical event can be found in a series of crises where its energy accumulates. In England, that series of crises were John's combination of consistent military failures and the subsequent frequent and heavy taxation.[73] In Edward's time, the war with France was on the boundary of the homeland. Similarly, in China, constant failures in the

[69] Stubbs (1913), p. 480.

[70] Prestwich (1997), pp. 466–467.

[71] Congar (1980), p. 150.

[72] Fukuyama (2011), p. 328.

[73] Danziger and Gillingham (2004), p. 182: "During his reign royal revenue soared. In the 5 years from 1199 to 1203 when money was desperately needed for war against Philip of France, revenues audited at the English Exchequer averaged just over £27,000 a year. In 1210 and 1212 the same sources produced roughly twice as much as that and in 1211 three times as much. Moreover, in these same years, large sums were paid directly into the king's chamber—his household financial office—and were not subject to the regular Exchequer audit. A recent calculation estimates John's total revenue from England in 1211 at a staggering £145,000—six times as much as the Crown's average annual income at the beginning of the reign. Hardly surprising that he was described as 'the plunderer of his subjects.' Something had to be done about this kind of government. In this instance, that 'something' turned out to be rebellion and Magna Carta."

face of the invasions by foreign military forces gave rise to enormous unfair financial compensation.

Another similarity to be noted is the one between the promulgation of the Abdicant Rescript and the Magna Carta. In these historical moments relating to the redistribution of power, both emperors, Emperor Puyi (6 years old) and King Henry III (9 years old), were very young and lacked practical power. The Abdicant Rescript was issued in the name of the Empress Dowager Longyu under the pressure of Yuan Shikai, while the Magna Carta was issued with the aid of King Henry's consultant, William Marschal, Earl of Pembroke, in 1216 and 1217.[74] We tend to have the impression that in these historical moments, people who signed these documents were very determined to lead history in the right and progressive direction, but in fact, they were merely actors on a political stage, behind whom are some other interest groups. The historical facts are the results of the composition of forces. This is the same in the East and the West.

There was also an urgent need for the Chinese emperor to consult his subjects in parliament as much as possible. However, without the tradition of consensus, he, unlike the king of England, failed, and, as a result, a parliamentary republic was not established.[75] Thus, the practical need for consultants is obviously not self-evident to the appearance and existence of the parliament. The possible reason for this could lie only in the principle that guided the people's behaviors because of their differences, to which the diversified results could be attributed. In the second part of this thesis, I will further discuss in detail how the differences between *Quod Omnes Tangit* and Tianxia Wei Gong led to different results in the historical choice of the form of government in their respective nations.

3.3 Renaissance from Classics

Although this chapter follows the structure of the previous chapter, in which the two series of events and documents are compared, this does not imply that it is less important; rather, it is even more important for both sides because it explores their new interpretation by different people, such as scholars, emperors and popes. In this way, these two phrases gained various meanings, exercised more power and were reborn through new interpretations.

---

[74] Breay (2002), p. 44.

[75] Cheng et al. (1999), pp. 275–281.

3.3.1 Background of the Renaissance

Before explaining how the new interpretations came into being, it might be interesting and necessary to ponder why the two phrases were newly interpreted, who deemed it a necessity, under what circumstances they were needed again, and in which direction these new interpretations developed. The answer to these questions can be found in history: its theme is the conflict of power.

3.3.1.1 For Tianxia Wei Gong

The Qing Dynasty (1644–1912) was the last federal dynasty in Chinese history. The Opium War in 1840 indicated the beginning of modern China.[76] Consequently, the period from 1840 to 1912 was an eventful epoch in China. During that phase, conflicts arose between China and foreign countries. China had wars one after another with the United Kingdom, France, Russia and Japan.[77] These catastrophes compelled the Chinese to open not only the door to trade but also their minds to accept Western thinking. The rulers of the Qing Dynasty were not yet aware of their fate, but what they did know was that it was vital to embark on a reform to establish a modern state capable of assuring domestic order and protecting the borders.

Therefore, another conflict arose: the conflict between the royalty and the reformers. Conflicts such as these tend to be rather straightforward in terms of the parties involved as well as their alliances and goals: royals want to maintain their power while reformers try to overthrow them. However, in China's situation, the two sides split internally, and one half melted into the opposite side.

First, the royalty side should be inspected. Cixi, Emperor Xianfeng's wife, discussed political affairs with the emperor, read over the actual memorial to the throne and gradually took a position as a regent parallel to the following two emperors, Tongzhi and Guangxu, after Emperor Xianfeng's death in 1861.[78] She is a representative of conservatism, in contrast to Emperor Guangxu, who was a reformer. Emperor Guangxu was interested in reform and acted as the reformers' guard. Unfortunately, real power belonged not to him but to his aunt Cixi. This fact was not any more evident than it was during the Hundred-Days-Reform.[79] Emperor Guangxu was a supporter of the reform, led by Kang Youwei and Liang Qichao. It resulted in Emperor Guangxu being put under house arrest in the Summer Palace

[76]Some Scholars are against this point of view. However, this discussion is not the main point of this thesis.

[77]Fairbank (1978), p. 3.

[78]Spence (2008), pp. 269–270.

[79]The Hundred-Days-Reform was also called Wuxu Bianfa. Wuxu is a Ganzhi, like Xinhai, see Sect. 3.2.1.1 in this thesis.

because the Queen Mother, Cixi, was against the reform.[80] Cixi trusted neither the reformers nor the revolutionaries, both of whom were traitorous in her eyes.[81]

Next, the reformers' side should be checked. All Chinese intellectuals stood before a fork road at the end of the Qing Dynasty. They faced the choice between traditional thought and modernity or moderation. As Viren Murthy put it,

> [o]ne could separate the intellectual factions that emerged after China's loss in the Sino-Japanese War of 1895 into conservatives, reformers and revolutionaries. Each of these political groups encompasses complex ideological and political tendencies. Conservatives brought together an attachment to the Confucian tradition with a resistance to the importation of Western models of political governance. Reformers are famous for their attempts to unite readings of traditional figures such as Confucius with a political project for reform under the Manchu-led Qing dynasty government. Finally, revolutionaries united novel interpretations of figures in Chinese history with the political goal of overthrowing the Qing government and creating a modern republic ruled by the Han.[82]

Chinese intellectuals at that time promoted Western knowledge, emphasizing "statecraft" (经世Jingshi) and "practical studies" (实学Shixue): the reformers insisted on the "Chinese origins for Western knowledge" (西学中源Xi xue zhong yuan) and the Chinese "structure" or "essence" with Western "efficacy" or "usefulness" (中体西用Zhong ti xi yong), while the revolutionists upheld total westernization (全盘西化Quanpan xi hua).[83]

Currently, an increasing number of scholars try to avoid the modernization theory that all societies will modernize along the lines pioneered by the North Atlantic nations and that they take Western developments as normative. They seek to understand how Chinese elites came to an understanding of Western political philosophy and what they did with this knowledge. Even the series of words such as "influence," "cultural borrowing," "diffusion" or "absorption" slighted the active and creative nature of the process and the role that native tradition plays in the adaptations involved in confronting new ideas; rather, a balance should be struck between localized explanation and the translation of new concepts, between revolutionary nature and intellectual change, and between historical determinism and the novelty of new intellectual formulations.[84]

3.3.1.2 For *Quod Omnes Tangit*

It is impossible to understand the growth of Western constitutional thought without the recognition of ecclesiastical and political theory, especially the relationship

[80] Spence (2008), p. 286.

[81] Peter Zarrow's original text reads "[i]n the wake of 1898, the Qing treated both reformers and revolutionaries as equally traitorous." It is not accurate to generalize the attitude of "Qing" because of the different opinions of Cixi and Puyi, who both represented the "Qing". Zarrow (2012), p. 154.

[82] Murthy (2011), pp. 1–2.

[83] Jenco (2015), p. 13; Fairbank and Liu (1980), p. 274–283.

[84] Zarrow (2009), pp. 237–238.

between the church and the state. The author applauds the outline of the juridical foundation from 1150 to 1250 that Tierney sketched. This outline construed a logic chain that clearly illustrated the relationships among society, church, and law, which is the most important aspect of the social background for *Quod Omnes Tangit*.

First, what was unusual about Western society from the twelfth and thirteenth centuries onward? Tierney's answer excluded the Teutonic tradition, the ancient notions of customary law and popular participation in local assemblies, targeting the religious aspects of medieval civilization. However, Western Christianity has "coexisted happily" with absolutisms.[85] In that case, what was special about the Christian church in the organization of medieval society? He thought that was the "unusual duality of structure:" the struggle of medieval empire and papacy.[86] The ecclesiastical and secular powers were.

"always jealous of each other's authority, always preventing medieval society from congealing into a single monolithic theocracy. Ecclesiastical criticism diminished the aura of divine right surrounding kingship; royal power opposed the temporal claims of the papacy. Each hierarchy limited the authority of the other."[87]

One outcome of this dual structure is the authority limitation of both sides. In Danziger's words, "[c]hurch-state relations bristled with intractable problems that could only be managed in a spirit of compromise."[88] On the one hand, they achieved a balance at the cost of sacrificing each other's power range; on the other hand, they tried to extend their own authority by drawing support via other channels, one of which was the interpretation of *Quod Omnes Tangit*.

Under such circumstances, the legitimation of their power could be accomplished, but they also might obtain support from the third party when what the religious power needed was absent in their own canon law tradition but existed in Justinian Roman law. They then naturally tended to resort to Roman law when Gregor VII launched the Renaissance of Roman law to corroborate pontifical authority and build a comprehensive canon tradition.[89] Innocent studied in Bologna,[90] which enabled him to achieve the goals mentioned above through Roman law.

A further question must be raised: how did constitutional ideas come into existence? Although absolutism was passively avoided, why did another way of thinking positively emerge? Tierney ascribed this emergence to the frequent interexchange of the staff and the growth of corporative associations.[91] The author questions this statement. When the growth of corporative associations could even be accepted as a reason for the appearance of constitutional ideas, the interexchange of the staff was possibly not a reason because only when something comes into

[85] Tierney (1982), p. 9.

[86] Tierney (1982), p. 10.

[87] Tierney (1982), p. 10.

[88] Danziger and Gillingham (2004), p. 139.

[89] Ullmann (1972), pp. 162–164.

[90] Tierney and Painter (1983), pp. 345–346.

[91] Tierney (1982), p. 10.

existence can it then be exchanged. How did the later interexchange give rise to the emergence of that object? Tierney himself wrote that constitutional thought.

> often emerged first in the academic writings of the medieval canonists; but the canonistic doctrines themselves grew from a fusion of secular and religious ideas, and trained canonists staffed the chanceries of kings as well as the bureaucracy of the church.[92]

Thus, it could be safely concluded that this kind of interexchange was not the reason for the formation of constitutional thought, although it seemed to be an interesting phenomenon that attracted much attention. The reason, rather, may be the one opportunity offered by the church's bureaucracy to the trained canonists to apply their knowledge, including constitutional thought.

Tierney presented that it was common to see medieval jurists, "as masters in universities or as members of cathedral chapters or religious orders,"[93] participating in the activities of corporative groups, depicted with the generalized term *universitas*[94] in Roman law, whose phenomenon, namely, their daily practices, shaped their envisagement of social and political structure.[95] Even the barons of England regarded themselves both as members of a feudal hierarchy and as a corporate entity, the *universitas regni*.[96] People confirmed their responsibilities according to the realm and collegiality and distinguished the case in which two opposite sides had to participate from that in which everyone took part in only for himself or herself.[97] It is worth noting that *Quod Omnes Tangit* was reinterpreted at such a time. The rudiment of representation was thus already formed.

Without these social aspects, it is difficult to understand the thought itself. Nevertheless, we cannot overstate the importance of preventing intellectual history from falling into social history. Moreover, there are still some social aspects left to explore, the meaning of which may be easier to grasp after having investigated the interpretation of the maxim.

3.3.1.3 Comparison

Chances were high that the reallocation of power would follow the trend and model of democracy. One might be inclined to ask why this point in time turned out to be the pivotal moment, which requires more clarification. Danny Danziger and John Gillingham noted,

> [h]ad there been an active heir to the throne in 1215, those who opposed John would have turned to him; there would have been no Magna Carta.

[92]Tierney (1982), pp. 10–11.

[93]Tierney (1982), p. 11.

[94]Gierke (1868), p. 648.

[95]Tierney (1982), p. 11.

[96]Tierney (1982), p. 11.

[97]Congar (1980), p. 119.

> In other ways too, family politics played its part in the making of the Magna Carta.[98]

As in the West, it can be found how much family politics exercised their influence on the Oriental royal family's decisions. The Battle of Bouvines, taking place 1 year before the issuing of the Magna Carta, is noteworthy in its potential influence on the charter.[99] Danziger and Gillingham put forth a brilliant hypothesis:

> [h]ad John's troops and allies won, he would have returned to England in triumph, ready to launch a new expedition to reconquer his ancestral lands in France and punish those barons who had refused to help his war effort. Now he was in no position to do either.[100]

These hypotheses help us to understand the situation. Due to the defeat suffered in battle, the barons serving John became increasingly unsatisfied, which contributed to the drafting of the Magna Carta in the following year. As the historian Sir James Holt put it more sharply, "[t]he road from Bouvines to Runnymede was direct, short, and unavoidable."[101] The reason may be the series of battles: the loss of lands resulted in the loss of revenue, and fewer subjects were burdened with providing more support for John's war, forming a vicious circle.[102] The same was true in China: warfare is an expensive undertaking, forcing the ruler to divert funds from domestic resorts and thus causing unrest among the populace, culminating in people demanding change.

A curious phenomenon happened both in the East and the West: once both documents came into effect, there were efforts to invalidate them. However, like the phoenix rising from the ashes, they ultimately persevered. The Magna Carta had been legally valid for only 10 weeks after it was sealed in June 1215 because John knew well that the Pope would be against the charter, "he sent envoys to Innocent III seeking an annulment of the charter", and the Pope did not disappoint John, issuing a papal bull to declare the charter "null and void," stating that Magna Carta was "as unlawful and unjust as it is base and shameful."[103] In China, Wuxu Bianfa lasted for only one hundred days.[104] Nevertheless, the Magna Carta underwent a process of constant reissue, transforming "from a document wrung from a king facing civil war into the standard royal declaration of the law and custom of the country."[105] In

---

[98] Danziger and Gillingham (2004), p. 104.

[99] Danziger and Gillingham (2004), p.117.

[100] Danziger and Gillingham (2004), p. 168.

[101] Holt (1992), p. 100.

[102] Breay (2002), p. 12.

[103] Breay (2002), p. 40.

[104] Because of that, Wuxu Bianfa is also called hundred-days-reform.

[105] Breay (2002), pp. 44–45: "In 1225, Henry III made the most significant reissue of the charter...In 1297 the text of the 1225 reissue was copied on to the first statute roll...The issues addressed by Magna Carta retained their importance and in 1253 a document was issued at Westminster Hall declaring that anyone who broke its terms was to be excommunicated. Orders were made for it to be read twice a year in county courts from 1265, and twice yearly in cathedrals from 1297. It was routinely read and confirmed at the opening of each parliament, and in 1341 parliament required the officers of state to swear to observe its terms."

China, however, there was never a complete document with only minor modifications being inherited but rather a principle running throughout many decades.

In addition, there were two tensions within one hierarchy. For the West, Tierney pointed out that "century central feudal barons resisted royal centralization in the secular world while feudally minded bishops resisted papal centralization in the ecclesiastical sphere."[106] For the East, we have discussed the conflict between and within the royal side and the reformer's side. Hence, the social context for reinterpretation tends to witness tensions and conflicts.

3.3.2 New Interpretation

3.3.2.1 Tianxia Wei Gong

3.3.2.1.1 From Kang Youwei (1858–1927)

Kang Youwei exerted his influence through his books, teachings and political activities.[107] Kang Youwei's *magnum opus*, the Book of Great Harmony, also called Da Tong Shu, directly adopted the chapter name of Tianxia Wei Gong in Liji, depicting the utopia in his mind.[108] Da Tong Shu, or Ta T'ung Shu, was first incompletely published in 1913.[109] Liang Qichao, the only one who mentioned both Tianxia Wei Gong and *Quod Omnes Tangit*, was Kang Youwei's student, who helped with the publication.[110] Kang Youwei was also one of the leaders in the late Qing reformation activities.[111] The following paragraphs will continue elaborating the three perspectives.

Canton is located on the seaside in eastern China. After the Qing government signed a series of unequal treaties, several trading ports were forced to open, some of which were located in Canton. This unpleasant measure objectively promoted the external exchange of Canton with the outside world. Many reformers or revolutionaries were Cantonese, which is no coincidence because the Cantonese "had direct contact with Westerners in Hong Kong and Shanghai,"[112] with Canton Province being the closest province to Hong Kong. A school called "Yue Xue," the study of Canton, flourished. Hao Chang identified that "Yue Xue" dominated the academic

[106]Tierney (1982), p. 10.

[107]Kang (1958), pp. 14–23.

[108]Kang (1958), pp. 26, 27.

[109]Kang (1958), p. 26.

[110]Kang (1958), pp. 14, 26.

[111]Kang (1958), pp. 14–18.

[112]Teng and Fairbank (1979), p. 147.

field of Canton Province in the nineteenth century.[113] This school also had a far-reaching impact on Chinese intellectual history.

To a large extent, this effect would be exercised through Kang Youwei. Born in Canton Province in 1858, Kang Youwei, as a descendant of a high official, started to nurture his intellectual ability at the age of five, after which time, in the following years, he utilized the enormous family library to learn about Confucius.[114] When he was 18 years old, he started to study under the most learned scholar of the Canton School, Zhu Ciqi.[115]

Zhu Ciqi is an important scholar who has not received enough attention from researchers. In his time, he was very famous and highly respected. One could argue that he is so to this very day owing to his students, especially Kang Youwei. Nevertheless, Kang Youwei was admittedly so much influenced and enlightened by his tutor that the thinking of his teacher is the source not only of his theory but also of his methodology. A compatible attitude toward different kinds of knowledge is the common point of all forerunners in modern China. Zhu Ciqi is no exception. Chang found that Zhu Ciqi combined Han and Song Learning with the Ancient and the New Text, which were two distinct schools of Confucius.[116]

This kind of thinking to consolidate differences can be clearly traced in Kang Youwei's *magnum opus*, *Confucius as a Reformer* 《孔子改制考》*and the Book of Great Harmony* 《大同书》. In the first article, Kang tried to combine the theory of Confucius with the logic of reform.[117] In *the Book of Great Harmony*, also called *Da Tong Shu*, he pursued an extreme unity—the Great Harmony, Da Tong, which is the utopian world of Tianxia Wei Gong. Kang thought only in this way would all differentiae be eradicated and a utopia emerge. In this book, Kang Youwei interpreted Tianxia Wei Gong in detail. The *Da Tong Shu* consisted of ten sections, each numbered with a traditional Chinese tally,[118] and the first section, acting as a skeleton, described the suffering engendered from nine kinds of boundaries: the boundaries between nations, classes, races, sex, family, livelihood, administration, kinds and suffering.[119] He attributed all these kinds of sufferings to the existence of boundaries. The following nine chapters elaborate how to separately abolish the boundaries and to achieve utmost happiness.[120] Some of his analyses about the potential or the existing problems within a union are meaningful today, for example, to the EU or UN. In Kang's review,

> [t]here are six difficulties in united states

[113]Chang (1987), p. 22.

[114]Thompson (1958), pp. 11–25; Fairbank and Liu (1980), p. 283.

[115]Yang (2005), p. 7.

[116]Chang (1987), p. 22.

[117]Opitz (1969), pp. 20–21.

[118]甲乙丙丁戊己庚辛壬癸, 10 characters as Tiangan in Chinese number system Ganzhi, see the first footnote in Sect. 3.2.1.1 in this thesis.

[119]Kang (1958), p. 31.

[120]Kang (1958), pp. 31–33.

(In sum, the six difficulties standing in the way of union are:

1. Conflicting self-interests of states.
2. Unwillingness of states to surrender their sovereignty.
3. Even after the establishment of a strong union, the unwillingness of member states to submit to laws of the overall government conflicts with their individual interests.
4. The disparity between large and small states raises problems of proportional representation in the legislature.
5. Problems of reaching agreement on legislation in view of the number of states whose opinions are to be harmonized.
6. Even after the union has been in effect for some time and is firmly based, the possibility of some serious differences arising would lead to a rupture, as in the case of the American Civil War.)[121]

Kang's method seemed not to aim at regulation design but rather at thoroughly eliminating the trigger as well as all kinds of boundaries for all this suffering.

Kang's envisaged world seemed to be as follows:

1. the entire world would be governed by a single government and divided into different regions;
2. both central and regional governments would be popularly elected;
3. any man or woman cannot cohabitate more than one year, the mate of which must be switched regularly;
4. pregnant women would learn to nurse in institutions for prenatal education;
5. according to children's age, they would go to school from kindergarten up;
6. government would assign different work in agriculture, industries and other productive enterprises to adults;
7. hospitals and nursing homes would be established for the sick and old;
8. there would be public dormitories and dining halls for the enjoyment of all classes depending on their working income;
9. special rewards would be given to inventors, discoverers, and so on;
10. the dead would be cremated and fertilizer factories erected in the neighborhood of the crematoria.[122]

Kang Youwei revised his manuscript of the *Universal Principles* in 1887, envisaging the establishment of the world language institute, the world parliament, a world army, and so on. *Da Tong Shu*, as a work of utopian socialism, was not published and only available for his students because Kang thought that the contemporary age was merely a disordered epoch and not Da Tong.[123] He himself was aware of the distance between ideality and reality, saying that.

"[g]oing from winter's cold to summer's heat, we must pass through spring's warmth before we can arrive; going from the level plain to the mountain peak, we must pass by the foothill-slopes before we can ascend. . . Thus, given the conditions of the present, we must [start by forming] alliances, disarming, and establishing a

[121] Kang (1958), p. 87.

[122] Adapted from Hsü (2000), p. 366.

[123] Hsü (2000), p. 366.

universal legislature, and after [these have been accomplished] we will be able gradually to attain One World."[124]

Thus, Kang tried to solve the urgent social and political problem by taking other actions. From 1888 to 1898, Kang presented 10 memorials over many institutional obstacles to the throne, suggesting how to make the country prosper and people cultivated.[125] Among the 10 memorials, in 1895, Kang and his student Liang Qichao organized "the first 'mass political movement' in modern China,"[126] Gongche Shangshu 公车上书, during which they drafted a 10,000-word treatise and gathered the signatures of more than 600 provincial graduates to protest the Treaty of Shimonoseki[127] with Japan.[128]

In addition to 公车上书Gongche Shangshu, the Wuxu Reform seems to be mentioned in every research paper on modern China, and for good reason, as it signaled an act of courage in the process of the reform.

> For 103 days, from June 11 to September 20, some forty to fifty reform decrees were issued in rapid succession in the areas of education, government administration, industry, and international cultural exchange.[129]

Private citizens were encouraged to submit suggestions on the reform directly to government offices. Kang might have suffered too much from the block of the way of opinions toward the emperor. However, "[a]t the age of forty, K'ang had captivated the emperor and become the leader of a radical reform."[130] He and his students, Liang Qichao, who will be discussed in the next chapter, "have been identified as two central figures in this movement."[131] In addition, their roles were three-dimensional: intellectual, social and political.

Hao Chang revealed that Liang recognized Kang's role as a religious leader and the "Martin Luther of Confucianism."[132] It is because of Kang's tremendous influence and, with his new interpretation of Neo-Confucianism, the ideal of Da Tong that Tianxia Wei Gong has become a heritage and seen a revival.

---

[124] Kang (1958), p. 87.

[125] Immanuel Chung-Yueh Hsü's text concerned more about the activity of Kang Youwei *per se* vis-à-vis the corresponding part in *the Cambridge history of China* edited by Fairbank John K., with the latter adding various interactivities of Kang Youwei with other Chinese intellectuals. Hsü (2000), pp. 367–372. Cf. Fairbank and Liu (1980), p. 291–300. Cf. Mühlemann (2006), p. 146.

[126] Hsü (2000), p. 367.

[127] Opitz (1969), p. 9.

[128] Hsü (2000), pp. 366–367.

[129] Hsü (2000), p. 375; Sievers (1972), pp. 55–81.

[130] Hsü (2000), p. 372.

[131] Kwong (1984), p. 227.

[132] Chang (1987), p. 65.

3.3.2.1.2 From Liang Qichao (1873—1929)[133]

Liang Qichao is the only scholar whose work explained both Tianxia Wei Gong and *Quod Omnes Tangit*, albeit in Chinese, because he could not speak or write in English. He is thus also the only Chinese scholar who has quoted the term *Quod Omnes Tangit*.[134] Until now, only he has enabled the observation of the coexistence and interplay between *Quod Omnes Tangit* and Tianxia Wei Gong. His works concerning our two maxims will be studied in detail after a short biographical introduction, which is based on several selected studies.[135]

Liang was born in 1873, like Kang Youwei, in Guangdong Province. Very brilliant at an early age, Liang started his Confucian learning with his grandfather and father. The four classics were his first learning material. At first, Liang tried to launch a typical career like all Confucian scholars, attending a series of exams to pave his way for becoming an official in the imperial system. Things went smoothly until 1890, when he failed the metropolitan examination. On his way home, he found many great works of Western thinking in the city of Shanghai, which were published by the Translation Department of the Jiangnan Arsenal. At that moment, his attention to Western thought was aroused by Western learning. After he returned to Guangdong Province, Liang was informed of Kang Youwei's reputation and introduced to him to be his student. Under Kang's instructions, Liang dipped not only into Song-Ming Neo-Confucianism and Gong-Yang Confucianism but also into the political theories and institutions of both China and the West.[136]

"Liang Ch'i-ch'ao in the early twentieth century became the most influential of all Chinese publicists."[137] Regarding Liang's fame and popularity, despite its length, it is necessary to quote the passage written by Andrew J. Nathan:

"'Even Napoleon at the height of his power could not have captivated a larger number of men in his armies than the numberless youths whom Liang held under the influence of his pen,' one of Liang's translators contended. A man who later became a diplomat recalled that Liang's 'sharp pen and overflowing emotion deeply moved me.' He 'stimulated my patriotic fervor,' said a later government official; he was a

---

[133] Liang Ch'i-ch'ao, the cantonised form of pronunciation, equals Liang Qichao in Mandarin. Hummel (2010).

[134] For quoting *Quod Omnes Tangit*, the original text of Liang Qichao is "我住在此地, 就要管此地的事。为什么呢?因为和我有利害关系", meaning "I live here, so I'll govern the local affair, because it touches my interest", see Liang (2014), p. 44; Liang (2015), p. 18. Liang's work quoting *Quod Omnes Tangit* was first published in 1919, see Liang (2014), p. 221.

[135] In order not to interrupt the fluency of Liang Qichao's biography, the author chooses to draw a sketch of his early life from the following literatures and organize the materials into the following paragraph. Shen and Wu (2015), p. 27; Huang (1969), pp. 61–105; Shin (1980), pp. 105–106; Liang (1959), pp. 98–102; Spengler (1974), pp. 110–127.

[136] In order not to interrupt the fluency of Liang Qichao's biography, the author chooses to draw a sketch of his early life from the following literatures and organize the materials into this paragraph. Shen and Wu (2015), p. 27; Huang (1969), pp. 61–105; Shin (1980), pp. 105–106; Liang (1959), pp. 98–102; Spengler (1974), pp. 110–127.

[137] Teng and Fairbank (1979), p. 220.

'fountain of wisdom' (a college dean); his writings 'completely capped the times' (a historian). A general wrote that he had decided to enter the military profession after reading Liang; a Buddhist leader resolved to 'save the world through Buddha' after reading him; a literary critic writing in the 1950s claimed that 'every Chinese intellectual in the last fifty years has been influenced by Liang Qichao.' The philosopher Hu Shi wrote that Liang's essays were 'capable of making us dance, of making us weep, of arousing us to a determined enthusiasm.' For the Chinese in the first years of this century, Liang's writings were the window on all that was modern and foreign and might be used to save China. He introduced new ways of thinking about literature, history, international relations, science, religion, language, the races of mankind, and the meaning of life. For political thinkers, his work defined the tradition within which later Chinese debates over democracy took place."[138] Nathan's words are not as exaggerated as they seem to be.

Now we move to the part that concerned *Quod Omnes Tangit*. The context of Liang's quoting Quod Omnes Tangit was Liang's expedition with several other scholars to Europe by sea from 1918 to 1920,[139] during which Liang recorded what he saw and thought. The following re-emergence of this context is based on Liang Qichao's works.[140] Liang was a little surprised that the scene he saw during the trip was identical to that on the Chinese continent, especially in Canton Province and Fujian Province, the two coastal provinces. In Singapore, he found that the miner, the worker in rubber plantation, the salesman and the beggar were all Chinese people. The total number was several million, or, put in other words, even outweighed the number of the earliest migrants to the Americas. To his dismay, these Chinese people did not establish a new country, although their motivation was the same as that of the migrant to the Americas, as it was hard to sustain a life in the homeland, so they went overseas to seek a new life.[141] Liang and the other scholars regarded this as shameful. Furthermore, the people in the mainland, where the population amounted to 40 billion, as Liang Qichao wrote, had never thought of establishing their own country, not to mention these several million outsiders.[142] The only reason, Liang Qichao concluded, was grounded in a principle he once mentioned, that is, "I live here, so I'll govern the local affairs, because it touches my interest."[143] This narration resembles the content of *Quod Omnes Tangit*. However, Liang Qichao, like many other Chinese scholars, including his teacher Kang Youwei, wrote their essays in a quite casual style—involving not their attitude but the sense of academic standardization. There were quotation marks but no sources or references, and as such, any possible clue leading to Codex Civil or Magna Carta

[138] Nathan (1985), pp. 47–48.

[139] Liang (1992), pp. 429–452.

[140] Liang (2006), pp. 429–452; Liang (2006), pp. 290–291.

[141] Liang (1992), pp. 429–430; Liang (2006), pp. 290–291

[142] Liang (1992), p. 430; Liang (2006), p. 291.

[143] Liang's original Chinese text is "我住在此地，就要管此地的事。为什么呢?因为和我有利害关系". Liang (1992), pp. 429–430; Liang (2006), pp. 290–291.

was lost. Nevertheless, it could be confirmed that Liang adopted this principle from Europe, and this principle exercised great influence on his thinking. In Liang's eyes, the Chinese had never known or recognized this principle; otherwise, they might have already founded a number of countries. With regards to the domestic affairs, it was more of the responsibilities of the people in mainland, the reason lay also in this principle: "I live here, so I'll manage the local affairs, because it involves my interest."[144] Liang pointed out that it could possibly be a lifelong mission of some ambitious youth to spread this thought, which was a great way to serve the motherland.[145]

Not only did Liang Qichao mention this principle in this essay, but he also referred to it in another essay in the same book during the same tour, in which he chose 13 subtitles under the theme, such as the self-awareness of the Chinese people, to discuss current affairs at that time. The tenth, local autonomous rule or self-government, he narrated as follows:

> The tenth, a home truth, is the local self-government. Not until I traveled to Europe and investigated it on the spot this time did I know that European countries had achieved 'city government' and magnified the power of the government. Originally speaking, people are entitled to the rights to participate in local public affairs, and the right extends to centralization; thus, it becomes the democratic politics of the whole country. They bear a doctrine in mind: 'I live here, and I must manage the local affairs. Why? Because it involves my interest.' It is the same to a local government, also to the central authority. Therefore, the interest in and the sense of responsibility for politics is generated naturally and automatically – patriotism is not to be taught.[146]

Liang Qichao then compared the situation in China with that in Europe. Thinking about how unaware the Chinese people were about their own rights, he let out a heartfelt sigh.[147] From these two essays, it could be concluded that the principle Liang Qichao mentioned was a written creed originating from Europe because when he referred to it twice, he used quotation marks, and the words were the same. In addition, Liang Qichao fully realized the importance of the principle for political development in Europe and its contribution to democracy.[148] Considering the meaning of this principle, it is very likely to be *Quod Omnes Tangit*. Nevertheless, not only can the source of the principle mentioned by Liang Qichao not be confirmed, but the exact meaning of *Quod Omnes Tangit* and the other principle also slightly differ: *Quod Omnes Tangit* declares the rights of all from the macro level, while the other expresses the right of individuals from the micro level. However, it can be inferred that these two separate principles are, in fact, only one owing to their striking resemblance and the background information presented.

---

[144] Liang (1992), pp. 429–430; Liang (2006), pp. 290–291.

[145] Liang (1992), p. 430; Liang (2006), p. 291.

[146] Liang (2006), P. 281.

[147] Liang (2006), pp. 290–291.

[148] Liang (2006), p. 281; Liang (2006), p. 291.

Liang plays an indispensable role not only in this thesis but also in Chinese history.[149] Although, on the one hand, the style of Liang Qichao's articles is not purely academic, this contributed, on the other hand, to the feasible and wide acceptance from the common people.[150] Liang is such "a powerful and emotional writer"[151] that some of his big and empty words may seem to be somewhat absurd today, but it may well be the reason why at those special moments, when they were confronted with the crisis of their nation, the patriotic sentiment sleeping at the bottom of the common people's hearts was thoroughly awakened and echoed what he had written.[152]

Liang mentioned not only *Quod Omnes Tangit*, as already illustrated, but also Tianxia Wei Gong. As a master of Chinese classics, there is no doubt that Liang Qichao was familiar with Li Gi. In his completed works, *Yin Bing Shi He Ji*[153] quoted Tianxia Wei Gong to promote a more open and tolerated attitude toward foreign countries.[154]

In addition, he mentioned "Tianxia Xingwang, Pifu You Ze" in Volume II to argue for the establishment of schools for women.[155] In Volume I, he quoted Gu Yanwu to argue for the necessity to establish schools for children, writing that "Gu Tinglin has once said, the prosperousness or the collapsing of Tianxia, although ordinary men have only low social status, they share the responsibility [Pifu You Ze], too."[156]

In Volume 33,

> The key to wiping out our national shame lies in changing mindset...There are a lot of people. If we have to change everyone, it is almost impossible. I should not ask other ones. I should only ask myself. This is what Gu Tinglin said, Tianxia Xingwang, Pifu You Ze.[157]

---

[149]Teng and Fairbank (1979), p. 220.

[150]Teng and Fairbank (1979), p. 220.

[151]Teng and Fairbank (1979), p. 220.

[152]Teng and Fairbank (1979), p. 220.

[153]Yin Bing Shi is the name of Liang Qichao's private library, where he daily studies and writes, thus he was sometimes called the Host of Yin Bing Shi 饮冰室主人. Many Chinese scholars have such libraries with a name having a meaning that can represent their noble characters. Their works will thus also be named after their libraries.

[154]Liang (2015), vol. 2, p. 181: "天下为公, 选贤与能, 讲信修睦。" (Tianxia was for common good and owned by all. Able and virtuous personage was selected, and man kept promise and peace. Trans. by the author).

[155]Liang (2015), vol. 2, pp. 151, 152: "天下兴亡, 匹夫有责, 昌而明之, 推而广之。" (The prosperousness or the collapsing of Tianxia, although ordinary men have only low social status, they share the responsibility, too. [This spirit should be] explained and advocated. Trans. by the author.).

[156]Liang (2015), vol. 1, p. 45: "顾炎武曰, 有亡国, 有亡天下" (Gu Yanwu said, there is the collapsing of a nation and the collapsing of Tianxia. Trans. by the author) Liang Qichao thought that if Children Education were not promoted, it would be catastrophic.

[157]Liang (2015), vol. 12, p. 3273: "今欲国耻之一洒, 其在我辈之自新......夫我辈则多矣。欲尽人而自新, 云胡可致。我勿问他人, 问我而已。斯乃真顾亭林所谓天下兴亡匹夫有责也。" ("The key to wipe out our national shame lies in changing mindset...There are a lot of

Gu Tinglin; more famous by another name, Gu Yanwu; was a significant intellectual in the late Ming Dynasty[158] who profoundly influenced Liang Qichao and Sun Yat-sen. In this book, Liang Qichao clearly referred to Gu Yanwu as the author's name. However, to some degree, Liang Qichao has also changed and newly interpreted the words of Gu Yanwu, at least the original focus of the author. Gu Yanwu wrote in one of his most famous works ("Ri Zhi Lu", with English translation as "Record of Daily Knowledge"):

> There is the collapsing of a nation and the collapsing of Tianxia. How to distinguish them? The change of dynasties with the altering of the name of the nation are called the collapsing of a nation; when justice and humanity degenerate, beasts are led to eat humans and even human take their own species for food, which can be called the collapsing of Tianxia...To defend a nation is the responsibility of the Kaiser and his officials; to safeguard Tianxia, ordinary men, despite the commonness of whom, all share responsibilities.[159]

Liang Qichao's interpretation elaborated on the differences and collapses of nations and Tianxia but concentrated on civilians' participation in public and political affairs,[160] which was emphasized by both scholars. The reasons why Liang did so stem from the fact that he wanted to reserve a possibility for the remains and consistency of the Qing dynasty and to integrate it into his thinking system of a constitutional monarchy.[161] What he found more urgent was the enhancement of the Chinese people's awareness of politics and the improvement of individual quality; otherwise, he would not have chosen the name of Xinmin (enlighten the people)[162] for one of the newspapers edited by him.[163]

---

people. If we have to change everyone, it is almost impossible. I should not ask other ones. I should only ask myself. This is what Gu Tinglin said, Tianxia Xingwang, Pifu You Ze." Trans. by the author.) Liang (2015), vol. 5, p. 2778; Chen (2015), http://www.cssn.cn/wx/wx_bh/201506/t20150605_2023840.shtml Accessed 27 Feb 2018.

[158] Gu (2017), p. 1.

[159] Gu (1990), p. 590. "有亡国, 有亡天下, 亡国与亡天下奚辩?曰:易姓改号, 谓之亡国;仁义充塞而至于率兽食人，人将相食，谓之亡天下......保国者，其君其臣、肉食者谋之;保天下者，匹夫之贱，与有责焉耳矣!"Trans. by the author. For another translation, see Gu (2017), pp. 103–104: "There is loss of the kingdom and there is loss of [the moral basis] of the world. How may these two things be distinguished? It is said that a change in the family name of the emperor and in the reign period constitutes loss of the kingdom. However, when ren 仁 [loving-kindness, benevolence, humanity] and yi 義 [right action, righteousness, duty] are entirely obstructed, it comes to a point where beasts are led on to devour men and men to devour one another. It is this that is referred to as loss of the moral basis of the world...For this reason, it is necessary to know how to protect all under heaven before it is possible to know how to protect the state. Protecting the state is something that is planned by the ruler, ministers, and high officials. Protecting all under heaven is the responsibility of every man, even the meanest."

[160] Teng and Fairbank (1979), p. 220.

[161] Teng and Fairbank (1979), p. 220.

[162] "Xinmin", adopting Pinyin system, equals "Hsin-min" (Wade-Giles system) in Teng and Fairbank's book. Teng and Fairbank (1979), p. 220.

[163] Teng and Fairbank (1979), p. 220.

Liang Qichao devoted his lifetime to contemplating the following question: Which form of government should China adopt? Influenced by his mentor, Kang Youwei, he supported a constitutional monarchy from 1895 to 1898.[164] However, after the emperor abdicated, he fled to Japan and read many Japanese versions of Western works and became a supporter of the parliament republic.[165] It was maybe then that he encountered the concept of *Quod Omnes Tangit* for the first time. At any rate, *Quod Omnes Tangit* and his new interpretation of Tianxia Wei Gong, Tianxia Xingwang, and Pifu You Ze became part of his thinking and exercised great influence on his future works and thus on the common people at that time.

3.3.2.1.3 From Sun Yat-Sen (1866–1925)

Sun, the Father of Modern China, was one of the most important interpreters of Tianxia Wei Gong.[166] He integrated Tianxia Wei Gong into his political thinking and left many calligraphic works writing the four characters of Tianxia Wei Gong.[167]

Sun Yat-Sen led the Xinhai Revolution and successfully toppled the Qing Dynasty in 1911. Consequently, he was conceived as the father of modern China both in the mainland and in Taiwan. His impact, however, is not confined to the effect of revolution. The political leaders of the Chinese Communist Party and of Taiwan both claim to have developed his "The Three Principles of the People."[168] Sun's thinking has also influenced political leaders in other Third World countries such as Indonesia, Vietnam and the Philippines.[169] Schiffrin gave a reason why Sun became a revolutionist, with which Viechtbauer and Wegmann also agreed, stating that Sun did not initially belong to the elite class; hence, he wanted to unite the working-class Chinese overseas first and saw hope in revolution instead of in petition.[170]

Sun could be regarded as one of the most significant figures who supported the principle of Tianxia Wei Gong. In his speech in 1924 on the theme of Three People's Principles, he narrated that the real three people's principles lay in the world of the Da Tong, which is an ideal society and was first described by Confucius: When the Grand Course was pursued, a public and common spirit ruled all under the sky.[171] It is unlikely that the maxim was more than a rhetorical ornament in Sun's speech because his ideal, goal, and basic spirit are truly condensed in the maxim. Tianxia Wei Gong also seemed to be his favorite phrase in his life, which Sun wrote 32 times

[164] See also Teng and Fairbank (1979), p. 220.

[165] Teng and Fairbank (1979), p. 220.

[166] Sun (1986), p. 262; Sun (1942), p. 106.

[167] Sun (1986), p. 262; Sun (1942), p. 106.

[168] Teng and Fairbank (1979), p. 260.

[169] Wells (2001), p. xi, 171.

[170] Schiffrin (1968), p. 40; Viechtbauer and Wegmann (1969), p. 115.

[171] Wang (2003), p. 57.

as the calligraphic works sent to the privileged.[172] It is no exaggeration to say that Tianxia Wei Gong is the lifelong pursuit of Sun, which could be tracked both in his theory and practice.[173]

Sun's most significant political theory is Three Principles of the People 三民主义. They are the principle of nationalism, the principle of democracy and the principle of livelihood, corresponding to the Chinese words Minzu 民族, Minquan 民权 and Minsheng 民生.[174] "Min" 民 in Chinese means "the people"; thus, the theory was called the Three Principles of the People, basically entailing the main points about which the people were most concerned: the reconstruction of the political and social system in a postrevolutionary time.

With regard to liberty, Sun meant to provide a solution or a target to enable China to become an equal of the great powers in the world, independent and free from harassment outside.[175] The first maxim of the Three People's principle is also related to the maxim of Tianxia Wei Gong because each country should be equal as well, and no one should be dominated by others. Sun did not explicitly lay the focus of Tianxia Wei Gong on nations, but, in fact, the concentration of his interpretation transferred from individual to nation. As such, this indicated a trend that one could resort to China's ancient virtues to illustrate the essence of some modern Western political principles. In his lecture on nationalism delivered on March 2, 1924, Sun retrospectively reviewed China's ancient virtues, such as loyalty, kindness, love, honesty, justice, harmony and peace, stating that they should not be discarded.[176] Only in this way could China revive the national spirit in the process of modernization, which would qualify China as a great world power with ancient morality and love for peace.[177]

Specifically, Sun Yat-sen adopted Tianxia Wei Gong to elaborate the second maxim of the Three People's Principle. It is in his lectures about the principle of democracy that he explicitly quoted the maxim, saying "When the Great Doctrine prevails, all under heaven will work for the common good."[178] Moreover, he embedded the maxim with concrete meaning so far as to bridge a gap between theory and practice. Although it is not enough, he certainly and made it more maneuverable than ever before in a way that was unprecedented. In his first lecture about the principle of democracy, he raised the concept of "Minquan," meaning the power of people.[179] He elaborated upon power as sovereignty and argued that a unified body of men was called 'a people' and that sovereignty was the power to execute orders and to regulate public conduct. It was not until then that 'Tianxia'

---

[172] Wang (2003), p. 57.

[173] Zhou and Liu (2008), pp. 39–42.

[174] Sun (1986), pp. 183–184; Sun (1942), p. 3; Cf. Wells (2001), pp. 61–97.

[175] Sun (1986), p. 184; Sun (1942), p. 3; Wells (2001), p. 62.

[176] Sun (1986), pp. 241–247; Sun (1942), p. 76–83; Wells (2001), p. 67.

[177] Sun (1986), pp. 251–253; Sun (1942), pp. 88–92; Wells (2001), pp. 67, 68.

[178] Sun (1986), p. 262; Sun (1942), p. 106.

[179] Teng and Fairbank (1979), p. 259.

was, for the first time, explained as sovereignty, and the subject to exercise this power was defined as all people. With this explanation, 'Tianxia' is no longer ambiguous. He harbored a belief that in 1924, the world was bound to move into an era of democracy, and republicanism was the only way to unite China. Regarding people, equal political rights should be given to everyone. Thus, his chief concern consisted of improving the lives of the disadvantaged and inspiring people with great ability to serve others with their talents; however, not all citizens were aware of that. To solve this problem, Sun provided a solution: the distinction between sovereignty and ability,[180] which was, at the time, treated as a defect. He also compared the government to the chauffeur of an automobile and people to the owner of the automobile.[181] Moreover, government being an executive machine, there should be a five-power constitution consisting of executive, legislature, judiciary, censorship, and civil service examinations, the last of which was duplicated by Great Britain.[182] At the same time, the people must have the four popular rights: suffrage, recall, initiation of legislation and referenda, functioning as people's right to confine direct democracy.[183]

Weaknesses in this thinking can be easily perceived. Difficult questions for Sun would be raised effortlessly; for instance, how could the owner of a vehicle know better where to go when he himself has no idea about the traffic condition? In fact, if only the chauffeur knows how to drive, how could the owner of an automobile restrict the behavior of the chauffer? These insoluble questions suggest innate conflicts inside Sun's mind, which remained unsolved until his death, the paradox of elitism and populism. Audrey Wells thought that on the one hand, Sun was totally excited about the idea of equal rights and would like to advocate the entitlement of the rights as election, initiation of legislation, referenda and recall to everyone, including the Chinese coolies and peasants; on the other hand, Sun granted in the Program for National Reconstruction the four sovereign rights to the National Assembly or People's Congress, composed of representatives from each district.[184] Chester Tan commented that in the end, the People's Congress was able to grab sovereignty from the people, which Sun meant to delegate to the people through direct democracy.[185] The distinguishing and separation of sovereignty and ability resembled the differentiation of capacity in civil rights and civil conduct. Every mentally healthy adult should have both, even at the national level. Thus, this theory of Sun's has proved to be in error.

His simple metaphor showed how he tried to make his theory comprehensible to his uneducated audience. Audrey Wells provided three factors that may result in the deficiency of his theory: first, the narrations about the Three Principles of People

[180] Sun (1986), pp. 331, 347; Sun (1942), pp. 195, 214.

[181] Sun (1986), p. 331; Sun (1942), p. 195.

[182] Sun (1986), p. 352; Sun (1942), p. 220.

[183] Sun (1986), p. 352; Sun (1942), p. 220.

[184] Wells (2001), pp. 82–84.

[185] Tan (1971), p. 133.

were delivered in Sun's 16 lectures; then, the manuscript was destroyed by a bombardment of Sun's headquarters in Guangzhou; third, Sun's cancer harmed his thinking and expression as a lecturer.[186]

With all these obstacles and due to the inner fault of Sun's San Min Zhuyi, it is not surprising that some scholars treated Sun's theory dismissively. Donald W. Treadgold thought Sun's slogan was derived from the West as a hodgepodge[187]; Schiffrin seemed to have a balanced assessment.[188] It is necessary, however, to admit that regarding Sun's Three Principles of the People, as Marie-Claire Begère pointed out, they have "never been rated as one of the great works of contemporary Chinese thought."[189] In contrast, Audrey Wells thought "it is likely that Sun's ideas have significance even now and not just for China."[190] Richard Wilhelm referred to Sun's thought as follows:

"The greatness of Sun Yat-sen rests, therefore, upon the fact that he has found a living synthesis between the fundamental principles of Confucianism and the demands of modern times, a synthesis which, beyond the borders of China, can again become significant."[191] No matter how the impact of the three principles of people will be measured, it is clear that with Sun's interpretation Tianxia Wei Gong became more famous and embraced more implications. In addition, the maxim found itself again revived in history. The research on Sun Yat-sen and his thinking seems to have no end, as seen in the life of the maxim Tianxia Wei Gong.

3.3.2.1.4 From Huang Zongxi (1610–1695)

Huang Zongxi was one of the most prominent Chinese thinkers in the seventeenth century[192] and wrote on political themes, although the Qing government did not approve of scholars doing this.[193] It is heatedly debated whether his thinking could already have been subordinate to democracy. This is not discussed here; rather, his interpretation of Tianxia Wei Gong is concentrated on. In his representative work, Min I Dai Fang Lu[194]《明夷待访录》, the tenets of this work originated from two classics: one of them is a thesis of Mencius, "Min Gui Jun Qing" 民贵君轻, saying that the people are more important than the ruler[195]; the other is Tianxia Wei Gong in

[186] Wells (2001), p. 61.

[187] Treadgold (1973), p. 95, cited in Wells (2001), p. xiii.

[188] Schiffrin (1980), p. 26; Schiffrin (1968), pp. 1–9; cited in Wells (2001), p. xiv.

[189] Begère (1998), p. 381; cited in Wells (2001), p. xiv.

[190] Wells (2001), p. xv.

[191] Wilhelm (1931), p. 8, cited in Wells (2001), p. xiii.

[192] Xu (2011), p. 137. For Huang's introduction, see Hummel (2010), pp. 351–354.

[193] Schmidt-Glintzer (1990), p. 451; Xu (2011), p. 137.

[194] Huang (1993), p. 5.

[195] Mencius (1895), p. 483.

the Book of Rites, Liji.[196] He raised the point that "Tianxia Wei Zhu, Jun Wei Ke" 天下为主, 君为客, "In ancient times all-under-Heaven were considered the master, and the prince was the tenant," meaning that the prince should serve the people.[197] At the very beginning of one of the articles in his book, "On the Prince"原君, he wrote, "[i]n the beginning of human life each man lived for himself and looked to his own interests."有生之初, 人各自私也, 人各自利也。[198] Furthermore, "[i]f there had been no rulers, each man would have provided for himself and looked to his own interests."向使无君, 人各得自私也, 人各得自利也。[199] Even if the prince can try very hard, "still the cleverness of one man is no match for the greed of all."一人之智力不能胜天下欲得之者之众。.[200]

In Li Gi, the meaning of Tianxia Wei Gong was rather ambiguous. It is by the interpretation of Huang Zongxi that this maxim, for the first time, runs clearly against the emperor. However, it can still be argued that Huang Zongxi opposed only the emperor, not the monarchy. Regardless of this limitation, he has undoubtedly taken one step forward.

3.3.2.1.5 Gu Yanwu (1613—1682)

The time in which Gu Yanwu[201] was born, the Ming Dynasty, witnessed a historical change in which traditional Chinese society started to experience early modernization. The place where Gu Yanwu lived, the region of Jiangnan, belonged to the most developed area from the perspective of the commodity economy and withheld the strongest sprout of modernization elements.[202] The most prominent characteristic of that epoch is Tianxia Dashi Pianzhong Zai Shang, 天下之势偏重在商, the trend of the world leads to commerce.[203]

Under such an atmosphere, citizens were united with intellectuals in Jiangnan to fight against the ruler exploiting their interests. Donglin Party is organization stemming from them.[204] In 1604, several intellectuals revived Donglin College, gathering every month to discuss academic problems and political affairs.[205] The motto of Donglin College is quite famous in China: "the sounds of wind, rain, and reading come all into our ears; the affairs of home, state and the world are all taken

[196] Confucius (1994), p. 815, ch. 9. Cf. Teng and Fairbank (1979), pp. 7–8.

[197] Huang (1993), p. 92; Huang (1995), pp. 466–467.

[198] Huang (1993), p. 91; Huang (1995), pp. 466–467.

[199] Huang (1993), p. 92; Huang (1995), pp. 466–467.

[200] Huang (1993), p. 93; Huang (1995), pp. 466–467.

[201] For Gu Yanwu's life, see Gu (2017), pp. 1–11; Hummel (2010), pp. 421–426.

[202] Xu (2006), p. 3.

[203] Shen (2002), p. 664.

[204] Bary and Bloom (1999), pp. 916–919; for a detailed introduction of Donglin Academy, see Busch (1949), pp. 1–163; Xu (2006), p. 16.

[205] Hu (2015), pp. 119–121; Elman (1989), pp. 379–418.

care of by us."[206] It is not that hard to read out the sense of responsibility of the Donglin Party, and what they mean is not that far away from the message of *Quod Omnes Tangit*. If their motto were not convincing enough, the points they raised to explain their political pursuit and debate with the court officials would be identical to *Quod Omnes Tangit*, even more than that of Tianxia Wei Gong, because they expressed that 以众论定国是, which means state affairs should be decided by all people. 众论means "what most people said." On this subject, the members of the Donglin party debated heatedly with the court officials. Zhao Nanxing proposed that the only standard by which to judge and decide state affairs is public opinion—what most people said, regardless of whether this opinion matches the emperor's own thought. Without public opinion there are no state affairs. The emperor is not entitled to choose the public opinion that most satisfies him.[207] Miu Changqi put it even further, which should have inspired the people in early modern China and even today. In his opinion, all affairs have right and wrong. When two sides are involved in a discussion, one side can be right, the other wrong, but in this situation, the result can only be called "different," not Gong, public; the other possibility is that two sides are either right or wrong, but it still cannot be called Gong, rather "the same." Therefore, the emperor's opinion cannot substitute that of the officials or the public. For Miu Changqi, the truth lies in the opinion of 愚夫愚妇, the "foolish men and women." The officials should be the delegates of the citizens.[208] Gu Xiancheng argued that what the official said to support the rules was merely aimed at banning public opinion to realize one person's private goods.[209] He attached much importance to the communication tunnel, which was lacking in the concept of Tianxia Wei Gong. He argued that the unobstructed traffic of opinions was essential to solving state affairs.[210]

As Gu Yanwu was against the Qing Dynasty and always tried to restore the old Ming Dynasty, his interpretation of Tianxia Wei Gong tended to be nationalism: "保国者, 其君其臣、肉食者谋之；保天下者, 匹夫之贱, 与有责焉耳矣。".[211]

> Protecting the state is something that is planned by the ruler, ministers, and high officials. Protecting all under heaven is the responsibility of every man, even the meanest.[212]

It is a pity that sometimes the phrase would be translated into "Everyone has a duty to his country." The better translation would be "for the prosperousness or the collapsing of Tianxia, although ordinary men have only low social status, they share the responsibility, too." Gu Yanwu differentiated the fall of a country and

[206] Chinese original text: 风声、雨声、读书声, 声声入耳;家事、国事、天下事, 事事关心。.

[207] Zhao (1985), p. 8.

[208] Miu (1637), pp. 391–392.

[209] Gu (2002), p. 11.

[210] Gu (1987), p. 10.

[211] Gu (1990), p. 590.

[212] Gu (2017), p. 104.

that of the whole world.[213] As explained before, 天下means the world. In Gu's mind, the collapse of a dynasty is not that dramatic; it is merely the change of the name of a dynasty, which should be cared for by officials; it is the collapse of the world that counts, whose responsibility should be shared by all people, even by the people in the lowest social class.[214]

3.3.2.1.6 Lü Kun (1536–1618)

Lü Kun was an official in the Ming Dynasty who was born in 1536.[215] He went to Sishu, the school in ancient China, in the sixth year, showing his extraordinary competence to comprehend intricate and obscure books. His early well-educated years of life paved the way for him to be an official.

The main idea of Lü Kun's political thinking is 以理抗势, meaning adopting the truth to defend against power.[216] 势means the power the emperor and the other nobles have; 理 means political principles and the public willingness of all people, similar to 礼 in ancient times, which also embraces a moral character. He emphasized that principles are decided through the public, whose power should be shared with everyone.[217] For Lü Kun, principle rather than power is the utmost priority in judging everything. Principle legitimates the power of the emperor. When the power of the emperor conflicts with principles, the latter precedes the former. Not only 儒者, intellectuals of Confucianism, but also 匹夫匹妇, the most common men and women, should carry on this principle because it is the people who grasp the rightness and truth in their hands who are the most noble.[218] When it comes to truth, there is nothing more respectable or humble. Truth can genuinely convince people, while power can merely coerce people into executing commands, the latter of which is no different than a robber.[219]

It is worth considering that truth overriding power was not first proposed by Lü Kun but consisted of the thinking of Confucius. Confucius raised the point in Lun Yu, one of the Four Books, that the ministers should execute the commands of the emperor under the instruction of principles.[220] Mencius put forward this opinion as "以德抗位," adopting morality to resist power from higher positions.[221] However,

---

[213] See also Bell (2014), pp. 33–54.

[214] Gu (2017), pp. 103–104.

[215] Ma (2011), p. 1.

[216] Ma (2011), p. 63.

[217] Lü (1991), p. 43: The Tao, the public principle of the ancient and modern worlds, in which everyone has a share. ("道者, 天下古今公共之理, 人人都有分底。").

[218] Lü (1991), p. 64; See Ma (2011), p. 65: "Only those who know the Tao are the most noble in heaven and earth." ("天地间人惟得道者贵"。).

[219] Lü (1991), p. 43.

[220] Confucius (1980), p. 124, ch. 11. Ma (2011), p. 67.

[221] Ma (2011), p. 67.

as the author of Lü Kun's biography put it, the above ideas sound developed and precious compared with other Feudal ideology but are practically weak and naïve.[222]

Hence, the right that common people are also entitled to decide what truth is constituted a significant contribution of Lü Kun to the development of political thought in Chinese history. He agreed with the opinions of the Donglin Party, saying "以天下人行天下事",[223] which is also quite similar to *Quod Omnes Tangit* because it means that it should be the responsibility of all people under heaven to manage affairs under heaven.

The thinking of Lü Kun had a great influence on that of the other intellectuals both at his time and in the future. Liang Qichao was also influenced by him and commented that the thinking of Lü Kun was characteristic of the Luo School, prosperous in Henan Province, and had, to some degree, innovated the Luo School.[224]

3.3.2.1.7 Wang Tao (1828–1897)

Wang Tao,[225] the Chinese assistant to James Legge (1815–1897, the first English translator of the Confucian classics),[226]

> had been in contact with Westerners in Shanghai and Hongkong from 1848, and formed a close association with the leading British missionary sinologist Walter H. Medhurst (1796–1857), William Muirhead and James Legge.[227]

---

[222] Ma (2011), p. 68.

[223] Xu (2006), p. 35.

[224] Ma (2011), p. 350: "Henan, or Zhongzhou, is the cradle of the nation's culture. In the Song Dynasty, Kang Jie and the two Chengs were born, and the discipline of "Luo Studies" was born. In the Yuan Dynasty, there was Xu Luzhai, and in the early Ming Dynasty, there was Xue Jingxuan, both of whom were from the same hometown and continued this line of scholarship. That is why Zhongzhou was called the capital of Lixue. After the rise of Yaojiang and Baisha, the center of the academy shifted to the southeast. In the late Ming Dynasty, there was Ningling Lv Xinwu Kun who revived the school of Luo. In ancient times, Ningling was called Sha Sui, the hometown of the two Chengs. Therefore, Ming Dao, Yichuan and Xinwu were also called 'successive Sha Sui scholar'. Xinwu's study, cultivated deeply, but specializes in the plain place. He was good at understanding things, very courageous in action, and very clever in response. It was very different from the last stream of Wang's school, which was fond of harangue. However, it was also influenced by the times, and its argument was not as roundabout as the two Chengs'. Xinwu's Luo Studies is also the new Luo Studies."("河南, 中州也, 实全国文化最初发源地。至宋, 康节、二程生焉, 于是有'洛学'之目。元则许鲁斋, 明初则薛敬轩, 咸以乡人衍其绪。故中州称理学之府焉。姚江、白沙学兴, 学界重心移于东南矣。及晚明则有宁陵吕新吾坤复兴洛学。宁陵古沙随, 即二程故里。故明道、伊川与新吾亦称'先后沙随先生'云。新吾之学、持养绵密, 而专向平实处致功。善察物情, 而勇于任事, 妙于因应。与当时王学末流之好高谈大言者异撰。然亦受时代影响, 持论不如二程之迂。新吾之洛学, 盖新洛学也。").

[225] About Wang Tao's life, see Bauer (1990), pp. 543–552; Hummel (2010), pp. 836–839.

[226] Bauer (1990), p. 546.

[227] Teng and Fairbank (1979), p. 135.

In 1867, James Legge invited Wang Tao to Scotland, after which he spent the next 2 years in Europe: in 1868, Wang Tao gave a speech at Oxford; in 1870, he returned to Hong Kong and became a famous editorial writer.[228] Among his many writings, a passage in *A Note on the British Government* is worth special attention here.[229] Although Wang Tao did not mention either *Quod Omnes Tangit* or Tianxia Wei Gong, he clearly pointed out the mysterious connection between the same epochs in two different cultures. He wrote that,

> [t]he real strength of England, however, lies in the fact that there is a sympathetic understanding between the governing and the governed, a close relationship between the ruler and the people ... My observation is that the daily domestic political life of England actually embodies the traditional ideals of our ancient Golden Age [lit., the Three Dynasties and earlier].[230]

The ancient Golden Age, the three dynasties, is exactly what Confucius said, the time "[w]hen the Grand Course was pursued."[231] Wang Tao recognized that English parliament had realized the spirits of *Quod Omnes Tangit* and Tianxia Wei Gong. Fairbank commented on him as the "[a]mong the writers who prepared the way for institutional reform in China, one of the most interesting and quixotic,"[232] with which the author cannot agree more.

It is not an easy task to search for the feeble flame of the connection between *Quod Omnes Tangit* and Tianxia Wei Gong in the writings of Chinese scholars in history, but what Liang Qichao and Wang Tao have written shone throughout the murky fog of history. The former has received sufficient attention to his thinking and his life story, while the latter should have been given more importance in academic research.

3.3.2.1.8 He Qi (1859—1914) and Hu Liyuan (1847—1916)

He Qi, a modern Chinese thinker, had an intellectual father, He Futang, who was the second Chinese priest in Christian history.[233] He Futang, also the assistant of James Legge like Wang Tao, helped the British intellectual to translate Chinese classics into English. The elder sister of He Qi, He Miaoling, married Wu Tingfang (1842–1922), the first Chinese person in history to acquire the doctor's degree in law.[234] Growing up in such a family deeply entrenched in the learnings of the West, He Qi followed his brother-in-law, becoming the second to obtain the degree of doctor in law from a Western country in Chinese history. He Qi graduated from

228 Teng and Fairbank (1979), pp. 135, 136.

229 Teng and Fairbank (1979), pp. 139–142.

230 Teng and Fairbank (1979), p. 140.

231 Confucius (1885), pp. 364–366.

232 Teng and Fairbank (1979), p. 135.

233 The biography of He Qi is based on Zhang (2011), pp. 22–29.

234 Wu (2018), p. 90.

Hong Kong College, whose name changed to Victoria College in 1889 and Queen's College in 1889. At the age of 13, he was an extraordinarily intelligent student and went to England to further his education. Three years later, He Qi entered the University of Aberdeen and spent 4 years there to attain a master's degree in medicine. Afterward, he went to study law in Lincoln's Inn and completed his studies at the age of 23 with the doctor's degree in law.[235] With such talent and a remarkable educational background, it is no wonder that He Qi could leave his mark in Chinese intellectual history.

Before elaborating upon the thinking of He Qi, another person must be mentioned: Hu Liyuan, who was a close friend of He Qi. Their relationship, in the author's view, was similar to that between Karl Marx and Friedrich Engels. Hu Liyuan once studied at Hong Kong College, too, but when he went there, he was already 15 years old.[236] Although he was enrolled in Hong Kong College at an older age, compared with He Qi, he wasted no time in the early years of his youth and immersed himself in the Chinese Classics, which laid a good foundation for cooperation with He Qi in the future. He Qi was an expert in Western learning but a layman in Chinese Classics, and he needed someone who could write better in Chinese than himself and who, at the same time, had an idea of Western learning because only in this way could more Chinese people understand him.[237] Hu Liyuan was undoubtedly a suitable candidate who was also willing to cooperate. Thus, from 1887 to 1900, He Qi and Hu Liyuan published a series of articles on contemporary political affairs, which attracted wide attention and aroused heated debate, including the one with Kang Youwei.[238]

One of the main ideas of Hu Liyuan's thinking is Da Tong. Li Henan, a friend of Hu, once wrote that Hu viewed Da Tong as truth and adhered to it for decades in writing books and giving speeches.[239] Hu Liyuan's ideal of Da Tong was not as systematic and intact as that in Kang Youwei's thinking since it was rather fragmental. He did not publish an academic work to elaborate upon Da Tong as Kang Youwei did in a complete book. Thus, Kang Youwei is more frequently studied by later scholars related to the ideal of Da Tong. Nevertheless, one scholar thought that Hu Liyuan should be seen as the first scholar to promote the ideal of Da Tong in modern China because he studied the ideal of Da Tong earlier than Kang Youwei; at the same time, the content of Hu Liyuan's Da Tong had not lost its comprehensiveness and profoundness as one theme under Kang Youwei's pen. Hu Liyuan, like Kang Youwei, also did something more than the inheritance of the ideal of Da Tong; he specified the ideas of Da Tong into these ideas of changing the political system in

[235] This paragraph is based on Zhang (2011), pp. 25–29.

[236] Zhang (2011), p. 125.

[237] Tsai (1981), p. 201.

[238] Zhang (2011), pp. 148–155.

[239] Hu (1975), p. 1, cited in Zhang (2011), P. 240.

China, realizing primary globalization and, in the end, achieving the utmost happiness of human beings.[240]

According to Zhang Liheng, in addition to the Da Tong Ideal, He Qi and Hu Liyuan also challenged the status of Kang Youwei as the first Chinese to promote the concept of civil rights. Wang Rongzu spoke highly of the contributions made by He Qi and Hu Liyuan to the emergence and development of civil rights in China.[241] According to the textual research of some scholars, the origin of "civil rights" in its Chinese version neither exists in ancient Chinese books nor is it the brainchild of Kang Youwei. Rather, it came from the Japanese translation of "democracy," revealing the connotation of "the rights of the people."[242] Zhang Liheng pointed out that two scholars, Wang Fang and Wang Renbo, questioned that opinion and held the point that there is no doubt that 民权 came from Japanese, but it is not accurate to conceive it as the Japanese translation of democracy. As is universally acknowledged and proved by a Japanese scholar, democracy is translated as 民主.[243] Thus, it is inappropriate to perceive 民权 as the translation of democracy. The question of where the word民权comes from remained unsolved until Zhang Liheng pointed out that He Qi and Hu Liyuan once provided the answer, which had not attracted the attention of the Chinese intellectual world for a long time. He Qi and Hu Liyuan wrote in 1899 that the Chinese word 民权 is the translation of "liberty."[244] They understood the word in the sense of "legal liberty." When they explained 民权, they rendered the word with some annotations with characteristics that are from typical Western thinking; on the other hand, they took the idea of 民本 from traditional Chinese thinking to decrease the tension emerging from this brand-new thinking.

They were not alone in doing so, but it was then a turning point from the whole history of the new interpretation of Tianxia Wei Gong to see that the concept of "right" was added to complete and explicate its meaning. He Qi and Hu Liyuan declared that:

天子之权, 得诸庶民。

This means that the rights of the emperor come from the people. The reason why we consider the addition of the concept of right to the maxim Tianxia Wei Gong as a turning point lies in the comparison of that maxim with *Quod Omnes Tangit*. "Right"

---

[240] Zhang (2011), pp. 243–245.

[241] Wang (1983), p. 40.

[242] Wei and Chen (1995), p. 24.

[243] Sanetou (1983), P. 338.

[244] Hu (1975), pp. 21–22: "The translation of 'liberty' as 'freedom' began in Japan. Although the meaning of the western language is not exhausted, it can be said that the word 'liberty' is included with the word 'civil rights'. It is a pity that the translator of the word 'liberty' is not able to investigate the commonality between the Chinese and the foreign reasoning, so that the reader may mistakenly guess the meaning of the word." ("'里勃而特'译为自由者, 自日本始。虽未能尽西语之意, 然以二字包括之, 亦可谓能举其大由。自由二字而译为民权者, 此必中国学士大夫读日本所译者为之, 其以民权二字译'里勃而特'一语, 吾无间然, 独惜译之者于中外之理未能参究其同, 阅之者或至误猜其意。").

is a rather abstract concept lying behind these two maxims and an even more abstract one in Tianxia Wei Gong. People failed to recognize it if it was not explicitly declared. Thus, He Qi and Hu Liyuan made a great contribution to the development of Chinese political thinking.

What they explained about 民权 conforms half to *Quod Omnes Tangit*, half to majority rule:

> Everyone has the tendency to adore the good and resent the evil, and everyone has the right to reward the good and punish the crime. However, when rewards and punishments are decided by one individual, there tends to be bias; when they are decided by the public, there is always justice. Thus, the right to decide rewards and punishments should be given to the public. Civil rights are the rights of the people.[245]

He Qi and Hu Liyuan not only raised the conception of rights but also envisaged how the institution could realize their political thinking, which is another ambiguous part of Tianxia Wei Gong. He Qi's 10 years as a foreign student in England allowed him to witness the growth of English parliament, which might have had a profound influence on his political thinking. Hence, He Qi and Hu Liyuan spared no effort to promote the establishment of a parliament. The following words can be found in their books:

"The promotion of new political measures must include the establishment of a parliament, and the senators must be elected by the public."[246] This thinking differentiates He Qi and Hu Liyuan from Yangwu Pai 洋务派,[247] whose slogan is 中体西用 (Chinese Learning as Substance, Western Learning for Application), arguing that China only needs Western techniques without a Western political system.

Referring to the election qualification, He Qi and Hu Liyuan said that "Any man older than twenty years old, except those who are disabled and illiterate, can be given the right of election,"[248] showing the advancement of their thinking to some extent.

In summary, the thinking of He Qi and Hu Liyuan belongs in the history of the new interpretation of Tianxia Wei Gong and Chinese politics. Hu Liyuan expressed Da Tong earlier than Kang Youwei did. Bearing the differences between China and

---

[245] Hu (1975), p. 22: "Everyone has a heart for good and evil, that is, everyone has the right to reward good and punish evil. However, if we consider individual opinion, it is easy to involve selfishness, but if we consider the opinion of all people, it is always fair. Therefore, if we want to exercise the right to reward good and punish evil with the heart of good and evil, it is better to seek the right of all people, and the people's right is the right of all people." ("人人有好善恶恶之心, 即人人有赏善罚恶之权。然就一人之见而定, 则易涉私心, 就众人之见而观, 则每存公道, 是故以好善恶恶之心, 行赏善罚恶之权者, 莫若求之于众, 民权者以众得权之谓也。").

[246] Hu (1975), p. 13: "新政之行必设议院, 而议员俱由民众公举。" ("The promotion of new political measures must include the establishment of a parliament, and the senators must be elected by the public.").

[247] For details of Yangwu Yundong 洋务运动, also called 自强运动, the Self-strenthening Movement, see Hsü (2000), P. 277–291.

[248] Hu (1975), p. 8: "All men over twenty years of age, except those who are dumb, blind, deaf, or disabled, and those who can read and understand, shall be given the right of public election." ("凡男子二十岁以上, 除暗哑盲聋以及残疾者外, 其人能读书明理者, 则予以公举之权。").

the West in mind, He Qi and Hu Liyuan clarified the abstract conception of "civil right" and envisaged an institution to realize their political ideals, which bridged the gap between Tianxia Wei Gong and *Quod Omnes Tangit*.

3.3.2.2 Quod Omnes Tangit

This chapter aims to collect as many figures, texts and occasions relating to *Quod Omnes Tangit* as possible, and this work has been given excellent examples by some scholars thus far, as mentioned in the literature review of this thesis. Nevertheless, two issues should be considered. First, scholars repeated some cases and neglected others. This is not necessarily negative because the cases chosen should naturally serve our own objective; thus, scholars can choose various cases according to their differentiated themes, yet it is inconvenient to sometimes read the same cases repeatedly and sometimes to have the other cases scattered in the texts of different authors. This thesis attempts to present a complete collection of cases mentioning *Quod Omnes Tangit*; however, given that this collection is not intact but well ordered, it will still be carefully referred to and relied on, preventing a waste of academic resources. The second issue is that almost all existing studies on *Quod Omnes Tangit* focus on how this principle, born from Roman law, evolved into a principle of consent and representation, which is important but lacks innovation. This thesis sorts the cases into two groups: pope and king quoting *Quod Omnes Tangit* and academics discussing *Quod Omnes Tangit*. The significance of this classification lies in later comparing *Quod Omnes Tangit* with Tianxia Wei Gong, showing already one difference that the figures quoting the principles had different social status.

3.3.2.2.1 From Pope and King

Innocent III (1198–1216) is a significant figure quoting *Quod Omnes Tangit*. Yves Congar, in his thesis focusing on the historical origin and development of *Quod Omnes Tangit*, documented three instances of Innocent III quoting the maxim.[249] In the opening, Congar introduced a decretal of Innocent III without an exact date, expressing that "the bishops alone can neither nominate nor dismiss a dean, instead, this kind of issue must be co-decided by bishops and archdeacons, because a dean is in charge of both prelates," the reason for which is "what touches all, must be agreed by all."[250] The second occasion of Innocent III quoting *Quod Omnes Tangit* was "in 1206 in the answer to Constantinople Latin patriarchs, recalling the postulate of every judicial department: no judge with the absence of invitation and conviction of

[249] Congar (1980), p. 115, 117, 122.

[250] C. 7, X, I, 23 (Friedberg, II, Col. 152); Potthast (1874), vol. I, Col. 5031, p. 442; cited in Congar (1980), P. 115. Trans. by the author.

parties, except for default."[251] The third occasion was the papal bull *Vineam Domini* on April 19, 1213, in which Innocent III invited bishops, abbots and priors to the Fourth Lateran Council.[252] Congar pointed out that Innocent III was, however, not the creator of this act, but Alexander III was, when he summoned the Third Lateran Council.[253] Innocent IV also commented on a decree of Alexanders III, saying "*Nam in transactione voluntaria sicut in compositione necessarius est consensus omnium quos res tangit.*" (A *compositio* over a tithe is valid when the two clerks making it do so with the consent of the bishop or archbishop.)[254] On April 25, 1222, Honorius III phrased his invitation for the king and the prelates, to an assembly about crusades in Verona as "*quod christianos tangit communiter universos cum deliberation in tanto negotio necessaria ordinetur*" (The Christian business touches all, thus deliberation in such a negotiation is a necessary arrangement.)[255] In the papal bull *Super muros Jerusalem* on January 28, 1225, Honorius III demanded from the French clergy that every cathedral or stift should reserve two benefices for the Roman curia.[256] These quotations from popes exerted a great influence on canonists, who followed the pope to quote *Quod Omnes Tangit*. This maxim found its way into the *Regulae Juris*, drafted by Dinus Mugellanus and published by Boniface VIII (1294–1303) in the *Liber Sextus*.[257]

Canonists were often consultants of the king. It is no wonder that Canonists' propositions affected the king. Congar asserted that Friedrich II, who had a canonist consultant, Petrus von Vinea, quoted *Quod Omnes Tangit* to justify the principle of representation.[258] Gaines Post deemed Henry de Bracton (1210–1268) the chief figure in England influenced by *Quod Omnes Tangit*, showing how Bracton's adoption of *Quod Omnes Tangit* influenced royal writs about summoning communities[259] in the reign from Henry III to Edward I.[260] In addition, King Rudolf of Habsburg summoned a general cleric of the empire in 1274.[261]

[251] C. 8, X, I, 33 (Friedberg, II, Col. 199, 200); Potthast (1874), vol. I, Col. 2860, p. 245; cited in Congar (1980), p. 117. Trans. by the author.

[252] Hauck (1920), pp. 465–482; Barker (1913), pp. 32–33; Tierney (1998), pp. 43–44; cited in Congar (1980), p. 122.

[253] Mansi (1759–1798), vol. XXII, Col. 212, cited in Congar (1980), p. 123.

[254] *Apparatus* to *Decr. Greg. IX*, I, 36, 2 Statuimus, cited in Post (1964), p. 173; Congar (1980), p. 118.

[255] Huillard-Bréholles (1852), p. 241, cited in Congar (1980), p. 124.

[256] Mansi (1759–1798), vol. XXII, col. 1207–1210, cited in Congar (1980), p. 126. Trans. from Congar by the author.

[257] Reg. 29, in *Corpus iuris canonici*, Friedberg, II, Col. 1122: *Quod omnes tangit debet ab omnibus approbari.* Cf. Congar (1980), p. 119.

[258] Weiland (1896), p. 186, No. 152; Huillard-Bréholles (1852), vol. 4, p. 390, see also Post (1943), p. 231; cited in Congar (1980), pp. 145–146.

[259] Post (1964), p. 165.

[260] Post (1964), pp. 235–238.

[261] Weiland (1896), p. 50; cited in Congar (1980), p. 147.

In the end, the famous parliament of 1295 should be given more attention. With a war between England and France breaking out in 1294,[262] Edward I strove to explain to his people the necessity of paying taxes to support the war despite underdeveloped communication in that age.[263] At the beginning of the war with France, prayers were demanded for the success of the king of England, and in January 1296, Edward I made a similar request, which acts led to the consequence that all congregations were made aware of the problems faced by the nation.[264] In 1295, Edward I urged the delegates of the community and the lower clergymen to join the parliament, which suggested that the French aimed to destroy England, revealing much of the dangers threatening the realm; hence, *Quod Omnes Tangit* was quoted explicitly in the same writ to emphasize the necessity of universal approval for the measures to be taken to cope with a common danger by a remedy.[265]

These were the general situations of popes and king quoting *Quod Omnes Tangit.*

3.3.2.2.2 From Godfrey of Fontaines (c. 1250 – c. 1309)

Born in approximately 1250, Godfrey of Fontaines studied liberal arts at Paris under the guidance of Thomas Aquinas from 1269 to 1272.[266] His series of 15 quodlibetal questions[267] are his most significant contribution to philosophical and theological literature,[268] one of which focused on whether the subjects are bound to pay for a tax, which the ruler claimed for common good with an obscure necessity.[269] Carl Watner stated that the essence of the disputes was "the hefty taxes imposed by King Philip the Fair (of France) in order to sustain his wars."[270] Tierney thought that Godfrey's text included an explicit argument about the right of contentment to taxation as an essential attribute of a free society:

> when anyone rulesd over free persons . . . he ought not to impose any burden on his subjects except with their consent. Because they were free persons the subjects ought not to be coerced. When they paid a tax, they should do so voluntarily because they underst[oo]d the reason for the imposition. It was not enough for the ruler to say that he was levying a tax for

[262] Prestwich (1997), p. 381.

[263] Prestwich (1997), p. 412.

[264] Burton (1985), pp. 368–371, 409–410, cited in Prestwich (1997), p. 412.

[265] Stubbs (1913), p. 480. Cf. Marongiu (1980), p. 185; Congar (1980), pp. 150–151; Prestwich (1997), p. 412.

[266] Wippel (1981), pp. xvi, xvii; Watner (2005), p. 76.

[267] Quodlibets, as its name indicates, mean that a question could be directed at the Master by anyone (*a quolibet*) about any reasonable topic (*de quolibet*), which open to other Masters, Bachelors, students and other attendees. Wippel (1981), p. xxi.

[268] Wippel (1981), p. xxi.

[269] Watner (2005), p. 76.

[270] Watner (2005), p. 76; Cf. Tierney (1995), pp. 78, 79.

> the common good or by reason of state necessity; if he did not seek consent of the subjects they were not obliged to obey.[271]

Watner perceived Tierney's interpretation of Godfrey's stance on the importance of "consent to taxation" as unqualified. At the same time, he found that other modern commentators have been more circumspect. For example, Marshall Kempshall analyzed that while

> Godfrey [was] certainly familiar with the Roman maxim 'what touches all must be approved by all,' (*quod omnes tangit ab omnibus comprobetur*), he [was] careful to keep his options open when it [came] to defining exactly how this approval [could] be registered.[272]

Additionally, Kempshall found that Godfrey argued that the recognized consent was not the only means to legitimize extraordinary taxation; rather, it was the common good that remains the ultimate measure of legitimacy.[273]

If we accept Kempshall's interpretation of Godfrey's thinking, *Quod Omnes Tangit* in Godfrey's thinking shares much likeness with Tianxia Wei Gong. Gong represents the common good. Although the historical background was different, these two maxims both pursue the common good.

3.3.2.2.3 From William Durant the Younger (1296–1330)

William Durant the Younger, once the bishop of Mende, was a learned jurist and an excellent mediator between pope and king.[274]

The most important work of William Durant the Younger is probably the reform of the church (*Tractatus Maior*),[275] in which *Quod Omnes Tangit* is referred to to support William Durant Younger's argument, responding to Pope Clement V's request for reform proposals to the Council of Vienne in 1311–1312:

> It would appear to be good advice for the republic and for said administrators of the republic [i.e., the pope and the secular rulers] to limit their power by reason, as has been established in

---

[271] Tierney (1995), p. 79; Cf. Watner (2005), p. 76, Watner mistook the last word of Tierney from "obey" to "pay"; Godfrey of Fontaines (2000), pp. 315–320.

[272] Kempshall (1999), p. 253.

[273] Kempshall (1999), p. 255.

[274] Constantin Fasolt provided plenty of works on William Durant the Younger and his thinking of high quality. Fasolt recommended more than once the biography of William Durant the Younger written by Viollet, "Guillaume Durant," as the best: "[Viollet] was the first to draw at least on excerpts from documents buried in the archives that cast new light on Durant's exercise of his official responsibilities as bishop in the diocese of Mende, and the first to establish with certainty that he died in July 1330 (60–1). However, even though his biography remains the best, it is by no means definitive. A thorough account of the life of William Durant the Younger remains to be written." Fasolt (2014), p. 206. Falsot himself wrote a short biography of William Durant the Younger, which supplied the research in this thesis, Fasolt (1991), pp. 73–100.

[275] Fasolt asserted that "[t]he best edition of the *Tractatus de modo generalis concilii celebrandi* is by Jean Crespin, published in Lyon in 1531 under the title *De modo generalis concilii celebrandi tractatus*." Fasolt (2014), p. 234.

> the preceding chapters, in such a way that the lord pope will not use the prerogative of his power without the considered advice of the lords cardinals, nor kings and princes their own without the advice of other good men – as it used to be observed in the republic before – particularly the power of making concessions contrary to councils and to laws approved by all, so that, contrary to said councils and other laws, they will not be able to enact or concede anything new unless a general council has been convoked, since what touches all must, according to the rule of both canon and civil law, be approved by all.[276]

Fasolt concluded that William Durant the Younger differentiated two kinds of councils: small and permanent councils, consisting of, e.g., the cardinals, dealing with the prerogative power of the rulers; and general councils, consisting of all people, dealing with conflicts with general laws, the reason for which is *Quod Omnes Tangit*.[277] Regarding the question of whether William Durant the Younger adopted *Quod Omnes Tangit* in a democratic way, scholars' opinions varied. Some scholars insisted that, in William Durant the Younger's opinion, the Pope was subjected to Church Law and was therefore not entitled to change canon law without summoning the General Council.[278] Fasolt claimed, however, that the summoning Council did not mean requiring consent from the people; rather, the General Council was designed only to limit the power of the supreme authorities.[279] Presenting the complexity of this question, both sides demonstrated logical arguments.[280] This demonstration itself has met the needs of this thesis. Scholars disagreed with each other about how far William Durant the Younger went in interpreting *Quod Omnes*

[276] Cited in Fasolt (2014), p. 235. The original latin text can be found in fn. 37: "Videretur esse salubre consilium pro re publica et pro dictis administratoribus rei publice quod sic sub ratione, ut premissum est in rubricis proximis, limitaretur potestas eorundem quod absque certo consilio dominorum cardinalium dominus papa, et reges ac principles absque aliorum proborum consilio, sicut hactenus in re publica servabatur, non uterentur prerogativa huiusmodi potestatis, potissime aliquid concedendo contra concilia et contra iura approbata commniter, et quod contra dicta concilia et iura nihil possent de novo statuere vel concedere [*sic*] nisi generali concilio convocato, cum illud quod omnes tangit secundum iuris utriusque regulam ab omnibus debeat communiter approbari." *Tractatus maior* 1.4, fol. 7[rb].

[277] Fasolt (2014), pp. 235–236.

[278] Tierney (1998), p. 173. Fasolt provided two more scholars who were of the same opinion as Tierney: Haller (1903), p. 65; Scholz (1903), pp. 222–223; Fasolt (2014), p. 238.

[279] Fasolt (2014), pp. 234–247.

[280] Examining the arguments regarding this question, Tierney's opinion seems more to touch the content of William Durant the Younger's text, while Fasolt focused on some *pro forma* points. Tierney explained that William Durant the Younger divided his work into three parts to address the role of the General Council: first, "a Pope alone could not override the legislation of previous Councils;" second, "a General Council should be summoned whenever laws were to be promulgated touching the 'common state of the Church;'" third, the General Council should be summoned "regularly every ten years." Tierney (1998), pp. 176–177.

Fasolt emphasized that William Durant the Younger "declared nowhere that according to already existing laws or principles the supreme authorities were obliged to consult with general councils. He rather considered this to be a new obligation which still needed to be ratified." Furthermore, "the council's right to consent, as supported by QOT, appears in a subordinate clause of Durant's proposal. In the main clause, he merely insists that councils should be convoked or consulted; he does not truly demand a right of consent for them at all." Fasolt (2014), pp. 236–242.

Tangit, but no one denied that he was an important interpreter of *Quod Omnes Tangit*.

Antonio Marongiu commented that the conciliar theory of Wilhelm Durant equipped the Council and church with great power over the Pope, the king and the chieftain by the adoption of such a plain, precise and explicit affirmation of the democratic principle, endowing the principle with profound meaning and great significance, an idea that seemed to be the forerunner in the fourteenth century.[281]

3.3.2.2.4 From Marsilius of Padua (c. 1275 – c. 1342)

Marsilius played a significant role in the conflict between Ludwig of Bavaria and Pope Johannes XXII, which was one of the most important historic events in European history of the Middle Ages.[282] His theory helped to legitimate Ludwig's coronation: since a "strong part" is as the entirety, the "strong part" of civil society can coronate Ludwig without the interference of pope from the ecclesia.[283] Marsilius used the concept of *pars valencior*, strong part, to refer to an organic body of the entirety, thus free from the quantity of majority.[284] This "strong part" has several differences from the "major part." First, the "strong part" is stronger than the "major part." Since the "strong part" is free from the method of agent or delegation, it is thus equalized with the whole.[285] Furthermore, this "strong part" does not represent the entirety but acts as a part of the entirety, at the same time and for the same sense as the entirety.[286] One important feature of this kind of representation is that it cannot be reversed. This kind of setup foresees the possible controversy of representation, avoids the imaginable dispute, guarantees and in fact expands the power of an acting body.[287]

The achievement of Marsilius of Padua could be represented, theoretically and practically, by his *magnus opus*, *Defensor pacis*, and his acceptance and function in Ludwig of Bavaria's court, whose life is not adequately explored. Godthardt has commented on research on the life of Marsilius over the past 130 years.[288] The year of his birth is unknown and may range from 1270 to 1290.[289] The first affirmed date

[281] Marongiu (1980), pp. 189–190.

[282] Hofmann (2003), p. 225.

[283] See also Hofmann (2003), pp. 210–228.

[284] Hofmann (2003), pp. 210–211.

[285] Marsilius of Padua (2005), pp. I. xiii. 2.

[286] Hofmann (2003), pp. 210–211.

[287] See Hofmann (2003), p. 216.

[288] Godthardt recorded a half-page long list of academic work on Marsilius. Godthardt (2006), p. 29.

[289] Godthardt (2006), p. 30.

is March 12, 1313, when *magister Marsilius de Padua* "was mentioned as rector of the University of Paris."[290]

Next, we come to June 24, 1324, when *Defensor pacis* was completed.[291] Marsilius of Padua quoted *Quod Omnes Tangit* in this work,[292] which will be elaborated upon after a short introduction of his life.

Marsilius lived precisely in an epoch of church-state conflict. In 1326, Marsilius, with his colleague John of Jandun, was not in Paris anymore and was accepted at the court of King Ludwig the Bavarian, whom they accompanied in the next year on an Italian expedition, when, in 1327, the Pope declared five sentences in *Defensor pacis* heretical and thus excommunicated Marsilius and John of Jandun.[293] In 1328, Ludwig seemed to appoint Marsilius *vicarius in spiritualibus* after they returned from Rome to Munich, where Marsilius spent his rest of life.[294]

This not only contributes to the adequate evaluation of his political theory but also leads to an interesting discovery that takes contemporary political thinking in Masilius' motherland and hometown into consideration. It is surprising to find an astonishing resemblance to what Confucius did when the thinkers in Italy were tempted to contrast the present with a golden age of civic peace and unity. Dante praised the good old days as "Florence within her ancient limit-mark. . .was chaste and sober, and abode in peace."[295] The author of a Ferrarese chronicle also writes that "[a]t that time, the Ferrarese republic was prospering, and its citizens were enjoying wealth and peace."[296] Mussato drew a similar picture of Padua in the thirteenth century as peaceful, subjecting its neighbors through love.[297] This picture resembles what Confucius describes in Li Gi, which is the utopia of Confucius. It is also the main concern of Marsilius of Padua that the tranquillity and peace of civil regimes, as the title of his *magnum opus Defensor Pacis* suggests.[298] As seen above, maintaining peace was also a concern of Italian thinkers during Marsilius' time.[299]

> For Marsilius, like contemporary Italian Aristotelians such as Remigius and Ptolemy, peace is the first and the last word in discussing political principles. It would not be excessive to say

---

[290]Denifle and Chatelain (1881) (eds) vol. 2, Part 1, no. 698, p. 158 "Honestati nostre ac tranquillitati totius studii diligentius attendentes, nos omnes et singuli magistri quatuor facultatum Prisiensis Universitatis ad congregationem generalem vocati per magistrum Marcilium de Padus, tunc nostre Universitatis rectore"; no. 699, p. 158–159, here p. 158: "Querentes que ad pacem sunt, nos omnes et singuli magistri quatuor facultatum Parisiensis Universitatis ad congregationem generalem vocati per magistrum Mersilium [sic!] de Padua, tunc nostre Universitatis rectore," cited in Godthardt (2012), p. 14; Godthardt (2011), p. 41; Godthardt (2006), p. 30.

[291]Godthardt (2006), p. 31.

[292]Marongiu (1980), p. 190.

[293]Godthardt (2006), p. 31.

[294]Godthardt (2006), p. 32.

[295]Rubinstein (2004), p. 113.

[296]Rubinstein (2004), p. 113.

[297]Rubinstein (2004), p. 113.

[298]Lee (2008), p. 99.

[299]Skinner (1978), pp. 56–57.

that he was entirely occupied by the issue of how to attain peace in a political community.[300]

Tranquility is a keyword in the thinking of both Marsilius and Confucius. For Confucius, Tianxia Wei Gong represents his utmost ideal of society, namely, the Grand Union, while the Small Tranquillity ranks merely the second best.[301] The differences in the two ideals lie in whether the people only care for their own family's good or for all others' good.[302] For how to arrive at the destination of the Grand Union, Confucius emphasizes the function of rites more than punishment.[303] Other than that, he has not provided any practical manual. In contrast, for Marsilius, the two interchangeable conceptions, peace and tranquility, are "a secular political concept" that has no relation to "psychological, moral, or spiritual 'concords.'"[304]

Since *regnum* constitutes the tranquillity, at first, Marsilius defined *regnum* as a polity or a plurality of cities.[305] Furthermore, Marsilius followed Aristotle by defining a political association as "the perfect community having the full limit of self-sufficiency, which came into existence for the sake of living, but exists for the sake of living well."[306] Unlike in the Aristotle or Augustinian tradition that "men 'commune' with one another morally and intellectually," nor like the other extreme that the community is "a mere trade association or military alliance which is not a state at all," Marsilius preferred the state to be "an individualistic and economic community, its members 'being able to seek out *for themselves* the various necessaries, and exchanging (*communicantes*) them with one another.'"[307]

Marsilius quoted *Quod Omnes Tangit* here:

> men gathered into a civil community in order to pursue their benefit and the sufficient life and to avoid their contraries. In addition, therefore, any convenience or inconvenience that can affect all ought to be known and heard by all, so that they can pursue their benefit and avoid its contrary.[308]

Marsilius thought that legislation should be contracted through the people, *civium universitas* or *valentior pars*, which represented everyone (*quae totam universitatem repraesentat*).[309] Antonio Marongiu commented that Marsilius found a way to

[300] Lee (2008), p. 99.

[301] Confucius (1994), p. 815, ch. 9; Confucius (1885), pp. 364–367; Hsü (2000), pp. 365–366; Chan (2014), pp. 5–6.

[302] Wilhelm (1994), pp. 56–70.

[303] Confucius (2010), p. 20, Lunyu ch. 2.3; see also Chan (2014), p. 13.

[304] Gewirth (1951), pp. 96–97.

[305] Marsilius of Padua (2005), pp. 11–12, I. ii. 2.

[306] Marsilius of Padua (2010), p. 665; Cf. Marsilius of Padua (2005), p. I. iv. 1; Cf. Aristotle (1995), p. 10, 1252b27.

[307] Gewirth (1951), pp. 97–98; Marsilius of Padua (2005), p. 21, I. iv. 5.

[308] Marsilius of Padua (2005), p. 71, I. xii. 7.

[309] Marsilius of Padua (2005), pp. 66–67, 549, I. xii. 3, III. ii. 9–10; Gewirth (1951), pp. 182–184; Lee (2008), pp. 110–114.

utilize and practice *Quod Omnes Tangit* as persuasive evidence, avoiding its being merely a beautiful scroll.[310]

The descriptions of an ideal society in Western and Eastern cultures resemble each other. In the face of Marsilius' sentences, it would be too difficult to recall the writings of Kang Youwei. However, it can be observed that there is an awareness of the individual as a member of a community in Western thinking, which does not arise in Oriental culture.

3.3.2.2.5 Wilhelm of Ockham (1287–1347)

Wilhelm of Ockham, "*Baccalaureus* of Oxford" or *venerabilis inceptor,*[311] renowned for the philosophy of Ockham's Razor, made a great contribution to the interpretation of *Quod Omnes Tangit*. He accumulated his personal experience in the English empire, whose order and constitution determined his conception about the ideal form for political and religious organizations.[312]

Congar concluded that in three ways, Ockham quoted the maxim, of which the first two were sporadically and the last one frequently: at first, he applied the maxim to verify the obligation of the cleric and to defend the empire, when the cleric quoted *Quod Omnes Tangit* as a tool to deal with taxation from the Pope or the feudal[313]; then, Ockham quoted the maxim to sustain the King's law to participate in the election of the Pope; although he did not express it explicitly, the meaning was indicated.[314] What he applied in most cases was closely associated with Christianity.

"He argued for the appointment of councils or parliament, which should be the direct or indirect representation of the members in Christendom: a delegation from not only clergymen but also laymen, because all people are equally touched and *quod omnes tangit ab omnibus tractari et approbari debet*."[315] Wilhelm of Ockham regarded this principle as an intelligent solution for proper organized community because, on one hand, the ruler, or the public force in general, could demand what is necessary for the operation of the institution but not undermine the citizen's freedom, property and rights; on the other hand, the citizens can defend themselves against the highest power and are entitled to launch a reform when requisite.[316] However, Wilhelm of Ockham was not a jurist, and he failed to discuss problems such as how to realize, establish and manage representation.[317]

---

[310] Marongiu (1980), pp. 191–192.

[311] Marongiu (1980), p. 192.

[312] Marongiu (1980), p. 192.

[313] Congar (1980), p. 170.

[314] Congar (1980), p. 171.

[315] Marongiu (1980), pp. 192–193. Trans. by the author.

[316] Marongiu (1980), pp. 194–195.

[317] Marongiu (1980), p. 195.

Furthermore, Tobias Speck expounded on Ockham's reception of *Quod Omnes Tangit*.[318] To acquire a proper insight into this theme, some concepts must be set forth at first: the universal church (*ecclesia universalis*),[319] consisting of all believers, whose counterpart is regional church (*ecclesia particularis*)[320];for example, the Pope and his court was only the church of Avignon (*ecclesia Avinionica*).[321]

Ockham applied the maxim *Quod Omnes Tangit* to the belief of all, namely, the belief of universal church,[322] to enforce their responsibility and to protect their belief, in the way of being informed of the official bulletin, which affected them.[323] All can take measures against the heresy and condemn the heretic.[324] For example, regarding the interference with a heretical Pope, the proper decision could not be made by a single one or a small committee but by all people who were touched:

> Quod Omnes tangit ab omnibus tractari debet: ita causa quae omnes tangit ab omnibus tractari debet: sed causa papae haeretici omnes tangit Christianos. Ergo per omnes Christianos vel congregationem, cuiusmodi est concilium generale, tractari debet. . . .[325]

Ockham listed the responsibility of church in church field, social field, and national field: to be interfered with by the people for the choice of Pope,[326] to guarantee welfare of the people and the defense of fatherland.[327]

Wilhelm Ockham included *Quod Omnes Tangit* in his work *Dialogus de potestate imperiali et papali* as basic principles for social life considering its political and ethical value.[328] For Ockham, this principle became his life's philosophy.

3.3.2.2.6 Bartolomé de las Casas (1484–1566)

Bartolomé de las Casas[329] was born in Seville.[330] Kenneth Pennington suggested that Las Casas must have witnessed Christopher Columbus's return from the New

---

[318] Speck (2009), pp. 75–85.

[319] Ockham (1974), p. 63, q.1 c.17. Speck (2009), pp. 75–76.

[320] Ockham (1974), p. 174, q.7 c.4. Speck (2009), p. 75.

[321] Ockham (1914a, b), p. 473.

[322] Ockham (1612), pars 1, lib. 6, cap. 31. Ockham (1974), p. 64, q.1 c.17. Ockham (1974), p. 119, q.3 c.12. Speck (2009), p. 76.

[323] Ockham (1612), pars 1, lib. 7, cap.18.

[324] Ockham (1612), pars 1, lib. 6, cap. 32. Ockham (1974), p. 60, q.1 c.17. Speck (2009), pp. 77–78.

[325] Ockham (1612), pars 1, lib. 6, cap. 70. See also Marongiu (1980), p. 195; Congar (1980), p. 174; Speck (2009), p. 153.

[326] Ockham (1974), p. 203, I.1 c.6. Speck (2009), p. 81.

[327] Ockham (1914a, b), pp. 443–444; Speck (2009), pp. 52, 82.

[328] Marongiu (1980), p. 195.

[329] Clayton (2012), p. 1; Parish et al. (1976), p. 397.

[330] Huser (2011), p. 20.

World when he went to Seville in 1493.[331] Cruel colonial domination followed the triumph on the South American continent. Las Casas devoted himself to protecting the indigenous Indians, writing essays to systematically argue that Indians are not savages but the same species as the European; because of such works and actions, he was known as the protector of the Indians.[332] He was skilled in adapting given legal rules to support natural rights, which can be observed both in the legitimation of Indians' sovereign rights and the interpretation of *Quod Omnes Tangit*.

Las Casas quoted the maxim in his *De thesauris*.[333] Kenneth Pennington summarized that *Quod Omnes Tangit* had been used to regulate "the legal relationship between a bishop and his chapter of canons" to support "the lesser members of the ecclesiastical hierarchy," to voice "in the governing of the church," to assist European kings to summon representative assemblies and to build "the theoretical basis for parliament,"[334] aside from which usage, Las Casas added, since a prince or a bishop were not supposed to rule over an unwilling people, neither should a king be given rule over a free foreign people.[335] Similarly, without the consent of the native people, the pope cannot grant the Spanish king *dominium* in the New World.[336] In this way, the legitimacy of the Spanish sovereign title of South America was denied. In addition to the substantial innovation of the maxim, Las Casas also set a precedent that valid ecclesiastical rules "ought to be valid in the secular polity," which immensely strengthened "the interplay between canon and Roman law in constructing the ideological framework for monarchical and constitutional government."[337] In both spheres, the canonists played a pivotal role in fashioning the terminology.

3.3.2.2.7 Nicolas of Cusa (1401–1464)

Nicolas of Cusa, whose Latin name is Nicolaus Cusanus, should be considered one of the greatest thinkers in Western intellectual history. With his name appearing in every series of philosophy history, Cusanus established himself first and foremost not in the ivory tower in university or library but in the political arena of the church.[338] He is not only a philosopher and a theologian but also a jurist and a churchman.[339]

[331] Pennington (2018), pp. 98–99.

[332] Clayton (2012), pp. 2–6.

[333] Las Casas (1992), vol.11.1, p. 232. Cf. Clayton (2012), pp. 82–85.

[334] Pennington (2018), p. 103.

[335] Las Casas (1992), vol.11.1, p. 232. Pennington (2018), p. 104.

[336] Las Casas (1992), vol.11.1, p. 236.

[337] Las Casas (1992), vol.11.1, p. 230; Pennington (2018), p. 104.

[338] Brösch et al. (2014), p. 31.

[339] Mandrella (2012), p. 37.

According to the inscription on his tomb in the church San Pietro in Vincoli in Roma, Cusanus was born in 1401 and died on Aug. 11, 1464 in his 63rd year of life.[340] His father might have been a businessman who sold ships, and the family was definitely wealthy.[341] According to his autobiographic note on Oct. 21, 1449, Cusanus took pride in his promotion into the highest rank of society, for as cardinal, his status equaled that of a prince.[342]

According to the university registration material Cusanus registered in the summer semester in 1416 at Heidelberg University.[343] He studied the Seven Liberal Arts, "septem artes liberals," for 1 year in Heidelberg, before he turned to Padua to study law, where he stayed from 1417 to 1423, earning the title of Doctor before his 22nd birthday and advocating for conciliar thinking: a council should supervise the Pope.[344] In addition, from 1394 to 1411, Cusanus was one of Francesco Zarabella's students, who emphasized the consent of the ruled as a premise for the legitimate administration of church and state.[345]

The principle *Quod Omnes Tangit* is of great significance in his theory of consent. Cusanus was aware of the importance of insisting on the people's rights of consent to the legitimate exercise of authority; "otherwise he would have vitiated the whole purpose of the *De concordantia catholica*, which was to justify conciliar action against the pope;"[346] thus, "according to divine and natural law, the power to enact legislation depends on common consent."[347]

3.3.3 Comparison

As they examined the problems of their society in conversation with ideas formed in the earlier, more sophisticated civilizations of either ancient China or Rome, later intellectuals "did not merely repeat them, parrot-like." The medieval intellectuals' interpretations used classical concepts to rethink the political experience of their own society, which is also what the Chinese intellectuals did.

Interpreter

Kang, Liang and Cusanus all played multiple roles: not only intellectual ones but also political. Heretofore, they are all called "reformers" rather than scholars. Kang presented his ten memorials and drafted the concrete scheme of reform, while Cusanus also drew up the first detailed plan of the reform.

---

[340] Brösch et al. (2014), p. 33.

[341] Kandler (1995), pp. 10–11.

[342] Brösch et al. (2014), p. 33.

[343] Brösch et al. (2014), p. 34.

[344] Kandler (1995), pp. 12–13.

[345] Kandler (1995), p. 13.

[346] Monahan (1994), p. 103.

[347] Sigmund (1963), p. 151.

It is worthwhile to note that the statuses of the eastern and western interpreters are similar but slightly different. The majority of interpreters were scholars, such as Kang Youwei and Liang Qichao in the East and Ockham and Marsilius of Padua in the west. In the western world, some of them were popes and emperors, while in the eastern world, only one of them had a comparative degree of power, namely, Sun Yat-sen. However, the range and effect of their powers was not the same because Sun Yat-sen never gained total control over the unrest situation. An adequate power could exercise a great influence on the effect of the principles. The more power is acquired, the greater the influence of the principle is. With sufficient power, the principle promoted by the official authority could reach more people and be better implemented; it would also be less frequently doubted or attacked.

The existence of a religious institutional system enables educated intellectuals to exercise their wisdom in the position of management.[348] Their knowledge and management experience interact with and strengthen each other. In China, not only in ancient times but also until now, intellectuals and officials have nothing in common.[349] Intellectuals prepare their descendants, operate colleges and recruit students, while at first, officials may make an effort to learn something to gain a position, but the position has nothing to do with knowledge anymore but rather has to do with establishing a complex interpersonal relationship network. Since knowledge and practice hardly coincide in most cases, some scholars raised the point of Jing Shi Zhi Yong,[350] emphasizing that knowledge should be applied to practice. However, in contrast with the West, it could be observed that the Western tradition is deeply rooted in their religious institutional system. Fairbank pointed out that the Chinese language is itself an institution of society instead of merely a tool.[351] Moreover, this results in another disadvantage: in China, the power of knowledge is not fully acknowledged by the ruler or the administrational system. Consequently, there should be a bridge from knowledge to practice to eliminate this gap between intellectuals and officials. In the West, there is no such gap: intellectuals and officials are united in one role and embodied by one person.

Scholars have since changed their opinions. As Monahan said about Nicolas of Cusa, "[o]ne aspect of his thought and career that makes him particularly interesting was his change of position regarding the relationship between papacy and council."[352] In his major work in the fall of 1433, *De concordantia catholica*, he

---

[348] See also Forke (1964), p. VI.

[349] See also Li (2001), p. 148.

[350] For details see Qing Philosophy, Stanford Encyclopedia of Philosophy (2022), First published 16 Apr 2019 https://plato.stanford.edu/entries/qing-philosophy/. Accessed 19 Mar 2021; Gu Yanwu, Encyclopaedia Britannica (2021b), https://www.britannica.com/biography/Gu-Yanwu. Accessed 19 Mar 2021.

[351] Fairbank (1967), pp. 60–63.

[352] Monahan (1994), p. 98.

immersed himself in the demonstration of the superiority of council over Pope.[353] However,

> [h]e formally took the papalism side on the issue of ultimate authority in the Church shortly after the final break between Basel and Pope Eugene IV, but had become anticonciliar in attitude even before the council ended. Apparently deeply disturbed by the rapidly growing anti-papal extremism at Basel, he went over to the papal side in 1437 and was described in 1439 by Aeneas Sylvius (later Pius II) as the 'Hercules of all the followers of Eugenius[']. [354]

Kang and Liang underwent a similar change in thinking.

Regarding the characters of the documents interpreting the principles, both Tianxia Wei Gong and *Quod Omnes Tangit* have been interpreted in academic work. In addition, *Quod Omnes Tangit* also appeared in a Papal Decretal, "a letter containing a papal ruling, more specifically one relating to matters of canonical discipline, and most precisely a papal rescript in response to an appeal."[355] Many Popes discussed the legal force of the Papal Decretal,[356] which once "achieved an authority equal to that of conciliar canons."[357]

In comparison with the documents of interpretation of *Quod Omnes Tangit* in the West, the characteristics of the documents of interpretation of Tianxia Wei Gong in China are often not very clear-cut or even controversial. Tianxia Wei Gong was often interpreted in the works of intellectuals rather than legal documents. Thus, its effect is much weaker. Although Kang Youwei's thoughts, including Tianxia Wei Gong, influenced the Emperor's thinking and behaviors and were indirectly reflected in the decree he issued, it is a question whether the decree itself can be treated as legislation because the Emperor had no real power.

Compared with the features of the edict of the Qing Empire and the Magna Carta, it is indisputable that the Magna Carta is a document that is constitutionally meaningful, but it is quite disputable whether the edict of the Qing Empire is such a document. Some scholars think that it is a constitutional document, a contract to transfer sovereignty.[358]

Moreover, there is a common failure among Chinese academics: their poetic casualness in academic research. Most of their articles were written in a style similar to essays where they adopted a number of metaphors and parallelism but few references. Most of their works were not systematic. Additionally, some of their theories were irrelevant to reality at that time, such as Kang Youwei's world of Da

---

[353] Monahan (1994), p. 100; Sigmund (1963), p. 121.

[354] Monahan (1994), p. 99.

[355] Duggan (2003), vol.4, p. 599.

[356] "The legal force of decretals was discussed by popes from the time of their earliest known use: on specific points by Siricius (385), Innocent I (405) and Zosimus (418); and as a general principle by Leo I in 443. Gregory I, Nicholas I, and Gregory VII are among the later Popes known to have repeated and defined this principle, in demanding obedience to apostolic precepts expressed in decretal letters." Duggan (2003), vol. 4, p. 600. See also Jasper and Fuhrmann (2001), p. 13.

[357] Jasper and Fuhrmann (2001), p. 17.

[358] Ling (2013), pp. 159–180; Gao (2011), pp. 26–36.

Tong. Nevertheless, in the West, there was a need for *Quod Omnes Tangit* to balance the power, as they already functioned like a well-oiled machine.

In addition, in China's situation, there was little daily politics because Chinese people would not think about any problem until it was already too late. Thus, all those interpretations aimed at extinguishing the metaphorical fire failed to receive attention in time.

References

Aristotle (1995) Politics (trans: Barker E). Oxford University Press, New York

Ban G (1962) Hanshu. Zhonghua Book Company, Beijing. (班固, 汉书, 中华书局, 北京, 1962年)

Barker E (1913) The Dominican order and convocation. At the Clarendon, Oxford

Bary WT, Bloom I (eds) (1999) Sources of Chinese tradition, vol 1. Columbia University Press, New York

Bauer W (1990) Das Antlitz Chinas. Carl Hanser Verlag, Munich

Begère M (1998) Sun Yat-sen. Stanford University Press, Redwood City

Bell AA (2014) Reconciling confucianism and nationalism. J Chin Philos 41:33–54

Breay C (2002) Magna carta. The British Library, London

Brösch M et al (eds) (2014) Handbuch Nikolaus von Kues: Leben und Werk. WBG, Darmstadt

Brundage JA (2013) Medieval Canon Law. Routledge, New York

Burton DW (1985) Politics, propaganda and public opinion in the reigns of Henry III and Edward I. Dissertation. University of Oxford, Oxford

Busch H (1949) The Tung-Lin academy and its political and philosophical significance. Monumenta Serica 14:1–163

Chan J (2014) Confucian perfectionism: a political philosophy for modern times. Princeton University Press, Princeton

Chang H (1987) Chinese intellectuals in crisis: search for order and meaning (1890–1911). University of California Press, Berkeley and Los Angeles

Chang YZ, Wang ZY (2019) On the ancient Chinese Gan-Zhi(干支) and decimal system and the period of the twelve-digit system. Central Plains Culture Res 3:15–23. (常玉芝, 王曾瑜, 中国古代的干支、十进位制和十二进位制纪时, 中原文化研究, 2019年第3期, 第15-23页)

Chen F (2015) Sources of two famous quotes. http://www.cssn.cn/wx/wx_bh/201506/t20150605_2023840.shtml. Accessed Feb 27 2018 (陈福康, 说两句名言的出处, 中国社会科学网, 访问时间:2018年2月27日)

Chen P et al (2012) A literature review of the research theme the abdicant of the Qing emperor in the late one hundred year. Qing History J 4:104–125. (陈鹏, 韩祥, 张公政, 百年"清帝逊位"问题研究综述), 清史研究, 2012年第4期, 第104-125页

Cheng P-K et al (eds) (1999) The search for modern China: a documentary collection. W. W. Norton, New York

Clayton LA (2012) Bartolomé de las casas: a biography. Cambridge University Press, New York

Confucius (1885) The Li Ki (trans: Legge J). Clarendon Press, Oxford

Confucius (1980) Lunyu (trans: Yang BJ). Zhonghua Book Company, Beijing. (杨伯峻 译注, 论语译注, 中华书局, 北京, 1980年)

Confucius (1994) Liji. In: Qian X et al (eds) Shisan Jing Jinzhu Jinyi. Yuelu Publishing House, Changsha. (孔子, 礼记, 钱玄, 等编, 十三经今注今译, 岳麓书社, 长沙, 1994年)

Confucius (1998) The analects of Confucius (trans: Ames RT, Rosemont H). Random House Publishing, New York. Another Chinese edition

Confucius (2010) The analects of Confucius (trans: Watson B). Columbia University Press, New York

Congar Y (1980) Quod omnes tangit ab omnibus tractari et approbari debet. In: Heinz R (ed) Die geschichtlichen Grundlagen der modernen Volksvertretung. Wissenschaftliche Buchgesellschaft, Darmstadt, pp 115–182

Couvreur S (1950) Mémoires Sur Les Bienséances Et Les Cérémonies. Cathasia, Paris

Danziger D, Gillingham J (2004) 1215, The Year of Magna Carta. Hodder and Stoughton, London

Denifle H, Chatelain E (eds) (1881) Chartularium universitatis Parisiensis: sub auspiciis consilii generalis facultatum Parisiensum, vol. 2. Ex typis fratrum Delalain. Université de Paris, Paris

Ding D (2014) Ding Ding talking about the classic and fashional traits of Li Ji. http://www.rmzxb.com.cn/c/2014-11-03/401857.shtml. Accessed Feb 26 2018. (丁鼎, 丁鼎谈《礼记》的"古典"与"时尚", 人民政协网, 访问时间:2018年2月26日)

Ding S (2020) Review and a new interpretation of the issue of "rites do not extend down to the common people; criminal Laws do not extend up to the senior nobles". Jianghan Acad 8(4): 92–101. (丁四新, "礼不下庶人, 刑不上大夫"问题检讨与新论, 江汉学术, 2020年8月第4期, 第92-101页)

Duggan C (2003) Decretals. In: Carson T, Cerrito J (eds) New Catholic encyclopedia, vol 4. Thompson/Gale, Washington, DC, pp 599–601

Elman BA (1989) Imperial politics and confucian societies in late Imperial China: the Hanlin and Donglin academies. Modern China 15:379–418

Encyclopaedia Britannica (2021a) Confucian learning in Jin, Yuan, and Ming, In: Confucianism. Britannica. https://www.britannica.com/topic/Confucianism/Confucian-learning-in-Jin-Yuan-and-Ming. Accessed Jun 29 2021

Encyclopaedia Britannica (2021b) Gu Yanwu. https://www.britannica.com/biography/Gu-Yanwu. Accessed 19 Mar 2021

Fairbank JK (1967) The Chinese written language. In: Schurmann F, Shell O (eds) Imperial China. Random House, Harmondsworth, pp 60–63

Fairbank JK (ed) (1978) The Cambridge history of China, vol. 10, late Ch'ing, 1800–1911, part 1. Cambridge University Press, Cambridge

Fairbank JK, Liu K-C (eds) (1980) The Cambridge history of China, vol. 11, late Ch'ing 1800–1911, part 2. Cambridge University Press, Cambridge

Fasolt C (1991) Council and hierarchy: the political thought of William Durant the younger. Cambridge University Press, Cambridge

Fasolt C (2014) Past sense: studies in medieval and early modern European history. Brill, Leiden

Feifel E (1982) Geschichte der chinesischen Literatur. Wissenschaftliche Buchgesellschaft, Darmstadt

Feng YL (1948) A short history of Chinese philosophy. The Free Press, New York

Feng S (2001) Archeoastronomy in China. Social Sciences Academic Press, Beijing. (冯时, 中国天文考古学, 中国天文考古学, 社会科学文献出版社, 北京, 2001年)

Forke A (1964) Geschichte der mittelalterlichen chinesischen Philosophie. De Gruyter, Hamburg

Fukuyama F (2011) The origins of political order. Farrar, Straus and Giroux, New York

Gao QX (2011) The Imperial edict of Abdicaiton by the Qing emperor in a political and constitutional view. Global Law Rev 5:26–36. (高全喜, 政治宪法学视野中的清帝《逊位诏书》, 环球法律评论, 2011年第5期, 第26-36页)

Gewirth A (1951) Marsilius of Padua: the defender of peace, vol. 1: Marsilius of Padua and medieval political philosophy. Columbia University Press, New York

Gierke O (1868) Das deutsche Genossenschaftsrecht. Weidmann, Berlin

Godfrey of Fontaines (2000) Are subjects bound to pay a tax when the need for it is not evident? In: McGrade AS et al (eds) The Cambridge translations of medieval philosophical texts. Cambridge University Press, New York, pp 315–320

Godthardt F (2006) The philosopher as political actor – Marsilius of Padua at the court of Ludwig the Bavarian: the sources revised. In: Gerson M-R (ed) The world of Marsilius of Padua. Brepols, Turnhout, pp 29–46

Godthardt F (2011) Marsilius von Padua und der Romzug Ludwigs des Bayern: Politische Theorie und politisches Handeln. V&R Unipress, Göttingen

Godthardt F (2012) The life of Marsilius of Padua. In: Moreno-Riano G, Nederman CJ (eds) A companion to Marsilius of Padua. Brill, Leiden, pp 13–56
Gu XC (1987) The Legacy of Jinggao. Shanghai Classic Publishing House, Shanghai. (顾宪成, 泾皋藏稿, 上海古籍出版社, 上海, 1987年)
Gu YW (1990) Rizhi Lu. Huashan Literature & Art Publishing House, Shijiazhuang. (顾炎武, 日知录, 花山文艺出版社, 石家庄, 1990年)
Gu XC (2002) Wanli Shuchao. Shanghai Classic Publishing House, Shanghai. (顾宪成, 万历疏钞, 上海古籍出版社, 上海, 2002年)
Gu YW (2017) Record of daily knowledge and collected poems and essays 1 (trans: Johnston I). Columbia University Press, New York
Haller J (1903) Papsttum und Kirchenreform. Weidmann, Berlin
Hauck A (1920) Kirchengeschichte Deutschlands. Hinrich, Leipzig
Head JW (2011) Great legal traditions: civil law, common law, and Chinese law in historical and operational perspective. Carolina Academic Press, Durham
Hoang P (1910) Concordance des chronologies néoméniques chinoise et éuropéenne. Imprimerie de la mission catholique, Shanghai
Hofmann H (2003) Repräsentation. Duncker & Humblot, Berlin
Holt JC (1992) The northerners. Clarendon Press, Oxford
Holt JC et al (eds) (2015) Magna Carta. Cambridge University Press, Cambridge
Hsü IC-Y (2000) The rise of modern China. Oxford University Press, Oxford
Hu LY (1975) Hu Yinan Xiansheng Quanji. Wen Hai Press, Taipei. (胡礼垣, 胡翼南先生全集, 文海出版社, 常州, 1975年)
Hu M (2015) China's transition to modernity: the new classical vision of Dai Zhen. University of Washington Press, Seattle and London
Huang PC (1969) Liang Ch'i-ch'ao. In: Opitz PJ (ed) Vom Konfuzianismus zum Kommunismus. List Verlag, Munich, pp 61–105
Huang ZX (1993) Waiting for the Dawn: a plan for the prince (trans: Bary WT). Columbia University Press, New York
Huang ZX (1995) Ming I Dai Fang Lu. Shanghai Chinese Classic Publishing House, Shanghai. (黄宗羲, 明夷待访录, 上海古籍出版社, 上海, 1995年)
Huillard-Bréholles J-L-A (1852) Historia diplomatica Friderici secondi, vol 2. Henricus Plon, Paris
Hummel AW et al (eds) (2010) Eminent Chinese of the Ch'ing period. Global Oriental, Folkestone
Huser P (2011) Vernunft and Herrschaft. LIT, Berlin
Jasper D, Fuhrmann H (2001) Papal letters in the early middle ages. CUA Press, Washington, DC
Jenco L (2015) Changing referents: learning across space and time in China and the west. Oxford University Press, New York
Jiang D (2011) Probe of doctrine of "Li" in Chinese traditional legal culture through analysis on the word "Li". Hebei law. Science 29:39–44. (姜栋, 从"礼"字管窥中国传统法文化中的"礼"的起源, 河北法学, 2011年第29期, 第39-44页)
Justinian (529-534) Digesta. In: Iustinianus Project. Alexandr K, Yves L. https://droitromain.univ-grenoble-alpes.fr/Corpus/digest.htm. Accessed 5 Dec 2022
Kandler K-H (1995) Nikolaus Von Kues: Denker zwishen Mittelalter und Neuzeit. Vandenhoeck & Ruprecht, Göttingen
Kang YW (1958) Ta T'ung Shu, the one-world philosophy of K'ang Yu-wei (trans: Thompson LG). George Allen & Unwin, London
Kempshall MS (1999) The common good in late medieval political thought. Clarendon Press, Oxford
Köbler G (2009) Zielwörterbuch europäischer Rechtsgeschichte, 5th edn. Arbeiten zur Rechts- und Sprachwissenschaft Verlag, Gießen
Kuang YM (1990) A critical biography of Confucius. Nanjing University Press, Nanjing. (匡亚明, 孔子评传, 南京大学出版社, 南京, 1990年)
Kwong LSK (1984) A mosaic of the hundred days: personalities, politics, and ideas of 1898. Harvard University Press, Cambridge

Kyoson T (1927) Contemporary thought of Japan and China. Williams and Norgate, London
Las Casas (1992) De thesauris in Obras completas. Alianza Editorial, Madrid
Lee H-Y (2008) Political representation in the later middle ages: Marsilius in context. Peter Lang Publishing, New York
Li X (2001) The Chinese cultural revolution. Revisited China Rev 1(1):137–165
Li L (2016) A warring states period Ganzhi instrument in the National Museum of China. J Natl Museum China 5:137–142. (李零, 中国国家博物馆藏战国错金干支仪, 馆藏文物研究, 2016年第5期, 第137-142页)
Liang QC (1959) Intellectual trends in the Qing period (trans: Hsü I). Harvard University Press, Cambridge
Liang QC (1992) In: Xiao XH (ed) Selected works of Liang Qichao. China Broadcast Film & Television Publishing House, Beijing. (梁启超, 梁启超文选, 夏晓红编, 中国广播电视出版社, 北京, 1992年)
Liang QC (2006) In: Hou YJ (ed) Selected works of Liang Qichao. Baihua Edition, Tianjin. (梁启超, 梁启超文选, 侯宜杰选注, 百花文艺出版社, 天津, 2006年)
Liang QC (2014) The experience of travel in Europe. The Commercial Press, Beijing. (梁启超, 欧游心影录, 商务印书馆, 北京, 2014年)
Liang QC (2015) Yin Bing Shi He Ji. Zhonghua Book Company, Beijing. (梁启超, 饮冰室合集, 中华书局, 北京, 2015年)
Liebs D (ed) (2007) Lateinische Rechtsregeln und Rechtssprichwörter. C. H. Beck, Munich
Ling B (2013) The legitimate foundation for the Nation Building. The Jurist 4:159–160. (凌斌, 从清帝逊位诏书解读看国家建立的规范基础, 法学家, 2013年第4期, 第159, 160页)
Loewe M, Shaughnessy EL (eds) (1999) The Cambridge history of ancient China: from the origins of civilization to 221 B.C. Cambridge University Press, Cambridge
Lü K (1991) Shenyin Yu. Yuelu Publishing House, Changsha. (吕坤, 呻吟语, 岳麓书社, 长沙, 1991年)
Ma T (2011) Critical biography of Lü Kun. Nanjing University Press, Nanjing. (马涛, 吕坤评传, 南京大学出版社, 南京, 2011年)
Mandrella I (2012) Reformhandeln und spekulatives Denken bei Nicolaus Cusanus: Eine Verhältnisbestimmung. In: Frank T, Winkler N (eds) Renovatio et unitas – Nikolaus von Kues als reformer: Theorie und praxis der reformatio im 15. Jahrhundert. V&R Unipress, Göttingen, pp 37–52
Mansi JD (1759–1798) Sacrorum conciliorum nova et amplissima collectio, vol 22/32. Expensis Antonii Zatta, Florence-Venice
Manthe U (2008) Corpus Iuris Civilis. In: Cordes A et al (eds) Handwörterbuch zur deutschen Rechtsgeschichte, vol 1/3, 2nd edn. Erich Schmidt Verlag, Berlin, pp S 901–S 907
Marongiu A (1980) Das Prinzip der Demokratie und der zustimmung (Quod omnes tangit, ab omnibus approbari debet) im 14.Jahrhundert. In: Rausch H (ed) Die geschichtlichen Grundlagen der modernen Volksvertretung, vol 1. Darmstadt, Wissenschaftliche Buchgesellschaft, pp 183–211
Marsilius of Padua (2005) The defender of the peace (trans and ed: Brett A). Cambridge University Press, New York
Marsilius of Padua (2010) The defender of peace. Hackett Publishing Company, Indianapolis
Mathews RH (1931) Mathews' Chinese-English dictionary. Harvard University Press, Cambridge
Mayali L (2015) The legacy of Roman law. In: Johnston D (ed) Cambridge companion to Roman law. Cambridge University Press, Cambridge, pp 374–395
Mencius (1895) The Chinese classics, vol. 2, The Works of Mencius (trans: Legge J). Clarendon Press, Oxford
Miu CQ (1637) The legacy of Congyetang. Shanghai Chinese Classics Publishing House, Shanghai. (缪昌期, 从野堂存稿, 上海古籍出版社, 上海, 1637年)
Monahan AP (1994) From personal duties towards personal rights. McGill-Queen's University Press, Montreal & Kinston

Moos P (2004) 'Öffentlich' und 'privat' im Mittelalter: Zu einem problem historischer Begriffsbildung. Universitätverlag Winter, Heidelberg
Mousourakis G (2003) The historical and institutional context of Roman law. Ashgate, Hampshire
Mousourakis G (2012) Fundamentals of Roman private law. Springer, Heidelberg
Mühlemann G (2006) Chinas Experimente mit westlichen Staatsideen. Schulthess, Zürich
Murthy V (2011) The political philosophy of Zhang Taiyan. Brill, Leiden
Nathan AJ (1985) Chinese democracy. Alfred A. Knopf, New York
Ockham (1612) Dialogus. In: Goldast M, Monarchia S (eds) Romani Imperii. Biermanni & confort, Hanovie
Ockham (1914a) An Rex Angliae Pro Succursu Guerrae. In: Scholz R (ed) Unbekannte Kirchenpolitische Streitschriften aus der Zeit Ludwigs des Bayern (1327–1354). Verlag Von Loescher & Co, Rom, pp 432–453
Ockham (1914b) De Imperatorum et Pontificum potestate. In: Scholz R (ed) Unbekannte Kirchenpolitische Streitschriften aus der Zeit Ludwigs des Bayern (1327–1354). Verlag Von Loescher & Co, Rom, pp 453–480
Ockham (1974) Octo Quaestiones. Manchester University Press, Manchester
Opitz PJ (1969) Vom Konfuzianismus zum Kommuinismus. Paul List Verlag, Munich
Parish HR et al (1976) The correct birth Dec 05 2022 of Bartolomé de las casas. Hisp Am Hist Rev 56:385–403
Pennington K (2018) Bartolomé de Las Casas. In: Domingo R, Martínez-Torrón J (eds) Great Christian jurists in Spanish history. Cambridge University Press, Cambridge, pp 98–114
Plessis P (2015) Borkowski's textbook on Roman law. Oxford University Press, Oxford
Poetzelberger B (1993) Tianxia und guojia bei Liang Shuming (1893–1988): Konsens und Konflikt im chinesischen Beitrag yu traditionellen Ordnungsvorstellungen. Dissertation. Universität Bonn, Bonn
Post G (1943) Plena Potestas and consent in medieval assemblies: a study in Romano-canonical procedure and the rise of representation, 1150–1325. Traditio 1:355–408
Post G (1946) A Romanon-canonical maxim, 'quod Omnes Tangit,' in Bracton. Traditio 4:197–251
Post G (1964) Studies in medieval legal thought: public law and the state, 1100–1322. Princeton University Press, Princeton
Potthast A (1874) Regesta Pontificum Romanorum, vol 1/2. Rudolphi de Decker, Berlin
Prestwich M (1997) Edward I. Yale University Press, New Haven
Richter AL (1939) Corpus iuris canonici (ed: Friedberg E), vol 2. Tauchnitz, Leipzig
Rubinstein N (2004) Studies in Italian history in the middle ages and the renaissance. Ediyioni Di Storia E Letteratura, Roma
Sanetou K (1983) The Chinese studying in Japan. SDX Publishing House, Nanjing. (实藤惠秀, 中国人留学日本, 三联书店, 北京, 1983年)
Schiffrin HZ (1968) Sun Yat-sen and the origins of the Chinese revolution. University of California Press, Berkeley and Los Angeles
Schmidt-Glintzer H (1990) Geschichte der chinesischen Literatur. Scherz, Bern
Scholz R (1903) Die Publizistik zur Zeit Phillipps des Schönen und Bonifaz' VIII. F. Enke, Stuttgart
Shang B et al (2008) History of Chinese Confucianism development. Lanzhou University Press, Lanzhou. (尚斌, 任鹏, 李明珠, 中国儒学发展史, 兰州大学出版社, 兰州, 2008年)
Shen YL (1967) Political documents of the years Xuantong. Taiwan Wen Hai Press Company, Taipei. (沈云龙主编, 宣统政纪, 台湾文海出版社, 台北, 1967年)
Shen Y (2002) Collected works of Luofanlou. Shanghai Chinese Classics Publishing House, Shanghai. (沈垚, 落帆楼文集, 上海古籍出版社, 上海, 2002年)
Shen DD, Wu TJ (2015) Critical biography of Liang Qichao. Baihuazhou Wenyi Press, Nanchang. (沈大德, 吴廷嘉, 梁启超评传, 百花洲文艺出版社, 南昌, 2015年)
Shin TSW (1980) The concept of state (Kuo-Chia) and people (Min) in the late Ch'ing, 1890–1907: the case of Liang Ch'i-Ch'ao, Tan Ssu-T'ung and Huang Tsun-Hsien. Dissertation. University of California, Oakland

Sigmund PE (1963) Nicholas of Cusa and medieval political thought. Cambridge University Press, Cambridge
Sievers GS-v (1972) Die Reformbewegung von 1898. In: Opitz PJ (ed) Chinas große Wandlung. C H Beck, München, p 55-81
Skinner Q (1978) Foundations of modern political thought, vol.1, the renaissance. Cambridge University Press, Cambridge
Song PJ (2019) The discovery of the Imperial edict of Qing emperor' abdication signed by Yuan Shikai and its significance for understanding the state system transformation in late Qing and early republican period. Literature Hist Philos 4:74–93, 166-167 (宋培军, 袁世凯手批清帝辞位诏书的发现及其对清末民初国体因革的认知意义, 文史哲, 2019年第4期, 第74-93, 166-167页)
Speck T (2009) Quod omnes tangit: Rezeption als ekklesiologisches Phänomen bei Matthäus Romanus und Wilhelm von Ockham. Dissertation. Universität Freiburg, Freiburg
Spence JD (2008) Chinas Weg in die Moderne. Carl Hanser Verlag, Munich
Spengler T (1974) Liang Ch'i-ch'ao. In: Opitz PJ (ed) Die Söhne des Drachen. List, Munich, pp 110–127
Stanford Encyclopedia of Philosophy (2022) Qing Philosophy. https://plato.stanford.edu/entries/qing-philosophy/. Accessed 19 Mar 2021
Stubbs W (1913) Charters and excerpts illustrative of the reign of Edward I. In: Davis H (ed) Select charters and other illustrations of English constitutional history. Clarendon, Oxford, pp 417–506
Sun Y-s (1942) San min Chu I. Ministry of Information of the Republic of China, Calcutta
Sun ZS (1986) Complete works of Sun Zhongshan, vol 9. Zhonghua Book Company, Beijing. (孙中山, 孙中山全集, 中华书局, 北京, 1986年)
Tan CC (1971) Chinese political thought in the twentieth century. Doubleday & Company, New York
Teng S-y, Fairbank JK (1979) China's response to the west: a documentary survey 1839–1923. Harvard University Press, Cambridge
The Codification Committee of the Great Compendium of Chinese Characters (1988) The great Chinese dictionary. Hubei Dictionary Publishing Company and Sichuan Dictionary Publishing Company, Wuhan and Chengdu. (汉语大字典编纂委员会, 汉语大字典, 湖北辞书出版社, 四川辞书出版社, 成都, 1988年)
Thompson LG (1958) Biographical Sketsch of K'ang Yu-wei. In: Kang YW (ed) Ta Tung Shu. George Allen & Unwin, London, pp 11–25
Tierney B (1982) Religion, law and the growth of constitutional thought 1150–1650. Cambridge University Press, Cambridge
Tierney B (1995) Freedom and the medieval church. In: Davis RW (ed) The origins of modern freedom in the west. Stanford University Press, Stanford, pp 64–100
Tierney B (1998) Foundations of the conciliar theory. Brill, Leiden
Tierney B, Painter S (1983) Western Europe in the middle ages 300–1475, 4th edn. Random House, New York
Treadgold DW (1973) The west in Russia and China, vol 2. Cambridge University Press, Cambridge
Tsai JF (1981) The predicament of the comprador ideologists: He Qi (Ho Kai, 1859-1914) and Hu Liyuan (1847-1916). Modern China 7(2):191–225
Ullmann W (1972) A short history of the papacy in the middle ages. Methuen, London
Viechtbauer H, Wegmann K (1969) Sun Yat-sen. In: Opitz PJ (ed) Vom Konfuzianismus zum Kommunismus. List Verlag, Munich, pp 107–148
Wang RZ (1983) The reform thinking in late Qing dynasty. Linking Publishing, Taipei. (汪荣祖, 晚清变法思想论丛, 联经出版事业公司, 台北, 1983年)
Wang CN (2003) Reading the inscription from Sun Zhongshan. People's Tribune 1:57–59. (王春南, 读孙中山题词——"天下为公"), 人民论坛, 2003年第1期, 第57-59页)
Wang E (2007) An investigation on the creation of the book of rites. Zhonghua Book Company, Beijing. (王锷, 礼记成书考, 中华书局, 北京, 2007年)

Wang N (2009) Ancient Chinese. Beijing University Press, Beijing. (王宁 主编, 古代汉语, 北京大学出版社, 北京, 2009年)

Watner C (2005) Quod Omnes Tangit: consent theory in the radical libertarian tradition in the middle ages. J Libertarian Stud 19:67–85

Wei JT, Chen XC (1995) Exploring the civil rights thinking of Sun Zhongshan. Guangxi Normal University Press, Guilin. (韦杰廷, 陈先初, 孙中山民权主义探微, 广西师范大学出版, 桂林, 1995年)

Weiland L (1896) Constitutiones et acta publica imperatorum et regum inde ab a. MCXCVIII usque ad a. MCCLXXII (1198-1272). In: Monumenta Germaniae Historica(MGH). Harrassowitz Verlag, Wiesbaden

Wells A (2001) The political thought of Sun Yat-sen-development and impact. Palgrave, New York

Wilhelm R (1931) Preface. In: Tai TT (ed) Die geistigen Grundlagen des Sun Yat Senismus. Würfel Verlag, Gießen, p 8

Wilhelm R (ed) (1994) Li Gi, das Buch der Riten, Sitten und Bräuche. Eugen Diederichs Verlag, München

Wippel JF (1981) The metaphysical thought of Godfrey of Fontaines: a study in late thirteenth-century philosophy. CUA Press, Washington, DC

Wu K-C (1928) Ancient Chinese political theories. The Commercial Press, Beijing

Wu G (2018) Striving for democracy: confucian political philosophy in the Ming and Qing dynasties. In: Ames RT, Hershock PD (eds) Confucianisms for a changing world cultural order. University of Hawaii Press, Honolulu, pp 252–262

Xiao GQ (1998) The history of Chinese political thought. Liaoning Education Press, Shenyang. (萧公权, 中国政治思想史, 辽宁教育出版社, 沈阳, 1998年)

Xiao WY (2017) The westerners' translation toward Chinese sixty cycle. J Graduates Sun Yat-Sen Univ 38:25–36. (肖文远, 西方人对干支纪年的转译, 中山大学研究生学刊, 2017年第38期, 第25-36页)

Xu S (1979) Shuo Wen Jie Zi. Zhonghua Book Company, Beijing (许慎, 说文解字, 中华书局, 北京, 1979年)

Xu SM (2006) Critical biography of Gu Yanwu. Nanjing University Press, Nanjing. (许苏民, 顾炎武评传, 南京大学出版社, 南京, 2006年)

Xu DB (2011) Critical biography of Huang Zongxi. Nanjing University Press, Nanjing. (徐定宝, 黄宗羲评传, 南京大学出版社, 南京, 2011年)

Yang XY (2005) Research on Zhu Ciqi's scholarstic concepts. Master thesis. East China Normal University, Suzhou. (杨翔宇, 朱次琦学术思想研究, 华东师范大学硕士论文, 2005年)

Zarrow P (2009) Chinese conceptions of the state during the Late Qing Dynasty (1860–1911). In: Shogimen T, Nederman CJ (eds) Western political thought in dialogue with Asia. Lexington Books, Lanham

Zarrow P (2012) After empire: the conceptual transformation of the Chinese state, 1885–1924. Stanford University Press, Stanford

Zhang LH (2011) Critical biography of he qi and Hu Liyuan. Nanjing University Press, Nanjing. (张礼恒, 何启 胡礼垣评传, 南京大学出版社, 南京, 2011年)

Zhao NX (1985) Collected works of Weibozhai. Zhonghua Book Company, Beijing. (赵南星, 味檗斋文集, 中华书局, 北京, 1985年)

Zhou L, Liu G (2008) Tianxia Wei gong: the life pursuit of Sun Yat-Sen in his theory and practice. J Lit History 6:39–42. (周莉莉, 刘桂兰, 天下为公:孙中山毕生追求的理想和实践, 文史杂志, 2008年第6期, 第39-42页)

Chapter 4
Differences

It is natural and self-evident that two principles, evolving from totally diverse cultures, differentiate from each other, but they actually bear remarkable similarities when examined over time. Thus, their differences need to be unmasked and contemplated. In addition, it is their differences that may explain why the two principals have led to distinct results in history.

First, the principles themselves will be studied and examined by an analysis of the possible reasons for their own differences at the microlevel. In the following chapter, the differences in their characteristics and their developmental processes overlap at the macro level. In the last chapter, further discussion will be explored by examining some background information.

4.1 Inner Character

4.1.1 Inner Methodology

Although *Quod Omnes Tangit* and Tianxia Wei Gong have many common traits, which have been discussed in the previous chapter, these two maxims embrace different inner methodologies. Through the following introduction, explanation and comparison, it can be seen that except for the universal values such as freedom, equality and justice that they share, *Quod Omnes Tangit* and Tianxia Wei Gong reflect the different choices of the East and the West through some other values. To make a comparison between the different mechanisms in the two maxims, we will first show that our maxims have a close linkage with their separate inner mechanisms.

Y. Shang, *A Historical and Legal Comparison between Tianxia Wei Gong and Quod Omnes Tangit*, Ius Gentium: Comparative Perspectives on Law and Justice 110,
https://doi.org/10.1007/978-3-031-46467-6_4

Representation is a concept that has gained the most sophisticated meaning after a long-term reinterpretation.[1] This section will first review some literature on representation, then elaborate on the kind of representation most relevant to *Quod Omnes Tangit*, and finally analyze the relationship of this concept with Tianxia Wei Gong.

Although representation is one of the most important political concepts, the amount of literature dealing with this theme is largely less than it should be, especially compared with other themes such as democracy.[2] Hanna Pitkin's book of representation belongs to one of the most significant works on representation.[3] Unlike Pitkin's approach of "conceptual analysis," Hofmann adopted an approach evolving more elements, such as historical and cultural background.[4]

Hasso Hofmann raised a unique concept in European legal history, identity representation.[5] The special type of representation that *Quod Omnes Tangit* relates to, identity representation, was used to solve the problem of continuity in Italian communes in the middle ages during the transition from the governance of republic aristocracy to absolutism.[6] The case of Germany was different: the federal republic of Germany was not identical to the German empire but only represented it; this does not necessarily mean abandoning continuity but rather abandoning identity in the one-state form.[7]

In researching representation for this thesis, its etymological meaning was often explored, including its translations in Latin, English, French and German.[8] In Chinese, the word for representation is 代表, composed of two characters, with each having its own meaning. Interestingly, the first character 代 means substituting, and the second character 表 means presenting. Considering all the meanings of representation, no hint shows that Tianxia Wei Gong has any coinciding point with representation. A gap exists between Tianxia Wei Gong and representation. In contrast, *Quod Omnes Tangit* is closely related to representation, especially as a maxim of identity representation.[9] This accounts for a major difference between Tianxia Wei Gong and *Quod Omnes Tangit* from the perspective of inner methodology.

The traditional cosmological view of Chinese differs from that of Westerners. Highlighting an organic whole, the Chinese think highly of a harmonious relationship with everything else, since all things relate to each other and are reciprocal, which constitutes a sharp contrast with egotism held by Westerners. Chen Lai

[1] Pitkin (1967), pp. 2–6; Mulieri (2016), p. 128.

[2] Runciman (2006), p. 165.

[3] Pitkin (1967), pp. 1–6.

[4] Pitkin (1967), p. 7; Hofmann (2003), p. 35.

[5] Hofmann (2003), p. 216.

[6] Hofmann (2003), pp. 216, 217.

[7] Hofmann (2003), p. 218.

[8] Mulieri (2016), pp. 128, 129.

[9] Hofmann (2003), p. 216.

concluded the opinions of several sinologists as follows.[10] French socialist and anthropologist Marcel Granet mentioned in the 1930s that one of the main characteristics of the thinking habit for Chinese people is that they regard everything as correlating existence.[11] In the 1970s, American Sinologist Frederick Mote addressed this from another perspective: the Chinese are the single population lacking a creation myth, so the Chinese believe the world and the human species were not born from the hand of God but rather on their own.[12] Mote thought that Creation by God came from the conception of causality, while the Chinese believed in synchronicity.[13] Hence, the ancient Chinese would deem that it sufficed to comprehend the cosmologic mechanism with the balance between inner harmony and the organic part of the world; a God would be redundant.[14] It is not accurate to say that the Chinese people have no mythology, bearing in mind that they widely recognize Pan Gu, creator of the universe, whose body turned into various fragments of the world; such as the skin into the ground, the eyes into the sun and moon.[15] This story, however, also helps to support the Mote's argument. In the words of Joseph Needham, Chinese thinking favors a networking relationship in which incidents can be put into a certain process, as described in the theory of Whitehead, while Westerners were affected by Newton and preferred individual and causal chains. Therefore, the former described the cosmologic process as a net knitting by correlated incidents, while the latter imagined the cosmos as a causal chain stringing together a cluster of incidents.[16] Some scholars, in contrast, thought that Chinese mythology took birth and breed as the origin of the world instead of creation, which could be attributed to the expression of agricultural civilization and, moreover, to the influence of worship toward ancestors.[17] Ernest Cassier emphasized the belief in the unification of life, which implies communication between various forms of life as individuals and relates all of them to one another.[18] The thinking that the world is not created by God results in the high status of man in comparison with heaven and earth.

Returning to the maxim of Tianxia Wei Gong, this also stresses the cooperation of everyone when living in the same world. There is no individual, no procedure, but rather a relationship network, which is in line with the characteristics of traditional Chinese philosophic thinking.

Chinese feudal society was a patriarchal society in which all kinds of social relationships were family-like. The central moral plank was the Three Bonds:

---

[10] Chen (2015), p. 25.

[11] Ames (2009), p. 202.

[12] Mote (1971), pp. 17–18; Mote (2009), p. 19.

[13] Mote (1971), p. 22: "causality" "synchronicity"; Mote (2009), p. 23: "因果性"和"同时性"。.

[14] Mote (1971), pp. 23–24; Mote (2009), p. 26.

[15] Mote also mentioned the legend but thought it not meaningful, Mote (1971), p. 18.

[16] Whitehead (1933), pp. 168–169; Needham (1991), (vol. 2) p. 292; cited in Mote (1971), p. 27.

[17] Schwartz (2004), p. 25.

[18] Cassirer (1954), pp. 112–115.

emperor-subject, parent–child, husband-wife.[19] Although this element of Confucius had to be abandoned in the late Qing, this trait was retained. In one family, all family members shared the resources and shouldered responsibilities together. The principle to manage a dispute was sentiment rather than law. Liang Shuming, a Chinese scholar, thought that the ethics-oriented society of China was born from patriarchal society.[20] Chen Lai wrote that since the Spring and Autumn, patriarchal orders in the political field have dissolved, but at the social level, they still exist, and the traits and spirits cultivated by patriarchal orders have been inherited.[21] Chen Lai also identified the core values of Chinese civilization, which can be found in Tianxia Wei Gong. They are the priority of responsibility to liberty, obligations to rights, collectivity to individual and harmony to conflict.[22] In morality textbooks at the beginning of the twentieth century in China, it was discussed that the old trope of the state was an extended family. The contrast between private/selfish (si私) and public good (gong 公) was adopted to emphasize that just as a family could not be "privatized", the state should not be so, either.[23] "The state is the common property of its people just as a family is the common property of its members. This implied a distinction between patriotism and loyalism."[24] Nevertheless, the goal is always harmony and has not ever changed. "[']The family is the basis of the state, and the relationship between husband and wife is the basis of the family. ['] And so, [']If there is harmony between husband and wife, then the country will be at peace. [']".[25]

The core value of Chinese civilization, according to the conclusion of Chen Lai, is highlighted by the responsibility shouldered by individuals toward other people, the community, and even nature. Responsibility requires individuals to prioritize the needs of others rather than their own. A series of norms of morality reflect such a relationship, for instance, Xiao, the responsibility toward parents; Zhong, the responsibility toward higher authorities; and Xin, the responsibility toward friends.[26] In the thinking of Confucianism, an individual is not an atom but an organic part of society.[27] Every time an individual relates to others, the other is more important than the self.

Comparing Tianxia Wei Gong with *Quod Omnes Tangit*, this trait seems to be evident. Tianxia Wei Gong underlines the responsibility of everyone toward the

---

[19]Zarrow (2009), p. 236.

[20]Liang (1982), p. 81.

[21]Chen (2015), p. 38.

[22]Chen (2015), pp. 51–56.

[23]Liu (1903), p. 1a-2a.

[24]Zarrow (2009), p. 245.

[25]Zarrow (2009), p. 245: 高步瀛(Gao Buying) and陈宝泉(Chen Baoquan), 通俗国民必读 (*Tongsu Guomin Bidu*) 1:1a-b. Zarrow made a mistake on the first author's name of Tongsu Guomin Bidu. The right name should be Gao Bulian, 高步濂.

[26]Chen (2015), p. 51.

[27]New World Encyclopedia contributors (2021) Confucianism. In: New World Encyclopedia. https://www.newworldencyclopedia.org/entry/Confucianism. Accessed Apr 9 2021.

world, while *Quod Omnes Tangit* emphasizes that everyone has the right to participate in a decision.

Liang Shuming, a famous Confucian in the twentieth century, after practicing self-governance in Shan Dong and He Bei provinces in China, said that to shoulder obligations to each other is the basic distinction of Chinese ethics.[28]

> When people are born, there will be other people who have various relationships with them. This is Tianlun; people will always be in relationships with each other. This is ethics. This kind of intimate and interconnected feeling arises from flesh and blood; even if all related people naturally have feelings, where there is friendship, obligations arise. The duty of the father is kindness, and the duty of the son lies in filial piety. The duty of the elder brother is to be friendly. The duty of the younger brother is to be deferential, and the couple and friends, and even all related people, have their due obligations. An ethical relationship represents an obligation. A person does not exist for himself, but he should respect the other person. People in modern Western countries, on the contrary, can see their own positionalism everywhere, and everything starts with the concept of rights.[29]

All Confucian virtues appear in the form of obligation, which translates the humanity of the self into co-humanity with others. Their goal is not to guarantee individual interest but to render social responsibility to individuals. Li, for example, is also a responsibility in the sense that it requires individuals to improve themselves.[30]

Both Tianxia Wei Gong and *Quod Omnes Tangit* have the same theme: how to decide and handle public affairs involving more than one person. These two maxims are similar to the two sides of one coin: Tianxia Wei Gong stresses the obligation side and *Quod Omnes Tangit* the side of rights.

Chinese civilization puts special attention on family, considering family as the first social unit when an individual relates to others. From the first social circle to the outside world, the nation, the world and so on serve as the second and third social circles. There is no abstract conception about community, with family, nation and Tianxia acting as representatives. It is worth noting that those following levels of social circle are also entitled to the value of family and are expected to embrace the characteristics of a family. Unlike Plato and Aristotle distinguishing family, state, domestic affairs and civil politics in ancient Greek society, and emphasizing that these two situations are not supposed to overlap; rather, politics have priority over family.[31]China, from ancient times to today, has always tied family and state together, as shown in these idioms: "one should work for the father in the family and for the emperor in the court," "cultivate one's moral character and manage the

---

[28]Thøgersen (2009), p. 11.

[29]Trans. from Chen (2015), p. 53: "人生必有其相关系之人, 此即天伦;人生将始终在人与人相关系中, 此即伦理。亲切相关之情, 发乎天伦骨肉;乃至一切相关之人莫不自然有其情, 情谊所在, 义务生焉。父义当慈, 子义当孝, 兄之义友, 弟之义恭, 夫妇朋友至一切相关之人莫不自然互有应尽之义。伦理关系即表示一种义务, 一个人撕不为其自己而存在, 而以对方为重。近世之西洋人反是, 处处形见其自己本位主义, 一切从权利观念出发。".

[30]Cheng (2016), p. 160.

[31]Plato (2012), pp. 449c–461e; Aristotle (1995), I.1252b, II1261a; for the difference of Plato and Aristotle on opinions family, see Goodsell and Whiting (2016), pp. 484–485.

family affairs well," and "protect our homes and defend our country."[32] Regarding family as the base is one of the major symbols of traditional Chinese ethics and morals. In addition, although mankind is worshipped in traditional Chinese culture more than any god, a single man can only realize his value as a member of his family. It is of far greater worth to be a father, a brother and a son than to be an individual.[33]

This may explain why *Quod Omnes Tangit* has experienced a development from *ius privatum* to *ius publicum*, but the public and private conception in Tianxia Wei Gong is always ambiguous. There is never a separation of the two and no turning point in its historical evolution. Individuals should treat others as their own family, even when dealing with public affairs. According to the values that Tianxia Wei Gong advocates, public welfare is constructed on the basis of everyone's sacrifice; according to *Quod Omnes Tangit*, public welfare is determined by everyone protecting his own interests.

Chinese civilization is noted for its tendency to equivocate conflict. Most Chinese people are shy and express themselves rather indirectly. Relating this trait to the comparison of Tianxia Wei Gong with *Quod Omnes Tangit*, Tianxia Wei Gong expresses the issue of decision-making very ambiguously, expressing the hope of maintaining harmony, but *Quod Omnes Tangit* emphasizes the importance of every individual's opinion without fear of confronting any possible conflict regarding their opinions.

The conception of Tianxia, according to the conclusion of Chen Lai, contains three meanings.[34] The first is a geographic perspective, meaning the world. The second refers to the domain ruled by the Chinese Emperor. The third means the world with China in the middle. Some scholars alleged that the Chinese were aware only of Tianxia rather than of a state; others declared that the Chinese thought of China as the whole world.[35] These statements make some sense but are far from exact, as the Chinese had established their conception of state during the Han Dynasty,[36] commencing in 221 AD.

Mutschler compared the tendencies of Sima Qian and Tacitus, two of the most significant historians in eastern and western history, finding that Sima Qian tended to represent the preservation of peace and harmony, while Tacitus placed greater value on campaigns of conquering and the expansion of dominion.[37] He thought that Sima Qian's description referred to the goal of establishing a peaceful and harmonious

---

[32]Li (2015), p. 56:"迩之事父, 远之事君", "修身齐家治国平天下", "保家卫国"。Trans. by the author.

[33]Li (2015), p. 113.

[34]Chen (2015), pp. 91–92.

[35]Chen (2015), p. 93.

[36]Yao (2010), p. 260.

[37]Mutschler (2008), pp. 127–128. Mutschler took Wendi (203 BC –157 BC), an emporer of Han Dynasty (206 BC–220 AD), as an example: "Several letters to and from the shan yu, the ruler of the Xiongnu, are quoted in full, whereas the reports on campaigns comprise never more than a few lines." In contrast, Tacitus was delighted to describe "the campaigns of Germanicus in Germany and blames Tiberius for not being engaged in expanding Rome's dominion."

relationship with these most dangerous barbarian tribes since the empire is conceived of as Tianxia, comprising the world as a whole, and there is no surrounding world but barbarian tribes.[38] This argument found its support in Peter Zarrow's note that it was not until Zheng Guanying (1842–1922) that it was confirmed that the world consisted of a plurality of independent states rather than "all under heaven."[39]

The attitude of the Chinese toward other countries is always under the guidance of rites and ethics, emphasizing a friendly relationship with neighbors and sparing no effort to maintain peace all around.[40] Before the first united nation of China, the Qin Dynasty, Tianxia was a synonym for the royal Zhou family, which was higher than any state.[41] Tianxia, at the same time, was more valuable than state. This perception continues to affect the political assumptions of Chinese. For instance, the peace of Tianxia is the utmost political pursuit, higher than a well-ruled state.[42] A nation barely belongs to the highest political conception in the mind of the Chinese, constituting their view toward the world.[43] There is one statement in Li Gi echoing this perspective: taking the world as one family, China as one man.[44] This kind of thinking never dies out in Chinese tradition; in contrast, it is well inherited and can be found even today. For instance, the slogan of the 2008 Beijing Olympic games was "one world, one dream," reflecting the thinking of Da Tong 大同as well.

Through this examination, two sets of mechanisms have been displayed.

4.1.2 Communications Canal

With the consideration of the target audiences of the two principles, there are the common people on one end and, on the other end, the decision-makers. The birth of the principles likely happened at the moment when the decision-maker was interacting with the common people. In this way, a major difference appears between the two principles.

In *Quod Omnes Tangit*, there is a communicative channel between the top and the bottom, a two-way channel.[45] Basically, two steps are needed to accommodate the requirements in *Quod Omnes Tangit*. First, the decision-maker or the common people themselves declare that something has touched all and all must consent to it. Second, the common people must consent to it.

---

[38] Mutschler (2008), pp. 127–130.

[39] Zarrow (2009), p. 241.

[40] Chen (2015), p. 66.

[41] Liu and Huang (2006), pp. 523–524; Zhao (2009), pp. 7–9.

[42] Wilhelm (1994), pp. 46–55. Chinese original text: "修身齐家治国平天下".

[43] Zhao (2011), p. 42.

[44] Feng (1982), p. 43: 礼记 礼运, "以天下为一家, 以中国为一人".

[45] See also Reilly (2020), p. 102.

In Tianxia Wei Gong, however, only the first step can be found. Moreover, not only does the after-phase make a difference, so does the content of the principle itself. Tianxia Wei Gong only declares that the rights belong to the people, but there is no such internal communicative channel that facilitates the achievement of these rights. There is nothing to bridge the gap between the decision-maker and the common people. Furthermore, the information flow is unidirectional. In China's situation, it always goes from top to bottom. The superior could or would not listen to the common people.[46] At least, from the perspective of this principle, this mechanism lacks this channel. Most likely due to this fact, in China, it must always be strongly emphasized to take the influence of the principle into consideration and to listen to the common people. However, the executive effect is never satisfied. After all, it is not a necessary part of the principle.

Zarrow locates this issue in late Qing time. He mentions that mediators responsible for connecting the emperors and the world are as important as the emperors themselves.

> The [']road of speech['] (yanlu) or, more prosaically, channels of communication to the emperor, was a time-honored political value. The classics, with their idealized yet often fallible kings, emphasized the importance of good and frank advice.[47]

Nevertheless, due to the lack of a communication tunnel in the principle of Tianxia Wei Gong, the road of speech has not continuously been a valued political principle and a right of the people, but rather a means of ruling, and the ruler can decide if it is necessary to put it into use or set it aside. The Empress Dowager Cixi closed the road in 1885, and it was reopened by Emperor Guangxu in 1898 and reclosed in the same year owing to the crush of the reform.[48] However, after that, the "road of speech" gradually produced "popular power" (minquan).[49]

The second step could be called political participation. According to Jack H. Nagel, participation refers to "*actions through which ordinary members of a political system influence or attempt to influence outcomes.*"[50] This character, the lack of communicative channels, leads to the custom that the Chinese people are relatively obedient and always hesitate to explain for themselves, not to mention the fight against the upper class. It can be witnessed not only in political life—they have no interest in election or other political affairs—but also in social phenomena. For example, in a university classroom, most Chinese students are timid and not encouraged to express their ideas. Teachers play the most important role in the classroom, while in the West, the students are empowered to answer questions; there are more courses in which not only do the teachers give lessons but the students also have many discussions. Details also matter: the students in the West do not need to stand

[46] See also Elvin (1998), pp. 213, 222.

[47] Zarrow (2012), p. 18.

[48] Zarrow (2012), p. 19.

[49] Zarrow (2012), p. 19.

[50] Nagel (1987), p. 1.

up to answer the teacher's questions, while it is a requirement in Chinese universities. Students still show different attitudes toward the upper class because the communicative channels offered are derived from different backgrounds. In the West, students are accustomed to this communicative tunnel as a daily occurrence, while Chinese students are quite cautious in the face of change. These distinct customs can be traced back to the differences between the two principles.

The communication canal enables dialogue. In the Occidental world, there is a dialogue-friendly history. Medieval thinkers examined conversations between Christians and non-Western interlocutors.[51] They believed that

> the tenets of Christianity, not to mention the lessons of philosophy and history, suggested that differences in belief ought to be addressed from the standpoint of patience and charity, manifested through dialogue and discussion.[52]

Opinion counts as a core element of dialogue, which contains much of the active character of individuals. The concept of opinion underwent a long and full development in Western history. Blaise Pascal once highly praised "opinion," saying that

> [o]pinion settles everything. . . . I would like very much to see that Italian work, of which I have heard only the title: [']Opinion, the Queen of the World. ['] It alone is worth many other books.[53]

This became a famous saying for Pascal, quoted by many academics.[54] Another notable saying comes from David Hume: "It is, therefore, on opinion only that government is founded."[55] It is quoted by John Durham Peters from J.A.W. Gunn, tracing this trail to James Madison, Jefferson, and all the way to Tacitus.[56] Peters concluded that "[t]he term has a strong collective sense: opinion has long referred to what passes among [']the many['] for truth."[57] He thought even "[c]hanges in the meaning of [']opinion['] clearly parallel the revolutionary changes in political institutions and ideas in this period,"[58] referring to the second half of the eighteenth century.

Plena Potestas means sufficient power. Together with *Quod Omnes Tangit*, it is able to construct a system of representation,[59] specifically the representational government. *Plena Potestas* can be traced back to Roman law and was already being applied and developed by canonists in the twelfth and thirteenth centuries.[60] Initially, *Plena Potestas* was adopted as a principle in private law, which defines the

---

[51] Nederman (2009), p. 46.

[52] Nederman (2009), p. 46.

[53] Pascal (1849), p. 96.

[54] Gunn (1983), pp. 264, 265; Peters (1995), p. 5.

[55] Hume (1788), p. 37.

[56] Gunn (1983), p. 20; cited in Peters (1995), p. 5.

[57] Peters (1995), p. 5.

[58] Peters (1995), p. 5.

[59] Tierney (1995), pp. 85–86; Tierney (1982), p. 23.

[60] Monahan (1987), pp. 125–126; Post (1964), pp. 91–110.

role of a lawyer as an agent for his principle in a lawsuit.[61] The application of *Plena Potestas* then expanded to business and politics.[62] What is the power in *Plena Potestas*? If the formula *Plena Potestas* was only a *pro forma* affirmation of royal decision, it would not entitle the user many rights; but if it was a substantial ratification, it would be able to help the user capture the royal authority,[63] and then it would become a mighty principle. Gaines Post discussed these two possibilities in detail.[64]

It can be concluded that *Plena Potestas*, together with *Quod Omnes Tangit*, has at least the potential to be the principle that can entitle or confine power. However, Tianxia Wei Gong has nothing to do with the entitlement of power. Thus, it did not give rise to the representation government, either.

In fact, *Quod Omnes Tangit* involves the idea of public opinion, whereas Tianxia Wei Gong hardly hints at it. "Public opinion implies communication."[65] In Glasser's opinion, communications research and opinion research mean two opposite directions of information flow: communications research from top to bottom and opinion research the other way around.[66] If we see the two maxims as principles in charge of information flow, then we can observe that in *Quod Omnes Tangit*, there are two directions of information flow, but in Tianxia Wei Gong, there are none, or at most, the information flows from top to bottom. There is a long history discussing the essence of opinion in the West, dating back to "Plato's contrast of *doxa* (opinion) from *epistêmê* (knowledge)," which follows Aristotle's argument for practical wisdom (*phronêsis*), a different kind of knowledge than *epistêmê*.[67] For the Greeks, *doxa* was "the decision reached in political assemblies: *doxa* thus also has the sense of consensus or views held in common;"[68] thus, it is also the result of *Quod Omnes Tangit*. In contrast, regarding Tianxia Wei Gong, no such nuances, thus far, have been noted or discussed.[69]

Participation

Quod Omnes Tangit invites participation.

As early as Aristotle's time, Western thinkers were concerned about participation. Aristotle has an interesting statement on the farming class participating in the constitution. He says that with their work taking all their time, they cannot enjoy any leisure, including the leisure to rule; as a result, they promote the law and confine the meetings to a minimum.[70] Regardless of the accuracy of this statement, it suffices

[61] Post (1964), p. 93; Tierney (1982), pp. 23–24.

[62] Post (1964), p. 103.

[63] Post (1964), pp. 91–92.

[64] Post (1943), pp. 355–408.

[65] Glasser and Salmon (1995), p. xxiii.

[66] Glasser and Salmon (1995), p. xxii.

[67] Glasser and Salmon (1995), p. 4.

[68] Kim (2016), p. 259; Peters (1995), p. 4; Gadamer (1990), pp. 371, 372.

[69] See the explanation of Tianxia in 3.1.1 of this book.

[70] Aristotle (1995), p. 147, 1292b21.

to prove the existence and significance of the theme of participation in Western political thought history, which is lacking in the historic context of the East.

4.1.3 Some Original Reasons for the Differences

Some natural and geographical conditions contribute to the divergence of the two maxims. China bears various mainland characters thanks to its continental geographical condition as opposed to the oceanic characteristics of Europe.[71] Confucius mentioned the ocean only once in Lunyu.[72] Ancient Chinese people dwelled on a semi-closed continent surrounded by dessert in the northwest, Chomolungma in the southwest and the Pacific in the east.[73] These geographical conditions shaped the worldview of the Chinese to such an extent that they thought China was the center of the world and that Chinese society was the sole civilization.[74] That is why Tianxia is also a synonym for "the world." In addition, inside this geological semicircle around the Chinese mainland, the conditions for the development of agriculture are optimum. The terrain is flat, the soil fertile, the climate agreeable and the water supply abundant. The land, the carrier of agriculture, bears the lifestyle and social structure of the people living on it. One of the most notable characteristics of agricultural society is its dependence on nature. In regard to the relationship between people and nature, the ancient Chinese showed more conformity to than conquest of nature. One example is the idiom "Heaven and man are one" 天人合一.[75] Peasants tend to spend a lifetime on their land cultivation without departing for long distances. Villages are alike and separated, under which circumstances they tend to focus more on unity than on individual rights[76] because the conflict of rights seldom arises. Villagers need a stable social environment to conduct their agricultural activities. Therefore, they tend to uphold unity and prioritize social harmony rather than individual rights. This kind of thought continues from ancient times to the "three people's principles" of Sun Yat-sen throughout Chinese history.[77]

---

[71] Feng (2017), p. 42.

[72] Shang et al. (2008), p. 2: "If the proposition is indeed impossible to implement, I would like to float overseas on a wooden raft. However, I am afraid that only Zhongyou will follow me?"("道不行，乘桴桴于海。从我者其由于。"(论语·公冶长)) See original text, Chinese Text Project (2022): https://ctext.org/analects/gong-ye-chang/zh?searchu=子曰:"道不行，乘桴浮于海。從我者其由與?" Accessed 11 Nov 2022.

[73] Liu and Huang (2006), pp. 517–518.

[74] See also Zhao (2009), pp. 9–11.

[75] Yao (2014), p. 570.

[76] Jiang (2012), p. 15.

[77] Sun (1986), p. 120, 185, 189, 238–240, 244; cited in Jiang (2012), p. 121; however, there were also opposition against the traditional Chinese patriarchal Clan system, see Jiang (2012), pp. 120–123.

Natural resources such as light and water were abundant enough to serve the demands of the ancient Chinese. There were even many hermits living in the mountains during the Weijinnanbei Dynasty. Thus, conflicts and negotiations were avoided. It was possible that when a conflict about the use of light and water arose, the person concerned could choose to make a concession and move away to another place with the same, equally satisfying supply. As a result, the ancient Chinese did not have to learn how to deal with the problem of the allocation of resources, which were too abundant to attract the attention of the people and were not so rare and cherished to be developed as an abstract concept of 'rights.'[78] In the case of the West, people had no other choice but to face the allocation of limited resources directly. Therefore, they had to develop a mechanism for solving this problem which arose frequently in their daily life.

These geographical conditions and lifestyles contributed to the patriarchal clan system.[79] People valued their consanguinity, placed much emphasis on family life and worshiped their ancestors instead of gods.[80] Thus, the state is structured to resemble that of a family, inside which the authority must be respected, and consociation is emphasized, aligning at the ultimate purpose of Tianxia Wei Gong.

It is obvious that for the two maxims, there are different carriers, as the languages used are not the same. Sometimes this difference is so sharp and simple that it conceals some possible subjects worth studying that may have an influence on the thinking methods and philosophy of these two maxims. Therefore, it is necessary to re-examine their linguistic traditions.

Latin was the language of reflective political discussion in the middle ages. By 1500, English had yet to be spoken, while Latin had a literary history of 900 years, with the 12 Tables of 450–400 B.C. being the first relevant record of Roman legal terminology.

The Chinese language uses no articles, no sex, no plural, no tense and no voice. How could the Chinese be able to describe, explain or understand each other? It all depends on context. Thus, there are plenty of unsaid things that one must comprehend. Tianxia Wei Gong also follows this style.

There is a striking difference between the learning materials of the East and the west. There were several arts in both, "six arts" or "seven liberal arts," by which the discrepancy could have already been explained. The so-called "seven liberal arts" consisted of the trivium (grammar, rhetoric and logic), the quadrivium (arithmetic, astronomy, geometry and music) and the students spending most of their time on logic.[81] Thus, it is not surprising that Western scholars thought more about methodology. How they were cultivated was quite different. The skills to handle weapons

[78]Or in China, the patriarchal clan system shouldered the responsibility of allocation of resource, see Jiang (2012), p. 153.

[79]Jiang (2012), p. 63.

[80]Jiang (2012), p. 7.

[81]Danziger and Gillingham (2004), p. 80.

and to fight on a horse were much admired and taught by fencing masters and weapons.[82] Similarly, this was the case in the east.

Thus, it could be observed that the main difference lies in the discipline of Rite (Li) and logic. Westerners are excellent in the design of various mechanisms but not in the judgment of them. For example, they created the mechanism of election but were not concerned about whether benign or vicious results emerged, at first. In contrast, the easterners would not design any mechanisms and only focus on the correctness of the ethical and moral aspects, although this concentration and advocation do not naturally enhance their level of morality or cultivate more virtuous people.

4.2 Development Process

The birth of *Quod Omnes Tangit* marks a turning point in law history that indicates several qualitative changes, inter alia, from *ius privatum* to *ius publicum*, from *ius naturale* to *ius positivum* and from religion law to secular law, which to some degree symbolize the modernization and civilization of law. Through the examination of Quod Omnes Tangit and Tianxia Wei Gong against this background, inspiring thoughts about the question of what the differences between the West and the East are and why emerge.

4.2.1 *From* Ius Privatum *to* Ius Publicum *or Vice Versa?*

The division between private law and public law could be treated as a basic character, which shows that the modern European law system is related to Roman law.[83] The definition originated from Ulpian.[84] However, the distinction between private and public laws played no important role at that time.[85] It was not until the sixteenth and seventeenth centuries that this distinction finally aroused attention in legal, practical and political fields.[86] *Ius Publicum*, the regulatory law of ruling, cannot be violated or bargained for by an individual; in contrast, *ius privatum*, a law that regulates the Private Autonomy of an individual, can be changed by contract.[87]

[82] Danziger and Gillingham (2004), p. 107.

[83] Landau (2013), p. 295.

[84] Dig.1.1.1.2: *Publicum ius est quod ad statum rei Romanae spectat, privatum, quod ad singulorum utilitatem*. See *Digest* (Justinian 2009), p. 1.

[85] Landau (2013), p. 295.

[86] Bullinger (1968), p. 16, cited in Landau (2013), p. 296; see also Stein (1995), pp. 499–504.

[87] Moos (2004), p. 16.

Landau commented on several academics' opinions about the separation of *ius publicum* and *ius privatum* as follows: Dieter Wyduckel comprehended *ius publicum* more from the source of law than from the goal set by the public utility, quoting more work from Kardinals Hostiensis than canon sources and could not determine to what extent a utilization of *ius publicum* could be reflected in the source and the references from those authors[88]; Hans Müllejans thought that the canon law was neither formally nor essentially divided according to the concepts of *ius publicum* and *ius privatum*.[89] There are, however, some doubts about the research results of Müllejans. Landau criticized that Müllejans missed the point that his historical results ultimately verified his systematic approach that the division of *ius privatum* and *ius publicum* may be essentially different.[90] Despite the dispute, the whole positive canon law should be deemed as *ius publicum*.[91]

Quod Omnes Tangit is a connection between public law and private law. It is a political principle that is meaningful in both private law and administrative law.[92] The maxim would be applied initially to private law but gradually to public law, as well. During the time of Justinian, it was applied to the co-exercise of a guardianship and the nomination of guardians. In the case of the construction of an aqueduct, the use of this maxim can be found, as well. Both situations fall into the realm of private law. The era of Innocent III witnessed two main uses of the maxim: procedure law and the general principle of consultancy,[93] both of which were geared to public law.

The ideal of *ius publicum* was based on common welfare, general obligation and what always prevailed.[94] The spirit of *Quod Omnes Tangit* matches the ideal of *ius publicum*. Although it had little connection to popular sovereignty, *Quod Omnes Tangit*, benefiting from the general trend of revival of legal science, entered the realm of medieval public law and politics.[95]

During the development of the concept of right, there was also a transition from the right being private to the right being public. Although aiming at analyzing the difference between *ius* and *dominium*, Richard Tuck found a case in point: "the Emperor Hadrian gave squatters on virgin land in his imperial domain of North Africa the [']ius to possess it, take its crop and transmit it to heirs[']."[96] This kind of property right is born private and bilateral but gradually becomes public, extending to every corner of people's lives.[97]

---

[88]Wyduckel (1984), p. 107, cited in Landau (2013), p. 296.

[89]Müllejans (1961), p. 1, cited in Landau (2013), p. 297.

[90]Landau (2013), p. 297.

[91]Landau (2013), p. 299.

[92]Marongiu (1980), pp. 186–187.

[93]Congar (1980), p. 117, Yves Congar deemed procedure law as private law, with which the author disagrees.

[94]Gierke (1868), p. 643.

[95]Fasolt (2014), pp. 228–229.

[96]Tuck (1979), p. 11; Frank (1959), p. 94.

[97]Tuck (1979), pp. 5–13.

Tianxia Wei Gong did not experience such a transformation from private law to public law. Moreover, it cannot be called a law but rather something similar to a law, albeit an incomplete one. If it were a law, it could only belong to public law since there was no private law in ancient China. It seems to be the conclusion that the law that does not derive from individuals will not take the protection of individuals into consideration in the process of transformation and development unless it adopts the concept from the outside because in the expression of Tianxia Wei Gong, there is only community rather than individual members. Nevertheless, this statement has not involved the entirety of Tianxia Wei Gong. In Liyun, it was explicitly expressed that special care should be taken of the old and the young.[98] However, it could be noticed that the principle was supplemented in a passive way, in which the allocation of obligations takes priority over the entitlement of rights.

As explained at the very beginning of this thesis, there is no counterpart of Tianxia in English or Gong. The synonymous meanings are public, common and general. However, Gong is a concept with many historical changes in the particular cultural context of East Asia, which entails various meanings with slight differences and some relevance.[99] This may help us to grasp the meaning of the phrase Tianxia Wei Gong, with related research on the exact meaning of Gong.

In Tianxia Wei Gong, the individual is not as revered as it is in *Quod Omnes Tangit*. In China, it has long been a tendency to advocate and uphold Gong and to derogate and dispraise Si, as will be shown in the quest for the origin of Gong. Shuowen Jiezi explained Gong as equal division and the opposite of Si.[100] However, Mizoguchi Yuzo revealed that in the world of Oracle bone script and Chinese bronze inscriptions, no explanation of Si existed.[101] Thus, we must rely on other documents. Lee Seung-hwan calculated how many times Gong appeared in several important Chinese classics as follows:

Yijing, The Book of Change six times
Shujing, The Book of Documents 75 times
Shijing, The Book of Poetry 95 times[102]

For example, in Yijing,

"六四:中行告公从, 利用为依迁国。"[103]
("Hexagram 42,
Six in the fourth place means:
If you walk in the middle
And report to the prince,
He will follow.

---

[98] Liyun is one chapter of Liji, see this thesis p. 22; Confucius (1885), pp. 364–367.

[99] Nylan (2009), p. 43.

[100] Xu (1981), p. 105: "公, 平分也, 从八从厶。八, 犹背也。韩非曰:背厶为公。" (Gong, equally dividing something, is composed of 八 and 厶. 八 means to opposite. Hanfei said, to opposite Si means Gong.)

[101] Mizoguchi (2011), pp. 232–237.

[102] Lee (2006), p. 105.

[103] Zhou (2015), p. 220: 益, 卦四十二, 风雷益 (Hexagram 42, 'Increase').

It furthers one to be used
In the removal of the capital."[104])

"六五:密云不雨, 自我西郊；公弋取彼在穴。"[105]

("Hexagram 62,
Six in the fifth place means:
Dense clouds,
No rain from our western territory.
The prince shoots and hits him who is in the cave."[106])

In Shujing,

"立太师、太傅、太保, 兹惟三公。论道经邦, 燮理阴阳。"[107]

("Establishing the positions of Taishi, Taifu and Taibao, called three Dukes, whose responsibilities are harmonizing Yin and Yang, educating the ruler of Zhou and assisting him to reign the country.")

"今予一二伯父尚胥暨顾, 绥尔先公之臣服于先王。"[108]

("Now I hope you, my uncles, can care for each other and follow your ancestor to carry out the service to the king."[109])

In Shijing,

"言私其豵, 献豜于公"[110]

("The boars of one year are for themselves;
Those of three years are for our prince."[111])

"雨我公田, 遂及我私"[112]

("May it rain first on our public fields,
And then come to our private!"[113])

"被之僮僮, 夙夜在公"[114]

("With head-dress reverently rising aloft,

---

[104] Chinese Classics (1977), p. 374. Cf. Chinese Classics (1882), p. 150.

[105] Zhou (2015), p. 315: 小过, 卦六十二, 雷山小过 (Hexagram 62, 'Preponderance of the Small').

[106] Chinese Classics (1977), p. 509. Cf. Chinese Classics (1882), p. 203.

[107] Chinese Classics (1980), p. 235.

[108] Chinese Classics (1980), p. 244.

[109] Cf. Chinese Classics (1865), p. 567: "Now do ye, my uncles, I pray you, consider with one another, and carry out the service which the dukes, your predecessors, rendered to my predecessors."

[110] Chinese Classics (2019), p. 412.

[111] Chinese Classics (1871), p. 230. Cf. Chinese Classics (1974), p. 98: "we keep for ourselves the young boars, we present the older boars to the prince."

[112] Chinese Classics (2019), p. 557.

[113] Chinese Classics (1871), p. 381; Cf. Chinese Classics (1974), p. 166–167: "it rains on our public field, and then comes to our private fields".

[114] Chinese Classics (2019), p. 45.

Early, while yet it is night, she is in the prince's *temple*"[115])

In Chunqiu Zuozhuan,

"[庄公]十有五年春，齐侯、宋公、陈侯、卫侯、郑伯会于鄄。"[116]

("Duke Zhuang, year 15, spring: The marquis of Qi, the duke of Song, the marquises of Chen and Wei, and the count of Zheng met in Juan.")

Pi Mimi proposed that in Shijing and Shujing, Gong and Si presented differences in high and low social status.[117] Du Hongyi concluded the tendency as "以公灭私" (adopt Gong to kill Si), "公正无私" (justice without selfishness), "先公后私" (put Gong before Si), "公而忘私" (conduct Gong and forget Si), and "公私分明" (clarify Gong and Si).[118] Liang Zhiping concluded Gong's meanings as justice, public and state-owned.[119] Lee Seung-hwan defined Gong as

"[t]he concept of *gong* in general entails at least three different yet closely related meanings: the sphere of political dominion and ruling institution; the universal ethical principle of impartiality, fairness, and justice; and the common good and communality."[120] Lee thought among all these meanings, the most fundamental one is to define Gong as the sphere of political dominion, with Gong appearing in terms of the feudal lords or dukes.[121]

In most cases, Gong refers to the political leaders and rulers or the lords of the feudal states; only sometimes does it mean the royal clan members, ancestors or offspring of the duke.[122] The meaning of Gong was expanded in the *Book of Poetry* to "the space where administrative works are done, the sphere where the ruler governs, as well as those public figures who were directly in control of ruling institutions."[123] Until then, the author suggests that Gong referred to public affairs; thus, it is no longer so different from the Western idea of the public. It is the same as ancient times when the citizens in Rome gathered in forums to discuss public affairs. Like the phrase, *Quod Omnes Tangit*, it has something to do with the context of "the space where administrative works are done, and the sphere where the ruler governs."[124] The only difference lies in whether the concept can refer to the person and

[115]Chinese Classics (1871), p. 22; Cf. Chinese Classics (1974), p. 8: "How ample is her head-dress – morning and evening she is in the palace".

[116]Chinese Classics (1980), p. 1771.

[117]Pi (2017), pp. 155–160; Schuessler (1987), p. 197.

[118]Du (2012), pp. 561–565.

[119]Liang (2014), pp. 68–70.

[120]Lee (2006), p. 104.

[121]Lee (2006), pp. 104–105.

[122]The Codification Committee of the Great Compendium of Chinese Characters (1988), p. 242, No. 6 of the meanings of Gong; Lee (2006), p. 105.

[123]The Codification Committee of the Great Compendium of Chinese Characters (1988), p. 242, No. 4 of the meanings of Gong, trans. by the author; Lee (2006), p. 105.

[124]Lee (2006), p. 105.

the politic leader.[125] Even if the antonym of Gong, the concept of Si, indicates private, personal, or selfish, the author would argue that this is only a superficial distinction, the imminent character. It is not these slight differences but the development process and the attitude toward Gong and Si that play an important role in the factors that result in the discrepancy between the East and the west. The development process is already explained at the beginning part of this chapter, so the attitude toward Gong and Si will now be discussed.

According to Chinese cultural tradition, people are ashamed of being considered Si, and Si often refers to negative things such as Sili, 私利 (expedience), Sitong, 私通 (improper intercourse between illicit lovers) and so on. The sage should be 大公无私Da Gong Wu Si,[126]which means much Gong and no Si. They thought it was best to erase all ideas associated with Si in one's mind. Tianxia Wei Gong is a case in point. This phrase helps to blur and alienize the concept and consciousness of an individual in common people's minds. Although it is different from the interpretation of Tianxia Xingwang, Pifu You Ze, it emphasizes the awareness of an individual and at the same time grants too much responsibility to common people. Unlike in the West, it has only covered private affairs rather than state affairs. However, as *Quod Omnes Tangit* was written in Codex Civil, the right and responsibility are equal and not overloaded. However, this custom to shoulder all the rights and responsibilities may be cultivated in this way and be carried forward to state affairs.

Lee adopted the phrase Tianxia Wei Gong in the *Book of Rites* as an example to illustrate another meaning of Gong: major interest and opinions, quoting Zheng Xuan, a famous commentator in the Han Dynasty, to demonstrate its relevance to the concept of Gong:

> The *Book of Rites* opens up opportunities for political participation to every competent person.... This phrase provides an important momentum in the conceptual evolution of *gong*: it denies that the king's throne is the private property of a family; instead, it argues that everyone with proper virtue could play the role of the sovereign.[127]

Originally, the concepts of public and private in the West had the same status as Gong and Si in the East. The Latin form of public is *poplicus*, relating to *populus* (people), and *pubes*, which means "the adult male population".[128] The Greek form of public is *to koinon*, private, and *idiom*, reminding us of "idiot."[129] Women and slaves work in the private space (household) to support the citizen living their public life on the battlefield and in the courts and assemblies.[130] Greek and Roman histories both praise the public and belittle the private, which is similar to the situation in the East.

[125] Mutschler (2008), p. 440.

[126] Du (2012), pp. 561–565; Lin (2017), p. 113.

[127] Lee (2006), p. 111.

[128] Hölscher (1979), p. 41. Cf. Peters (1995), p. 9.

[129] Peters (1995), p. 6.

[130] Saxonhouse (1983), p. 363–384. Cf. Peters (1995), p. 6.

However, a major difference lies in the concept of and attitude toward individuals and autonomy: in the West, individuals and autonomy are important, while in the East, they cannot find their place in the value system. Many Western philosophers value individuals. Aristotle defined a city as "a body of such people adequate in number for achieving a self-sufficient existence."[131] Aristotle asked the question, what kind of life is the best, as the premise of discussing the best form of constitution, commenting that "[a]s long as that is obscure, the best constitution must also remain obscure."[132] He then provided the answer for the best way of life as, for both individuals and cities collectively, the life of goodness.[133] In addition, he stated that the happiness of the city is the same as that of the individual.[134] Although people assemble to form a city, these individuals have not, merely because of that or any other reason, abandoned their self-sufficient existence. A city and its existence ought to produce mutual benefit; moreover, the best constitution must enable anyone to be at his best and live happily. Hobbes also wrote that "[i]t is therefore a *right of nature*: that every man may preserve his own life and limbs, with all the power he hath."[135] Ockham was a firm supporter of the value of the individual.[136] We can see here that the value of the individual is put forward, in contrast to the case in the East.

"To master the self and return to ritual"[137] is one of the most important propositions in Confucianism. "To master" was almost unable to convey the genuine meaning and tendency of Confucius. Instead of translating 克己 into "to master," we must understand it as to control, to restrain and to repress oneself. This might be the most relevant example to observe the attitude of Confucius toward individuals and the relationship between individuals and individual responsibility.

To our interest, the West stresses individuality and has established the democracy of majority rule, while the East worships community. One fact that deserves much attention is that the concept of sharing in Tianxia Wei Gong complies with the contemporary spirit of today, which is absent in *Quod Omnes Tangit*. When Confucius said, "[w]hat you do not want others to do to you, do not do to others,"[138] it was based on a quite individual perspective at this micro level. At the macro level, he advocated Tianxia Wei Gong, which attached much significance to community and unity. Joseph Chan believed that there was some autonomy in Confucian thinking, not personal autonomy but moral autonomy, suggesting its four elements: "the voluntary endorsement of morality," "a reflective engagement in moral life," "the

---

[131] Aristotle (1995), p. 87, 1275b13.

[132] Aristotle (1995), p. 251, 1323a14.

[133] Aristotle (1995), p. 251–253, 1323a14, 1323b36.

[134] Aristotle (1995), p. 254, 1324a5.

[135] Hobbes (1994), p. 79, XIV. 6.

[136] Speck (2009), pp. 86–87.

[137] Confucius (2010), p. 80. The Chinese original text is "克己复礼" (论语·颜渊, Lunyu, Yanyuan), Lunyu ch. 12.1.

[138] Confucius (2010), p. 80. The Chinese original text is "己所不欲，勿施于人" (论语·颜渊, Lunyu, Yanyuan). Lunyu ch. 12.2.

recognition of morality as self-legislation" and "the recognition of morality as radical free expression of the individual's will," with the former two presented in Confucian ethics and the latter two incompatible.[139]

In conclusion, *Quod Omnes Tangit* was born to solve private disputes. As it embodies the meaning of protecting personal rights, it was gradually quoted at the official level to guarantee individual rights. From this perspective, it has gone through a process from *ius privatum* to *ius publicum*. Referring to Tianxia Wei Gong, at the very beginning, it could hardly be called *ius* because it is not a law but something similar to a law. Subsequently, we can hardly know whether someone has ever adopted it to solve some disputes. What can be determined is that it remains more in written forms than in real life. Ever since its birth, it was and has been in a high position as a reason for the abdicate script of the emperor or for the awakening of the public awareness of public affairs.

Based on the analysis of this process of development, it can be concluded that it is better to strike a balance between the care of oneself and the public. Simply speaking, we have an instinct to be selfish. However, this desire must be restricted, and others should also be taken into consideration. Otherwise, the ideal of unselfishness, as described in Tianxia Wei Gong, cannot be fulfilled because the ideal is too far away from one's natural tendency. Everyone is born to care for himself; it is one's primary task and responsibility to satisfy one's own will. Nevertheless, human beings are social creatures, so one cannot be truly satisfied when one only lives for himself. This trend suggests that a good law must guarantee one's own rights first and then enable participation in public affairs.

The following passages will explore the gap between the oriental and occidental cultures from the perspective of sociological psychology, which may facilitate the research of the two maxims. First, a group of conceptions needs to be defined, the previous pair of which are individualism and collectivism.

Individualism is "[t]he concept of giving priority to one's own goals over group goals and defining one's identity in terms of personal attributes rather than group identifications," while collectivism gives "priority to the goals of one's groups (often one's extended family or work group) and defining one's identity accordingly."[140]

To most people in industrialized Western cultures,

> **individualism** prevails. . . .One's identity – as a unique individual with particular abilities, traits, values, and dreams – remains fairly constant.[141]

In contrast,

> [m]ost cultures native to Asia, Africa, and Central and South America place a greater value on **collectivism**. . .people are more self-critical and focus less on positive self-views.[142]

[139] Chan (2014), p. 132.

[140] Myers and Twenge (2017), p. 33.

[141] Myers and Twenge (2017), p. 33.

[142] Myers and Twenge (2017), p. 33; Heine et al. (1999), p. 766–794.

In contrast, there are another two concepts worth defining: the independent self and the interdependent self.[143] Independent, or individualistic, emphasizes personal identity, which is "defined by individual traits and goals," "personal achievement and fulfilment," and "my rights and liberties," whose illustrative motto is called "To thine own self be true."[144] In contrast, interdependent, or collectivist, stresses social identity, which is "defined by connections with others," "group goals and solidarity," and "our social responsibilities and relationships," whose motto can be illustrated as "No one is an island."[145]

Referring to the phrase of *Quod Omnes Tangit*, it is easy to observe how it emphasizes the importance of individuals who aim at the realization of their rights to decide affairs in terms of guaranteeing the partial rights of every individual. In contrast, individuals are quite ambiguous in the phrase of Tianxia Wei Gong, in which personal rights merge in the pursuit of an all-around justice.

From the perspective of modern social psychology, these differences between Western and Eastern cultures echo those between *Quod Omnes Tangit* and Tianxia Wei Gong. The cultural gap in this sense might emerge under the influence of the maxims over a long course of history. Nevertheless, the relationship between the cultural gap and the maxims is not unidirectional but is correlational and causational.

Correlation and causation refer to the fact that "[w]hen two variables correlate, any combination of three explanations is possible. Either one may cause the other, or both may be affected by an underlying [']third factor[']."[146] A case in point is the status-longevity question and achievement/self-esteem question. As Myers put it, "[w]hen two factors such as status and health go together, it is tempting to conclude that one is causing the other."[147] The cultural gap and the effect of our maxims could also be regarded as two such variables.

We must be cautious when we use the difference between *Quod Omnes Tangit* and Tianxia Wei Gong to explain the cultural gap between east and west because in their development process, it could be vice versa that the cultural gap between east and west influenced or caused some differences between *Quod Omnes Tangit* and Tianxia Wei Gong. In addition, as number (3) in the table shows, there could be a third factor that influenced this phenomenon.

According to the figures, element X and element Y could trigger each other. At the same time, it is possible that X and Y have nothing to do with causation but are merely correlated. For example, self-esteem and academic achievement could be correlated under the influence of intelligence and family social status,[148] but one does not necessarily cause the other.

---

[143] Myers and Twenge (2017), p. 36.
[144] Myers and Twenge (2017), p. 36.
[145] Myers and Twenge (2017), p. 36.
[146] Myers and Twenge (2017), p. 17.
[147] Myers and Twenge (2017), p. 16.
[148] Myers and Twenge (2017), p. 17.

The adoption of the methodology of causation and correlation may facilitate the discovery of the possible underlying elements that trigger the discrepancy between East and Occident by pointing out at first that the causal relationship between the maxims and cultural gap is superficial. Moreover, a third factor does exist. The problem of what the third factor is requires further research.

*4.2.2 From Godly Law to Human Law (***Ius Naturale** *to* **Ius Positivum***)*

It is not uncontroversial which camp *Quod Omnes Tangit* belongs to. Antonio Marongiu theorized that for Wilhelm Ockham, *Quod Omnes Tangit* is a principle in natural law because the heads of the community will be elected by the members themselves.[149] The author proposes that *Quod Omnes Tangit* falls into a period of transition.[150]

Some may raise the query that these two sets of concepts, godly law and human law, *ius naturale* and *ius positivum,* are entirely different. How could they be put together to describe the legal tradition trend that *Quod Omnes Tangit* bears and presents? There might be various definitions of these two sets of concepts; nevertheless, what needs to be emphasized in this paper is the twofold meanings in this subtitle. First, *Quod Omnes Tangit* is a mark signifying the transformation of godly law into human law because the substantial content is confirmed by all people instead of God. The law is legitimized not through God but rather through a procedure.[151] Second, this law comes from human nature. When solving human conflicts, this law is in line with human nature.

The concept of natural law currently enjoys abundant research resources dispatched from both western and eastern academics. Names such as Aristotle, Hobbes, St. Thomas Aquinas and Rousseau appear definitively in the contents. Whether Grotius, Hume and others also continue to make their contribution to these academic works depends on the various focuses of the authors. Some of them focus on the differences or improvements that natural law thinkers make, and others focus on the continuity that natural law thinkers maintain. Irrespective of these diverse angles, it may be confirmed that there is no need to restate the history of natural law in this thesis. The foreknowledge of the concept and the history of natural law is required to understand the following part.

The exact concept of natural law, even the corresponding concept of natural law, does not exist in Chinese legal or philosophical history.[152] However, the most

---

[149] Marongiu (1980), p. 196.

[150] Generally, for the Roman influence on medieval papacy and the increasing papal jurisdiction, see Müßig (2019), pp. 42–43.

[151] Flaig (2013), p. 147.

[152] See Hu (2013), pp. 119–122.

approximate one is Tiandao天道.[153] This reminds us of our maxim in its full version: Dadao Zhi Xing Ye, Tianxia Wei Gong. 大道之行也，天下为公。 ("When the Great Tao was in practice, the world was for common good and owned by all.") We note that there are two characters that are the same. The first is Tian 天, and the other is Dao 道. Liu provides an excellent conclusion about the meanings of Tian in Chinese philosophy, which will facilitate our analysis of our maxim and concept:

(1) It is the material heaven, the counterpart of earth, as in Zhuang Zi.
(2) It is nature, as in Xun Zi and Zhuang Zi.
(3) It means fate or destiny, referring to things that humans cannot do anything but accept, as in Confucius, Mencius, and Xun Zi.
(4) It is the set of objectively valid moral and political principles, as in Confucius, Mencius, and Neo-Confucianism.
(5) It is a superhuman power, which has its own will and legislates for humans, as in Mo Zi, and, mostly, in pre-Confucian literature.[154]

These names Liu refers to are all the names of ancient Chinese philosophers. It is worth noting that although some of these ancient Chinese philosophers belong to different schools, the way they adopt the concept of Tian does not exactly follow this classification; rather, as is typical in Chinese culture, the concept of Tian is adopted in a compact and compounded way. In short, every time the concept of Tian appears, it may contain some of or all five meanings, and only their proportions are different. If Tian is a picture, these five meanings are the primary colors. Bearing this in mind, we may start analyzing our maxim and the concept of Tiandao. In Tianxia Wei Gong, the principle color comes from the first meaning, namely, heaven, but it is also a light touch of the fourth and fifth meanings, namely, moral and political principles or a superhuman power. For Tiandao, we may see that the principle colors come from almost all five meanings except the first one.

In addition, what is Dao? Because of the differences between the Pinyin system and the Wade-Giles system in pronouncing Chinese characters, Dao, in the Mandarin Pinyin system, is the same as Tao in the Wade-Giles system. Tao, the core concept and the utmost pursuit of Taoism; which is another important school of philosophy in Chinese history in addition to Confucianism, with Laozi as one of its representatives; is one of the most mysterious concepts in Chinese culture.[155] Simply said, Tao means principle, pattern, law and rule.[156] We will not discuss this concept here. However, we can explain the concept of Tiandao: combining the separate preparatory work on Tian and Dao, Tiandao means the rule of nature, remarkably close to natural law.[157] In this regard, there is also another concept that matches

[153] Hu (2013), pp. 125–126.
[154] Liu (2001), p. 260.
[155] Hu (2013), pp. 125–127.
[156] See also Hu (2013), p. 125.
[157] See also Hu (2013), pp. 125–129.

human law, Rendao人道. Academics also discuss the relationship between these concepts.

However, unlike in the West, where the contents of natural law are relatively clear, Tiandao is thought to be unknowable, similar to agnosticism.[158] For example, Antigone thought that burying her brother was a natural law that is higher than the state law, which forbids burying a traitor.[159] In one of Grotius' works, *De Jure Praedae Commentarius*, Chap. II, he proposes nine rules and 13 laws as the foundation of natural law.[160] The second rule is what the common consent of mankind has shown to be the will of all, that is, law.[161] These examples show that the contents of natural law are not vague; rather, they are very clear. In addition, the contents are about the rules of the world of human beings. These are the rules of humans. In contrast, Tiandao is, in the east, obscure and mysterious. In the Analects of Confucius, one of his students said, "when Confucius talks about the essence of material and Tiandao, it is not knowable."[162] Laozi also thought that Tao cannot be explained; therefore, he thought human beings should be *laissez-faire,* do nothing and let the Tiandao be followed. In conclusion, Tiandao is, in the end, the law of nature; it is not the law of human beings.

Through the transition from natural law to human law, we can see that Westerners adopt the concept of natural law to reinforce the authority of some rules constituting human ethics and the political world. However, easterners drew a line between Tiandao and Rendao, letting the contents of natural law stay vague forever and limiting the action of human beings, leading Tiandao to fall into the field of metaphysics and agnosticism.

The possibility that people can have a choice to decide the outcome of something concerning themselves should have a name. In the west, this is referred to as a 'right;' in the east, a name failed to develop for such an abstract conception. Thus, it is obviously important to examine the history of the development of the concept of 'rights.'

Charles Reid concluded that, regarding the origin of the concept of rights, scholars' opinions mainly vary from the seventeenth century to the fourteenth century, as represented by C. B. Macpherson, Leo Strauss, and Michel Villey,

---

[158] Hu (2013), p. 172.

[159] Sophocles (2003), p. 73; see also Burns (2002), pp. 545–547.

[160] Grotius and van Ittersum (2006), pp. 19–50.

[161] Grotius and van Ittersum (2006), p. 25.

[162] Paraphrasing trans. by the author. Cf. Confucius (1980), p. 46 (Lunyu ch. 5.13) "老师关于文献方面的学问, 我们听得到, 老师关于天性和天道的言论, 我们听不到。" p. 73 (Lunyu ch. 7.26): "善人我不能看见了." Confucius (1998), p. 98 (Lunyu ch. 5.13): "We can learn from the master's cultural refinements, but do not hear him discourse on subjects such as 'natural disposition' and 'the way of tian'." Confucius (2010), p. 38 (Lunyu ch. 5.13): "Zigong said, The Master's views on cultural and emblematic matters—these we have heard. However, his views on human nature and the Way of Heaven—these we have never been able to hear!" The Chinese original text is "子贡曰:'夫子之文章, 可得而闻也;夫子之言星与天道, 不可得而闻也。'". (论语·公冶长), Chinese Text Project (2022), Lunyu ch. 5.13. https://ctext.org/zhs . Accessed Nov 11 2022.

with Richard Tuck alone, as an exception, insisting on the thirteenth century.[163] C. B. Macpherson announced that individual rights were born in the seventeenth century with Hobbes, who attempted to link them with the economic condition.[164] Leo Strauss also believed that Hobbes' theory resulted in the shift from duties to rights because Hobbes highlighted self-preservation in the war of all against all.[165] However, Charles Reid challenged these arguments, seeing Michel Villey's idea as more powerful.[166] Michel Villey argued that the Romans and the early glossators on Roman law did not possess any subjective concept of right.[167] Villey stressed that the concept of right was born in the fourteenth century with Ockham's voluntarism and nominalism.[168] However, this argument is still not perfect. Reid thought Villey's argument "ignores the professional boundaries between law and philosophy that existed in the middle ages."[169] Richard Tuck tried to trace the origin of rights to the thirteenth century.[170] Brian Tierney criticized Tuck's text "for their inconsistent terminology and chronology."[171] Charles Reid disagreed with Tuck's idea that distinction between *dominium directum* and *dominium utile* was important for the history of rights theories and noted that Tuck missed the fact that canonists already knew about the distinction between active and passive rights.[172]

Irrespective of the differences of these three times, one point can be ascertained: the concept of rights was born in the West and accompanied the development of Western thoughts at least since the seventeenth century, possibly as early as the thirteenth century. China, in contrast, has never specifically developed the concept of rights; rather, it imported the concept at the beginning of twentieth century, according to "*A Quantitative Study of China's Selective Absorption of Modern Western Ideas and the Origins of Certain Key Concepts(1840-1915).*"[173]

4.2.3 From Religious Law to Secular Law

This section displays two different development processes of the East and the West from religious law to secular law. We will show that in the West, the church system was based on the secular world and contains various rational elements. Moreover,

163 Reid (1991), pp. 46–59.
164 MacPherson (1962), pp. 46–70.
165 Strauss (1953), pp. 120–164.
166 Reid (1991), p. 51.
167 Villey (1946), p. 201.
168 Villey (1964), p. 971.
169 Reid (1991), p. 57.
170 Tuck (1979), pp. 5–31.
171 Tierney (1983), pp. 431–444, cited in Reid (1991), p. 58.
172 Reid (1991), pp. 58–59.
173 Jin and Liu (2004), pp. 52–66.

with the study and spread of classic political theories from Plato, Aristotle, etc., the canonists of the fourteenth century promoted the rationalization of the political system. In the case of the east, we see a different situation: kingship and theocracy continuously blended over the course of many centuries until the reinterpretation of Tianxia Wei Gong, even as late as in the nineteenth and twentieth centuries.

A council is an assembly of many people, coming from various ranks, professions and genders, who gather in one place, on behalf of the common welfare of the Christendom.[174] With the first famous council being the Apostolic council, the dogmatic councils in late antiquity fell in the time of the Patristic, from Nikaia (325) to Chalkedon (451).[175]

The Roman provincial gathering (concilia) was the role model for the synods and councils.[176] "A council could again be a role model for parliament."[177] This chain presents how the West had different political resources than the East. Marsilius identified Council in terms of structure and function with the highest representational and legislative organs.[178] Nicolas of Cusa declared that the council of consent must be open because freedom of speech must be dominant.[179] These ideas guided the development of political discussion, formed the political atmosphere and laid the foundation of the political system.

It is convenient to adopt some models that have already existed and worked. Although Confucianism was adopted as the official basis of the Han Dynasty, it never developed its own administrative institutions, not to mention its function as a counterweight to royal authority.

During the late 1100s and early 1200s, the canonists were engaged in the search for the answer to the question of who enjoyed the higher power, the Pope or the Council.[180] The conciliarists believed that the Council was the answer[181] and established precedents for the medieval world.[182] They recognized that the ruling of the church had to be based on the consent of the people who are ruled, which was the same with communities as with the church; thus, they adopted the principle for the first time not only in the church but also in the political community.[183] Under such circumstances, a pope could be dethroned through a general council.[184] Boniface VIII (1294–1303) governed in this way.[185] This principle of conciliar

[174] Vogel (2011), p. 228.
[175] Vogel (2011), p. 226.
[176] Hintze (1931), p. 6; for different opinion see Hofmann (2003), p. 56.
[177] Vogel (2011), p. 230. Trans. by the author.
[178] Marsilius of Padua (1993), pp. 39–43; Miethke (2008), p. 241.
[179] Nikolaus of Cusa (1968), p. 103; Sieben (1983), p. 91.
[180] Tierney (1966), p. 1–3; Tierney (1995), pp. 74–75.
[181] Tierney (1998), pp. 1–2; Pennington (1970), pp. 149–161.
[182] Watner (2005), p. 74.
[183] Oakley (1983), pp. 318, 322.
[184] Watner (2005), p. 74.
[185] Kempshall (1999), p. 285.

supremacy was explained in the Decret Sacrosancta in the Council of Constance. Chances were good that this principle spread from the ecclesiastical world to the secular world.[186] The Maxim of *Quod Omnes Tangit* could also be observed during the conciliar development. Historians have seen the meaning of *Quod Omnes Tangit* as early as April 19, 1213 in the brief *Vineam domini* .[187]

In 1415, the Konstanz Council declared its superiority over the Pope within the Dekret Haec Sancta.[188] Some scholars treated Haec Sancta as a turning point between the Middle Ages and the modern world, and some even believed that it drew the direct line between the Konstanz Council and the Glorious Revolution in 1688.[189] However, Cusanus held that the principle in the decree *Haec sancta* acknowledged by Konstanz Council was implausible because the decreasing participants of the Basel Council resulted in it being unqualified to represent consensus omnium, which also contains the Pope's consent as a significant part.[190]

Cusanus treated the church as a godly hierarchy institution: the Pope, bishops and the council stand together at the top of the church, but they are distinct by virtue of their power of governance.[191] The pope cannot rule without the supervision of the council representing the church; the church and the council of representatives can only function under the authority of the Pope in the hierarchy.[192] As the legate of Pope, Cusanus devoted himself to the establishment of a neutral German nation facing the conflict between Pope and the council, with a decisive contribution to the recognition of Pope Eugens IV in the Reichstag of Aschaffenburg in 1447 and to the termination of the Vienna Concordance in 1448.[193] Cusanus strived for concordance between the Pope and the council.[194]

It is unclear whether *Quod Omnes Tangit* and the conciliar priority over the Pope led to anarchy, but this did not prevent autarchy because in China's situation, no one and no community could rank higher than the royalty. The organization of the church and the world will be labeled as the analogous structure.[195] China did not have a comparable institutional form from which to borrow. Thus, this difference comprises an essential discrepancy between *Quod Omnes Tangit* and Tianxia Wei Gong.

Western scholars attached much importance to these methods and always engaged themselves in their reflection, design and development, while Chinese

---

[186]Tierney (1998), pp. 4–6.

[187]Monahan (1987), p. 107.

[188]Rathmann (2000), p. 119–121. Cf. Tierney (1998), pp. xxii-xxix.

[189]Laski (1936), p. 638; Figgis (1999), pp. 28–44; Oakley (1962), pp. 1–31; Oakley (1965), pp. 673–690; Cf. Blythe (1992), p. 258.

[190]Kandler (1995), p. 115.

[191]Kandler (1995), p. 116.

[192]Kandler (1995), pp. 114, 115.

[193]Kandler (1995), p. 115.

[194]Kandler (1995), p. 115.

[195]Blythe (1992), p. 117; Sigmund (1963), p. 121.

scholars spoke highly of metaphysics and the capability to feel and comprehend by themselves. This can be found in almost every field, for example, in language, traditional Chinese painting, and traditional Chinese medical science.

In the case of Tianxia Wei Gong, there is no such transformation from religious law to secular law. Conversely, kingship and theocracy merged; more precisely, the former gradually overwhelmed the latter. Nevertheless, it can be observed that there were two possible periods of time that might be categorized into the process from religion law to secular law. One was the duration from shamanistic ceremony to Li[196] in which the "law" fulfilled the process from religion law to secular law.

The other was the transformation of Confucianism in modern times.

Li Zehou, an academic interested in the origin of Chinese culture, summarized the combination of kingship and theocracy as Wu Jun He Yi巫君合一, "the unity of Shaman and Ruler."[197] He state that Yao, Shun, and Yu, the three kings mentioned at the beginning of chapter Li Yun in Li Gi, together with other ancient Chinese political figures, are all great Shamans combining kingship and theocracy.[198]

This argument provides a reasonable explanation to one of the core pursuits in this thesis—what led to the discrepancy of the two maxims and the different direction of historic development of the East and the West. This explanation is not unidirectional but works together with our two maxims. We could also say that the different wording of our maxims mirrors the primitive differences.

The book in which Tianxia Wei Gong was promoted for the first time, Li Gi, depicts many ceremonies of Shamanism, for example, dancing to pray for rain.[199] Shaman巫 and Li 礼 share some traits, which Li Zehou summarized as four points:

> "Wu and Li aim at serving people's affairs on the earth, embracing concrete practical targets and material benefits;
>
> Wu and Li comprise a holy ritual containing a battery of complicated activity, customs, figures and languages;
>
> Wu and Li function actively and affect or control the Geist, which is a difference between Shamanism and religion;

[196] Li (2015), p. 31. English version: Li (2018), pp. 40–46.

[197] Li (2015), p. 7. English version: Li (2018), p.13.

[198] Quoted from Li (2015), p. 7, 8; English version: Li (2018), pp. 13–16; Xu (1962), p. 76: 颛顼:"依鬼神以制义。" Zhuanxu: "make laws conform to the will of Geist."(大戴礼记·五帝德)"帝颛顼主要的事事命重、黎'绝地天通'……只有他(指重)同帝颛顼猜管得天上的事情。" "The most important duty of King Zhuanxu is to command Chong and Li to communicate the sky with the earth. Only Chong and King Zhuanxu are competent to manage the affairs in heaven." Trans. by the author. The name of Zhuanxu comes from a dancing man with branches and jade in his hand. Zhou (2009), p. 131.

[199] Confucius (551–479 BC), *Li Gi*, 'Yue Ling', 礼记·月令第六: "是月也, 命乐正入学习舞。乃修祭典。命祀山林川泽, 牺牲毋用牝。" English translation: "In this month orders are given to the chief director of Music to enter the college, and practice the dances (with his pupils). The canons of sacrifice are examined and set forth, and orders are given to sacrifice to the hills and forests, the streams and meres, care being taken not to use any female victims." Trans. by James Legge. https://ctext.org/liji/yue-ling/ens. Accessed Dec 12 2019.

In Wu and Li, there is an exposure of a zealous emotion and status."[200]

There were two key figures to rationalize Wu in history. One is Confucius, who explained the inner perspective of Wu as Ren; the other is Zhougong, the Duke of Zhou and the brother of the founder of the Zhou Dynasty (1046 BC—256 BC), who produced the other perspective of Wu as a system of rituals.[201] This process spares China from the phenomenon in which science is separated from religion and rationality and isolated from emotion; rather, it forms a mode of thinking that is compacted with belief, emotion, visuality and rationality.

At the beginning of this thesis, since Tianxia Wei Gong originated from Li Gi, we discussed some background of Li. The following paragraph serves as a supplement. Li originated from ceremonies of primitive tribes dating back from 3000 BC to 2000 BC.[202] In early times, Li was no different from Yi, the feather as decoration in dancing, or actual shamanistic ceremony, meaning the property of behaviors, exterior appearance and language.[203] Yi constituted the law, justice and obligation of primitive men. Through the ceremony, the shamanistic activities became the Li system that everyone was obliged to obey. The system as a whole, however, was not deemed the secular contract but the general legislation in the universe. Li still has those characters as communicating with the cosmos and deities.[204] Ethics and morality are the core of the whole Li system. After the Han Dynasty, Li and "law" combined to be the rule politic of the emperor.[205]

In addition, the unification of kingship and theocracy is the same as the unification of worship toward god and ancestors. According to the archeological discovery of Neolithic times, one of the most significant primary characteristics of Chinese civilization is worship toward ancestors.[206]

The reason to emphasize this point is that some scholars consider Confucianism to be religion.[207] Thus, it might also be reasonable to argue that the modernization of Confucianism witnessed the historical process of the transformation of religious law to secular law. There is abundant discussion about the question of whether Confucianism is a religion or not.[208] This question concerns how to define a religion.[209] The modern Western religious theory began to impact China in the second half of the twentieth century.[210] The early modern Confucianists faced the question of how to

[200] Li (2015), pp. 11–12, trans. by the author. English version: Li (2018), pp. 20–22.

[201] Li (2015), p. 31. English version: Li ZH (2018), pp. 40–46.

[202] Yang (2000), pp. 7, 13; Li (2015), p. 46. Li (2018), p. 60.

[203] Li (2015), p. 47. Li (2018), pp. 61, 62.

[204] Li (2015), pp. 51–52. Li (2018), pp. 63, 64.

[205] Li (2015), p. 61. Li (2018), pp. 73, 74.

[206] He (1996), pp. 93, 96–97.

[207] Chen (2013), pp. 71–84; Sun (2013), pp. 77–79.

[208] Zhu (2011), p. 1.

[209] Chen (2013), pp. 91–101; Liang (1982), pp. 104–106, cited in Zhu (2011), p. 21.

[210] Zhu (2011), pp. 8–9.

constitute the modern Chinese value conception system.[211] On the one hand, they affirmed the value of religion; on the other hand, they objected to incorporating religion into the Chinese value system.[212] Most of them tend to classify Confucianism as a philosophy rather than a religion, declaring that treating Confucianism as a religion violated its history and lowered the traditional value of Confucianism; however, at the same time, they attempted to adopt the reasonable elements of a religion during the reconstitution and modernization of Confucian philosophy.[213]

This issue will not be further discussed in this thesis; rather, it serves to note that the reason for the heated discussion must be that Confucianism does bear some characteristics of religion but not all of them.

In contrast, there are arguments that Confucianism is not a religion because Confucianism does not address the afterlife.[214] Moreover, in the classic texts of Confucianism, Lun Yu, there is no such wonder as in the Bible.[215] In addition, Confucianism does not prevent believers from following other religions. Max Weber also emphasized that Confucianism is completely different from Christianity, arguing that the ethics of Confucianism unconditionally affirm and adopt the secular world.[216]

This argument explains why there are two possible processes in China for law to transfer from religion to secularism. In the first phase, there was not yet enough transformation; therefore, Confucianism still bore some characteristics of religion.[217] During modern development, the process was not entirely completed. Hence, unlike in the West, there were two processes in China for the transformation of religious law to secular law.

During the second process, as modern society fundamentally changed, the bond of blood vanished, a sea of farmers rushed into the city, and the relationships among family members weakened.[218] It could be witnessed how Confucianism and the meaning of Tianxia Wei Gong also experienced the process of modernization.[219]

As Peter Zarrow states:

> [t]he late Qing view of the state displayed what might be called Weberian themes: bureaucratic and instrumental rationality, disenchantment (secularization), and the separation of society from the cosmos. Late Qing intellectuals saw the state in secular terms: it was a human artifact.[220]

---

[211] Chen (2013), pp. 46–47.

[212] Zhu (2011), pp. 10–11.

[213] Zhu (2011), p. 20.

[214] Nationalgeographic Contributor (2021) https://www.nationalgeographic.org/article/chinese-religions-and-philosophies/. Accessed Apr 11 2021. See also Yang (2000), p. 37–41.

[215] Li (2015), p. 64.

[216] Weber (1989), p. 296.

[217] Levy (1992), p. 15.

[218] Levy (1992), p. 17.

[219] Levy (1992), p. 15.

[220] Zarrow (2009), p. 236.

In this thesis, the interpretation of Tianxia Wei Gong from late Qing intellectuals is itself a process of the second phase moving from religious law to secular law.

References

Ames RT (2009) Seeking harmony not sameness: comparative philosophy and east-west understanding. Beijing University Press, Beijing. (安乐哲, 和而不同: 中西哲学的会通, 北京大学出版社, 北京, 2009年)

Aristotle (1995) Politics (trans: Barker E). Oxford University Press, New York

Blythe JM (1992) Ideal government and the mixed constitution in the middle ages. Princeton University Press, Princeton

Bullinger M (1968) Öffentliches Recht und Privatrech: Studien über Sinn und Funktionen der Unterscheidung. W. Kohlhammer Verlag, Stuttgart

Burns T (2002) Sopholcles' antigone and the history of the concept of natural law. Polit Stud 50(3): 545–557

Cassirer E (1954) An essay on man. Doubleday Anchor Books, New York

Chan J (2014) Confucian perfectionism: a political philosophy for modern times. Princeton University Press, Princeton

Chen Y (2013) Confucianism as religion: controversies and consequences. Brill, Leiden

Chen L (2015) The Core values of Chinese civilization. SDX Joint Publishing Company, Beijing. (陈来, 中华文明的核心价值, 三联书店, 北京, 2015年)

Cheng C-Y (2016) Transforming virtues into rights--the practical ability and potential of human in Confucian ethic. In: Liang T (ed) Virtues and rights, on confucianism and human rights from cross-cultural perspectives. China Social sciences Press, Beijing, pp 241–255. (成中英, 将儒家美德转化为权利——儒家伦理观中人之实践能力与潜能研究, 梁涛编, 美德与权利, 中国社会科学出版社, 北京, 2016年)

Chinese Classics (1865) The shoo king (trans: Legge J). At The Author's, Hongkong

Chinese Classics (1871) The book of Peotry. Lane (trans: Legge J). Crawford & Co., Hongkong

Chinese Classics (1882) The Yi king. (trans: Legge J). Clarendon Press, Oxford

Chinese Classics (1974) The book of odes (trans: Karlgren B). Museum of Far Eastern Antiquities, Stockholm

Chinese Classics (1977) The I Ching or book of changes. (trans: Wilhelm R, Baynes CF). Princeton University Press, Princeton

Chinese Classics (1980) Reprint of the thirteen classics, commented and annotated. Zhonghua Book Company, Beijing. (十三经注疏影印本, 中华书局, 北京, 1980年)

Chinese Classics (2019) The book of odes (trans: Zhou ZF). Zhonghua Book Company, Beijing. (周振甫 译注, 诗经, 中华书局, 北京, 2019年)

Chinese Text Project (2022) Lunyu. In: Chinese Text Project. https://ctext.org/zhs. Accessed 11 Nov 2022

Confucius (1885) The Li Ki (trans: Legge J). Clarendon Press, Oxford

Confucius (1980) Lunyu (trans: Yang BJ). Zhonghua Book Company, Beijing. (杨伯峻 译注, 论语译注, 中华书局, 北京, 1980年)

Confucius (1998) The analects of Confucius (trans: Ames RT, Rosemont H) Random House Publishing, New York. Another Chinese edition:

Confucius (2010) The analects of Confucius (trans: Watson B). Columbia University Press, New York

Confucius (551–479 BC) 礼记 - Liji. Chinese Text Project. https://ctext.org/liji/ens. Accessed Dec 05 2022. English editions

Congar Y (1980) Quod omnes tangit ab omnibus tractari et approbari debet. In: Heinz R (ed) Die geschichtlichen Grundlagen der modernen Volksvertretung. Wissenschaftliche Buchgesellschaft, Darmstadt, pp 115–182

Danziger D, Gillingham J (2004) 1215, The Year of Magna Carta. Hodder and Stoughton, London

Du H (2012) On the tendency towards the public and its social values of the early idea of the public and private. J Liaoning Normal Univ 35:561–565. (杜洪义, 早期公司观念的尚公取向及其社会价值, 辽宁师范大学学报, 2012年第35期, 第561-565页)

Elvin M (1998) Who was responsible for the weather? Moral Meteorol Late Imperial China Osiris 13:213–237

Fasolt C (2014) Past sense: studies in medieval and early modern European history. Brill, Leiden

Feng YL (1982) A new codification of Chinese philosophy history. People's Publishing House, Beijing. (冯友兰, 中国哲学史新编, 人民出版社, 北京, 1982年)

Feng YL (2017) A short history of Chinese history. Beijing Lianhe Publishing House, Beijing. (冯友兰, 中国哲学简史, 北京联合出版公司, 北京, 2017年)

Figgis JN (1999) Political thought from Gerson to Grotius: 1414–1625. Batoche Books, Kitchener

Flaig E (2013) Die Mehrheitsentscheidung: Entstehung und kulturelle Dynamik. Ferdinand Schöningh, Paderborn

Frank T (ed) (1959) An economic survey of ancient Rome, vol 4. Pageant Books, Paterson

Gadamer H-G (1990) Wahrheit und Methode. Mohr Siebeck, Tübingen

Gierke O (1868) Das deutsche Genossenschaftsrecht. Weidmann, Berlin

Glasser TL, Salmon CT (1995) Public opinion and the communication of consent. The Guilford Press, New York

Goodsell TL, Whiting JB (2016) An Aristotelian theory of family. J Fam Theory Rev 8:484–502

Grotius H, van Ittersum MJ (eds) (2006) Commentary on the law of prize and booty. Liberty Fund, Indianapolis

Gunn JAW (1983) Beyond liberty and property. McGill-Queen's University Press, Kingston and Montreal

He BD (1996) The culture of Chinese humanism: source, feature and significance. 21 Century 33: 91–101, 34: 88-101(何炳棣, 华夏人本主义文化:渊源、特征及意义, 二十一世纪, 第33期, 第91-101页, 第34期, 第88-101页)

Heine SJ et al (1999) Is there a universal need for positive self-regard? Psychol Rev 106:766–794

Hintze O (1931) Weltgeschichtliche Bedingung der Repräsentativverfassung. Hist Z 143:1–47

Hobbes T (1994) The elements of law, natural and politic (Gaskin JCA ed). Oxford University Press, New York

Hofmann H (2003) Repräsentation. Duncker & Humblot, Berlin

Hölscher L (1979) Öffentlichkeit und Geheimnis. Klett-Cotta, Stuttgart

Hu S (2013) English writings of Hu Shih. Springer, Heidelberg

Hume D (1788) Essays, moral, political, and literary. Bell & Bradfute, London

Jiang L (2012) The spatial formation and transformation of Chinese rural clan settlements. Dissertation, Bauhaus-UniversitätWeimer

Jin GT, Liu QF (2004) A quantitative study of China's selective absorption of modern Western ideas and the origins of certain key concepts (1840-1915). 21 Century 48:52–66. (金观涛, 刘青峰, 二十一世纪, 2004年第48期, 第52-66页。)

Justinian (2009) The digest of Justinian (trans: Watson A), vol 1/4. University of Pennsylvania Press, Pennsylvania

Kandler K-H (1995) Nikolaus Von Kues: Denker zwishen Mittelalter und Neuzeit. Vandenhoeck & Ruprecht, Göttingen

Kempshall MS (1999) The common good in late medieval political thought. Clarendon Press, Oxford

Kim J (2016) Phenomenology of public opinion. In: Jung HY, Embree L (eds) Political phenomenology. Springer, Cham

Landau P (2013) Europäische Rechtsgeschichte und kanonisches Recht im Mittelalter. Wissenschaftlicher Verlag Bachmann, Badenweiler

Laski H (1936) Political theory in the later middle age. In: Prévité-Orton CW, Brooke ZN (eds) The Cambridge medieval Hisroty, The close of middle ages, vol 8. Cambridge University Press, Cambridge, pp 620–645
Lee S-H (2006) A topography of Confucian discourse. Homa & Sekey Books, Paramus
Levy MJ (1992) Confucianism and modernization. Society 29:15–17
Li ZH (2015) From shaman to ritual, rooting in Ren. SDX Joint Publishing Company, Beijing. (李泽厚, 由巫到礼释礼归仁, 三联书店, 北京, 2015年) English edition
Li ZH (2018) The origins of Chinese thought: from shamanism to ritual regulations and humaneness (trans.: Carleo III R.A.). Brill, Leiden
Liang SM (1982) The key to Chinese culture. Le Jin BKS, Taipei. (梁漱溟, 中国文化要义, 里仁书局, 台北, 1982年)
Liang ZP (2014) The concept of Wei Gong. China Law Rev 2:66–86. (梁治平, "为公"的理念, 中国法律评论, 2014年第2期, 第66-86页)
Lin A-W (2017) Confucianism and civil society. In: Hon T-K, Stapleton K (eds) Confucianism for the contemporary World. Sunny Press, New York, pp 107–116
Liu JB (1903) Xiaoxue Xiushen Jiaokeshu. Wenmin Shuju, Shanghai. (刘剑白, 小学修身教科书, 文明书局, 上海, 1903年)
Liu XS (2001) Natural law outside the Christian world. In: Braybrooke D (ed) Natural law modernized. University of Toronto Press, Toronto, pp 258–294
Liu J, Huang D (2006) The evolution of Tianxia cosmology and 1st philosophical implications. Front Philos China 1(4):517–538
Macpherson CB (1962) The political theory of possessive individualism. Oxford University Press, Oxford
Marongiu A (1980) Das Prinzip der Demokratie und der zustimmung (Quod omnes tangit, ab omnibus approbari debet) im 14.Jahrhundert. In: Rausch H (ed) Die geschichtlichen Grundlagen der modernen Volksvertretung, vol 1. Darmstadt, Wissenschaftliche Buchgesellschaft, pp 183–211
Marsilius of Padua (1993) Marsiglio of Padua: Defensor minor and De Translatione Imperii (trans and ed: Nederman CJ). Cambridge University Press, Cambridge
Miethke J (2008) Politiktheorie im Mittelalter: von Thomas von Aquin bis Wilhelm von Ockham. Mohr Siebeck, Tübingen
Mizoguchi Y (2011) Gong and Si of China. SDX Joint Publishing Company, Beijing. (沟口雄三, 中国的公与私, 三联书店, 北京, 2011年)
Monahan AP (1987) Consent, coercion and limit, the medieval origins of parliamentary democracy. McGill-Queen's University Press, Montreal
Moos P (2004) Öffentlich' und 'privat' im Mittelalter: Zu einem problem historischer Begriffsbildung. Universitätverlag Winter, Heidelberg
Mote FW (1971) Intellectual foundations of China. Alfred A. Knopf, New York
Mote FW (2009) Intellectual foundations of China. Beijing University Press, Beijing. (牟复礼, 中国思想之渊源, 北京大学出版社, 北京, 2009年)
Mulieri A (2016) Hasso Hofmann and the polysemy of representation. Redescriptions 19(2):127–145
Müllejans H (1961) Publicus und Privatus im römischen Recht und im älteren kanonishen Recht. Max Hueber, Munich
Müßig U (2019) Reason and fairness. Brill, Leiden
Mutschler F-H (2008) The problem of 'Imperial historiography' in Rome. In: Mutschler F-H, Mittag A (eds) Conceiving the empire China and Rome compared. Oxford University Press, New York, pp 119–142
Myers DG, Twenge JM (2017) Social psychology. McGraw-Hill Education, New York
Nagel J (1987) Participation. Prentice-Hall, Englewood Cliffs
Nederman CJ (2009) Varieties of dialogue: dialogical models of intercultural communication in medieval inter-religious writings. In: Takashi S, Nederman CJ (eds) Western political thought in dialogue with Asia. Lexington Books, Lanham, pp 45–64

Needham J (1991) Science and civilisation in China. Cambridge University Press, Cambridge
New World Encyclopedia contributors (2021) Confucianism. In: New World Encyclopedia. https://www.newworldencyclopedia.org/entry/Confucianism. Accessed 9 Apr 2021
Nikolaus of Cusa (1968) De concordantia catholica. Meiner Verlag, Hamburg
Nylan M (2009) The rhetoric of 'empire' in the classical era in China. In: Mutschler F-H, Mittag A (eds) Conceiving the Empire China and Rome compared. Oxford University Press, New York, pp 39–64
Oakley F (1962) On the road from constance to 1688: the political thought of John Major and George Buchanan. J Br Stud 1:1–31
Oakley F (1965) Almain and major: conciliar theory on the eve of the reformation. Am Hist Rev 70: 673–690
Oakley F (1983) Legitimation by consent: the question of the medieval roots. In: Viator: medieval and renaissance studies, vol 14. University of California Press, Berkeley, pp 303–335
Pascal B (1849) Thoughts of Blaise Pasca. Gould, Kendall and Lincoln, Boston
Pennington K (1970) Bartolome de las casas and the tradition of medieval law. Church History 39: 149–161
Peters JD (1995) Historical tensions in the concept of public opinion. In: Glasser TL, Salmon CT (eds) Public opinion and the communication of consent. The Guilford Press, New York, pp 3–36
Pi M (2017) The moralization of Gong and Si. Modern Philos 7:155–160. (皮迷迷, "公"与"私"的道德化, 现代哲学, 2017年第7期, 第155-160页)
Pitkin HF (1967) The concept of representation. University of California, California
Plato (2012) Republic (trans: Rowe C). Penguin, London
Post G (1943) Plena Potestas and consent in medieval assemblies: a study in Romano-canonical procedure and the rise of representation, 1150–1325. Traditio 1:355–408
Post G (1964) Studies in medieval legal thought: public law and the state, 1100–1322. Princeton University Press, Princeton
Rathmann T (2000) Geschehen und Geschichten des Konstanzer Konzils. Wilhelm Fink Verlag, Munich
Reid CJ (1991) The canonistic contribution to the Western rights tradition: an historical inquiry. Boston Coll Law Rev 33:37–92
Reilly R (2020) America on trial: a defense of the founding. Ignatius Press, San Francisco
Runciman D (2006) The paradoxes of democracy and the paradoxed of representation. In: Faggioli M, Melloni A (eds) Repraesentatio: mapping a keyword for churches and governance. Lit Verlag, Berlin, pp 163–175
Saxonhouse AW (1983) Classical Greek conceptions of public and private. In: Benn SI, Gaus GF (eds) Public and private in social life. St. Martin's Press, New York, pp 363–384
Schuessler A (1987) A dictionary of early Chinese. University of Hawaii, Honolulu
Schwartz BI (2004) The world of thought in ancient China. People's Publishing House, Nanjing. (史华慈, 古代中国的思想世界, 江苏人民出版社, 南京, 2004年)
Shang B et al (2008) History of Chinese confucianism development. Lanzhou University Press, Lanzhou. (尚斌, 任鹏, 李明珠, 中国儒学发展史, 兰州大学出版社, 兰州, 2008年)
Sieben HJ (1983) Traktate und Theorien zum Konzil. Knecht, Frankfurt am Mein
Sigmund PE (1963) Nicholas of Cusa and medieval political thought. Cambridge University Press, Cambridge
Sophocles (2003) Antigone (trans and eds: Gibbons, Segal). Oxford University Press, New York
Speck T (2009) Quod omnes tangit: Rezeption als ekklesiologisches Phänomen bei Matthäus Romanus und Wilhelm von Ockham. Dissertation. Universität Freiburg, Baden
Stein P (1995) Ulpian and the distinction between ius publicum and Ius privatum. In: Feenstra R et al (eds) Collatio Iuris Romani: études dédiées à Hans Ankum à l'occasion de son 65e anniversaire, vol 2. J. C. Gieben, Amsterdam, pp 499–504
Strauss L (1953) Natural right and history. The University of Chicago Press, Chicago
Sun ZS (1986) Complete works of Sun Zhongshan, vol 9. Zhonghua Book Company, Beijing. (孙中山, 孙中山全集, 中华书局, 北京, 1986年)

Sun A (2013) Confucianism as a world religion. Princeton University Press, Princeton

The Codification Committee of the Great Compendium of Chinese Characters (1988) The great Chinese dictionary. Hubei Dictionary Publishing Company and Sichuan Dictionary Publishing Company, Wuhan and Chengdu. (汉语大字典编纂委员会, 汉语大字典, 湖北辞书出版社, 四川辞书出版社, 成都, 1988年)

Thøgersen S (2009) Revisiting a dramatic triangle. J Curr Chin Aff 38(4):9–33

Tierney B (1966) Medieval canon law and Western constitutionalism. Catholic Historical Rev 52: 1–17

Tierney B (1982) Religion, law and the growth of constitutional thought 1150–1650. Cambridge University Press, Cambridge

Tierney B (1983) Tuck on rights: some medieval problems. Historic Polit Thought 4(429):431–444

Tierney B (1995) Freedom and the medieval church. In: Davis RW (ed) The origins of modern freedom in the west. Stanford University Press, Stanford, pp 64–100

Tierney B (1998) Foundations of the conciliar theory. Brill, Leiden

Tuck R (1979) Natural rights theories: their origin and development. Cambridge University Press, New York

Villey M (1946) L'idée de droit subjectif et les systèmes juridiques romains. Revue historique de droit français et étranger 24:201

Villey M (1964) La genese du droit subjectif chez Guillaume d'Occam. Archiv de Philosophic du Droit 9:97

Vogel C (2011) Zur Rolle der Beherrschten in der mittelalterlichen Herrschaftslegitimation. Düsseldorf University Press, Düsseldorf

Watner C (2005) Quod Omnes Tangit: consent theory in the radical libertarian tradition in the middle ages. J Libertarian Stud 19:67–85

Weber M (1989) The religion of China: Confucianism and Taoism. Yuan-Liou Publishing, Taipei. (马克斯·韦伯, 中国的宗教:儒教与道教, 远流出版社, 台北, 1989年)

Whitehead AN (1933) The adventure of ideas. Simon & Schuster, New York

Wilhelm R (ed) (1994) Li Gi, Das Buch der Riten, Sitten und Bräuche. Eugen Diederichs Verlag, München

Wyduckel D (1984) Ius Publicum: Grundlagen und Entwicklung des öffentlichen Rechts und der deutschen Staasrechtwissenschaft. Duncker & Humblot, Berlin

Xu XS (1962) The age of legends in ancient Chinese history. Science Press, Beijing. (徐旭生, 中国古史的传说时代, 科学出版社, 北京, 1962年)

Xu S (1981) Shuo Wen Jie Zi Zhu. Shanghai Chinese Classics Publishing House, Shanghai. (许慎, 说文解字注, 上海古籍出版社, 上海, 1981年)

Yang ZG (2000) A research on Chinese rituals. East China Normal University Press, Shanghai. (杨志刚, 中国礼仪制度研究, 华东师范大学出版社, 上海, 2000年)

Yao D (2010) The wisdom of Reading history. Fudan University Press, Shanghai. (姚大力, 读史的智慧, 复旦大学出版社, 上海, 2010年)

Yao X (2014) An eco-ethical interpretation of Confucian Tianren Heyi. Front Philos China 9(4): 570–585

Zarrow P (2009) Chinese conceptions of the state during the late Qing dynasty (1860–1911). In: Shogimen T, Nederman CJ (eds) Western political thought in dialogue with Asia. Lexington Books, Lanham

Zarrow P (2012) After empire: the conceptual transformation of the Chinese State, 1885 – 1924. Stanford University Press, Stanford

Zhao T (2009) A political world philosophy in terms of all-under-heaven (tian-xia). Diogenes 221: 5–18

Zhao T (2011) The Tianxai system. China Renmin University Press, Beijing (赵汀阳, 天下体系, 中国人民大学出版社, 北京, 2011年)

Zhou CZ (2009) Research on the ancient shaman doctor and the 'six poems'. Shanghai Classic Publishing House, Shanghai. (周策纵, 古巫医与"六诗"考, 上海古籍出版社, 上海, 2009年)

Zhou PP (ed) (2015) I Jing. Joint Publishing House of Beijing, Beijing. (周鹏鹏 编译, 易经, 北京联合出版公司, 北京, 2015年)

Zhu W (2011) The religion thinking of early modern neo-Confucianism. Shanghai Classic Publishing House, Shanghai. (祝薇, 论早期现代新儒家的宗教观, 上海古籍出版社, 上海, 2011年)

Chapter 5
Conclusion

This thesis, as its title suggests, has conducted historical and legal research on two principles, namely, *Quod Omnes Tangit* and Tianxia Wei Gong. These two principles are of importance separately in European and Chinese political and legal history. The research on *Quod Omnes Tangit* is relatively abundant and sufficient, while a systematic examination of Tianxia Wei Gong is lacking. Thus, this thesis has filled this gap, although its limitations lie in the ways in which the research materials are fragmented and prepared for a comparative legal study. In addition, this thesis connects these two principles for the first time. The selection of these two principles is not random; rather, it is based on the present research and literature review. Three perspectives structure this thesis: similarities and differences, concepts and practice, and origin and development. Among these perspectives, some are static, and others are dynamic.

I start by examining the meanings and origins of the two principles. As Tianxia Wei Gong is in Chinese, I have examined its exact tones to define its meaning. Their meanings are the basic foundation and starting point of all comparisons. What is more important may be their origins. Tianxia Wei Gong originates from Li Gi, while *Quod Omnes Tangit* stems from Code Civil. Li Gi is a classic work documenting Confucian thought, while Code Civil is a compilation of Justinian's Roman Law. It is thought-provoking to compare Confucius and Justinian, Confucian school and Roman Law school, or even the Chinese Empire and the Roman Empire, but the last group of subjects extends beyond the research range of this thesis. Thus, only the first two groups were briefly compared.

After that, two monarchs quoting the principles at critical moments in history were put forward for comparison. For Tianxia Wei Gong, it was in the Abdicant Rescript of the last Chinese Emperor, Puyi, while for *Quod Omnes Tangit*, it was in the writ of Edward I to win the support of English people in the war against French. Furthermore, Edward I confirmed the Magna Carta in 1297, exerting great influence on constitutional history. This is the first time that these two principles have been compared, and it is also the first time that these two historical events have been

Y. Shang, *A Historical and Legal Comparison between Tianxia Wei Gong and Quod Omnes Tangit*, Ius Gentium: Comparative Perspectives on Law and Justice 110,
https://doi.org/10.1007/978-3-031-46467-6_5

compared because of these two principles. The East and the West have many similar critical moments in history, in which monarchs quote principles with similar meanings. This is a new finding in comparative legal history.

In addition, after their debut in the historical stage, these principles experienced similar development processes, which means that they experienced a Renaissance, with many academics reinterpreting them. In this section, the interpretations of individual academics are examined in detail. The compilation of their thoughts separately in relation to these two principles is relatively comprehensive. On account of the limitations of this research, the comparison of these interpretations remains general, with only a few concrete crossovers. Hence, future studies can focus on the crossovers based on these materials.

Among all the academics interpreting the principles, Liang Qichao is worthy of special attention. As stated before, he is the only one who mentioned both Tianxia Wei Gong and *Quod Omnes Tangit*. This is one of the most important findings of this research. The successful findings of the literature showing that Chinese scholars were influenced by *Quod Omnes Tangit* has proven the effectiveness of the selected research method, namely, to seek out the quotation of *Quod Omnes Tangit* in the literature of Chinese scholars in the period when Western thoughts were imported into China, although this process was not easy or short. Except for Liang Qichao, the thoughts of other Chinese scholars relating to Tianxia Wei Gong are also thought-provoking. These thoughts demand more attention, and their academic contribution can supplement Chinese legal and political history.

Before moving on to the dynamic development process, I summarize and extract some core values within these two principles, which allows for a deepening of connotations of their meanings. This part is, from the perspective of concept, closer to the first part of this thesis, namely, the meaning of these two principles; as compared with their debut in history and quotations by monarchs at critical historical moments, this part is relatively remote in relation to the first part. Furthermore, as the core values are extracted from the meaning and abstracted, their uniqueness is weaker than the contents written before them. It is highly possible that many other legal or political principles share these core values as well. Therefore, I arrange this part at the end of the chapter. When examining their similarities, any single core value, which both Tianxia Wei Gong and *Quod Omnes Tangit* embrace, can be effortlessly found in another legal or political principle, but all of them together, freedom, equality, democracy, oneness and justice, do constitute their own characters. To this end, I analyzed the reflection of these core values in these two principles with a simultaneous comparison.

Finishing the part of similarities, the opposite side, differences, was the next topic to be discussed. This chapter started with, again, the static element, the main difference lying in the concepts of these two principles, which is of great importance in explaining the difference between the East and the West. The original difference in their concepts is that the methodologies of the two principles to distribute and legitimize rights are different. *Quod Omnes Tangit* links a set of political concepts in the collective decision process: consent, representation, participation, majority rule and *pancta sunt servanda*. The philosophic and ethical basis of ancient Chinese civilization is harmonious and family-like, emphasizing the priority of responsibility to liberty, collectivity to the individual and harmony to conflict. These two principles are samples presenting the differences in value selection of the East and the West. This research has not stopped been by the presentation of difference but puts forward the possible factors causing the difference, which go beyond the research range of this thesis but welcome further study. In this section, I discuss the concept of Tianxia again, considering its relationship with the philosophic and ethical basis of ancient Chinese civilization.

Regarding the inner structure of these two principles' distributing and legitimizing rights, the existence of a communicational canal is of significance. In *Quod Omnes Tangit*, there is a two-way street. First, something touches all; second, all must consent. However, in Tianxia Wei Gong, there is merely one declaration that something belongs to all, with no space for any feedback. This analysis counts as one of the most important findings of this research, profoundly affecting the eastern and western modes of thinking; thus, it offers a legal explanation for the difference between the East and the West. This is also a response, from a legal and political perspective, to the phenomenon that the East and the West have different value systems.

Finishing the static elements in the part of differences, the dynamic part followed. I have summarized three processes regarding the development of *Quod Omnes Tangit*, namely, from *ius privatum to ius publicum*, from *ius naturale to ius positivum* and from religious law to secular law. Correspondingly, it has been examined and compared whether Tianxia Wei Gong has experienced the same process in Chinese legal and political history, and the answer to this question is negative. This is the reason why these contents appeared in the part of differences.

Through the analysis from various lenses—social psychology, ethics, anthropology and so on—the characteristics' difference between East and West is coincidental. This is the same case in the legal historical research in this thesis. Although the conclusion is no longer actual and established, it may become a slight contribution made to the symphony of all social scientific disciplines from the perspective of legal history.

In analyzing Tianxia Wei Gong and *Quod Omnes Tangit*, it can be concluded that although Tianxia Wei Gong lacks, on the one hand, the individualism and concrete channels to reach an envisagement of institutions, it provides more space for the comprehension and implementation of its immense ideas, which means that it may contain more tolerance when it is reinterpreted. In addition, the comparison of the two maxims offers an answer to the questions raised at the beginning of this thesis. With Tianxia Wei Gong as a root of the thinking of Confucianism[1] and its influence throughout thousands of years on Chinese society, Chinese people value collectivity more than individuals. If the world belongs to all, then it is reasonable to accept that supervision of our daily lives happens in public spaces. Similarly, with almost every query a Western citizen would raise about any social issue currently happening in

[1] See also Billioud (2007), p. 56.

China, if we think about Tianxia Wei Gong, *Quod Omnes Tangit,* and their differences, our understanding will increase.

In the late nineteenth and early twentieth centuries, Chinese thinkers, including reformers and revolutionaries, had to reconcile Chinese ethnocentrism with Enlightenment modernity, establishing new political and social institutions to replace old ones.[2] "Their self-conscious theorizations of that process offer not only important evidence of their agency in resisting and mediating such global phenomena but also one of the most sustained, literate, and self-aware discourses about how and why we should learn from differently situated others,"[3] which "offer[s] striking and instructive parallels to the situation we face in the twenty-first."[4]

Topics such as those in this thesis are not amenable to exhaustive treatment. It cannot be claimed to have examined every relevant document. Further research would certainly enrich the concepts and might alter the arguments.

References

Billioud S (2007) Confucianism, "cultural tradition" and official discourses in China at the start of the new century. China Perspect 3:50–65

Jenco L (2015) Changing referents: learning across space and time in China and the west. Oxford University Press, New York

[2]Jenco (2015), pp. 2–5.

[3]Jenco (2015), p. 2.

[4]Jenco (2015), pp. 4–5.

References

Primary Literature

Aristotle (1995) Politics (trans: Barker E). Oxford University Press, New York

Ban G (1962) Hanshu. Zhonghua Book Company, Beijing. (班固, 汉书, 中华书局, 北京, 1962年)

Bary WT, Bloom I (eds) (1999) Sources of Chinese tradition, vol 1. Columbia University Press, New York

Chinese Classics (1865) The shoo king (trans: Legge J). At The Author's, Hongkong

Chinese Classics (1871) The book of Peotry. Lane (trans: Legginese Text Proe J). Crawford & Co., Hongkong

Chinese Classics (1882) The Yi king. (trans: Legge J). Clarendon Press, Oxford46

Chinese Classics (1974) The book of odes (trans: Karlgren B). Museum of Far Eastern Antiquities, Stockholm

Chinese Classics (1977) The I Ching or book of changes. (trans: Wilhelm R, Baynes CF). Princeton University Press, Princeton

Chinese Classics (1980) Reprint of the thirteen classics, commented and annotated. Zhonghua Book Company, Beijing. (十三经注疏影印本, 中华书局, 北京, 1980年)

Chinese Classics (2019) The book of odes (trans: Zhou ZF). Zhonghua Book Company, Beijing. (周振甫 译注, 诗经, 中华书局, 北京, 2019年)

Chinese Classics (1046 BC – 771 BC) 诗经 – Book of Poetry. Chinese Text Project. https://ctext.org/book-of-poetry/ens. Accessed Dec 05 2022. English editions

Chinese Classics (Late 9th century BC) 易經 - Yi Jing. Chinese Text Project. https://ctext.org/book-of-changes/yi-jing. Accessed Dec 05 2022. English editions

Chinese Text Project (2022) Lunyu. In: Chinese Text Project. https://ctext.org/zhs. Accessed 11 Nov 2022

Confucius (1885) The Li Ki (trans: Legge J). Clarendon Press, Oxford

Confucius (1980) Lunyu (trans: Yang BJ). Zhonghua Book Company, Beijing. (杨伯峻 译注, 论语译注, 中华书局, 北京, 1980年)

Confucius (1994) Liji. In: Qian X et al (eds) Shisan Jing Jinzhu Jinyi. Yuelu Publishing House, Changsha. (孔子, 礼记, 钱玄, 等编, 十三经今注今译, 岳麓书社, 长沙, 1994年)

Confucius (1998) The analects of Confucius (trans: Ames RT, Rosemont H). Random House Publishing, New York. Another Chinese edition

Confucius (2010) The analects of Confucius (trans: Watson B). Columbia University Press, New York

Y. Shang, *A Historical and Legal Comparison between Tianxia Wei Gong and Quod Omnes Tangit*, Ius Gentium: Comparative Perspectives on Law and Justice 110,
https://doi.org/10.1007/978-3-031-46467-6

Confucius (551–479 BC) Yue Ling. In: Li Gi (礼记·月令第六). Chinese Text Project. https://ctext.org/liji/yue-ling/ens. Accessed 12 Dec 2019

Confucius (480 BC–350 BC) 論語 - The Analects. Chinese Text Project. https://ctext.org/analects/ens. Accessed 05 Dec 2022. English editions

Confucius (551–479 BC) 礼记 - Liji. Chinese Text Project. https://ctext.org/liji/ens. Accessed Dec 05 2022. English editions

Couvreur S (1950) Mémoires Sur Les Bienséances Et Les Cérémonies. Cathasia, Paris

De Las Casas FB (1992) In: Losada A, Moleres ML (eds) De thesauris in Obras completas. Alianza, Madrid

Denifle H, Chatelain E (eds) (1881) Chartularium universitatis Parisiensis: sub auspiciis consilii generalis facultatum Parisiensum, vol. 2. Ex typis fratrum Delalain. Université de Paris, Paris

Gadamer H-G (1990) Wahrheit und Methode. Mohr Siebeck, Tübingen

Gewirth A (1956) Marsilius of Padua: the defender of peace, vol. 2: the Defensor Pacis. Columbia University Press, New York

Godfrey of Fontaines (2000) Are subjects bound to pay a tax when the need for it is not evident? In: McGrade AS et al (eds) The Cambridge translations of medieval philosophical texts. Cambridge University Press, New York, pp 315–320

Grotius H, van Ittersum MJ (eds) (2006) Commentary on the law of prize and booty. Liberty Fund, Indianapolis

Gu YW (1613–1682) Tinglin Shiwenji. Chinese Text Project. https://ctext.org/wiki.pl?if=en&res=567076. Accessed 05 Dec 2022. English edition

Gu YW (1990) Rizhi Lu. Huashan Literature & Art Publishing House, Shijiazhuang. (顾炎武, 日知录, 花山文艺出版社, 石家庄, 1990年)

Gu YW (2017) Record of daily knowledge and collected poems and essays 1 (trans: Johnston I). Columbia University Press, New York

Habermas (1992) Faktizität und Geltung. Suhrkamp, Frankfurt am Main

Heidegger M (1967) Sein und Zeit. Max Niemeyer Verlag, Tübingen

Hintze O, Gilbert F (eds) (1975) The history essays of Otto Hintze. Oxford University Press, New York

Hobbes T (1994) In: Gaskin JCA (ed) The elements of law, natural and politic. Oxford University Press, New York

Hobbes T (1998) Leviathan. Oxford University Press, Oxford

Hu LY (1975) Hu Yinan Xiansheng Quanji. Wen Hai Press, Taipei. (胡礼垣, 胡翼南先生全集, 文海出版社, 常州, 1975年)

Huang ZX (1662) Ming Yi Dai Fang Lu. Chinese Text Project. https://ctext.org/wiki.pl?if=en&res=192095&remap=gb. Accessed Dec 05 2022. English edition

Huang ZX (1993) Waiting for the Dawn: a plan for the prince (trans: Bary WT). Columbia University Press, New York

Huang ZX (1995) Ming I Dai Fang Lu. Shanghai Chinese Classic Publishing House, Shanghai. (黄宗羲, 明夷待访录, 上海古籍出版社, 上海, 1995年)

Hume D (1788) Essays, moral, political, and literary. Bell & Bradfute, London

Justinian (2009) The digest of Justinian (trans: Watson A), vol 1/4. University of Pennsylvania Press, Pennsylvania

Justinian (529–534) Digesta. In: Iustinianus Project. Alexandr K, Yves L. https://droitromain.univ-grenoble-alpes.fr/Corpus/digest.htm. Accessed 05 Dec 2022. English edition

Kang YW (1913) Da Tong Shu. Chinese Text Project. https://ctext.org/wiki.pl?if=en&res=306261&remap=gb. 05 Accessed Dec 2022. English edition

Kang YW (1958) Ta T'ung Shu, the one-world philosophy of K'ang Yu-wei (trans: Thompson LG). George Allen & Unwin, London

Kant I (2016) Grundlegung zur Metaphysik der Sitten. Felix Meiner Verlag, Hamburg

Köbler G (2009) Zielwörterbuch europäischer Rechtsgeschichte, 5th edn. Arbeiten zur Rechts- und Sprachwissenschaft Verlag, Gießen

Las Casas (1992) De thesauris in Obras completas. Alianza Editorial, Madrid

Liang QC (1959) Intellectual trends in the Qing period (trans: Hsü I). Harvard University Press, Cambridge

Liang QC (1992) In: Xiao XH (ed) Selected works of Liang Qichao. China Broadcast Film & Television Publishing House, Beijing. (梁启超, 梁启超文选, 夏晓红编, 中国广播电视出版社, 北京, 1992年)

Liang QC (2006) In: Hou YJ (ed) Selected works of Liang Qichao. Baihua Edition, Tianjin. (梁启超, 梁启超文选, 侯宜杰选注, 百花文艺出版社, 天津, 2006年)

Liang QC (2014a) The experience of travel in Europe. The Commercial Press, Beijing. (梁启超, 欧游心影录, 商务印书馆, 北京, 2014年)

Liang QC (2015) Yin Bing Shi He Ji. Zhonghua Book Company, Beijing. (梁启超, 饮冰室合集, 中华书局, 北京, 2015年)

Locke J (1960) Two treatises of government. Cambridge University Press, New York

Lü K (1991) Shenyin Yu. Yuelu Publishing House, Changsha. (吕坤, 呻吟语, 岳麓书社, 长沙, 1991年)

Mansi JD (1759–1798) Sacrorum conciliorum nova et amplissima collectio, vol 22/32. Expensis Antonii Zatta, Florence-Venice

Manthe U (2008) Corpus Iuris Civilis. In: Cordes A et al (eds) Handwörterbuch zur deutschen Rechtsgeschichte, vol 1/3, 2nd edn. Erich Schmidt Verlag, Berlin, pp S 901–S 907

Marsilius of Padua (1993) Marsiglio of Padua: Defensor minor and De Translatione Imperii (trans and ed: Nederman CJ). Cambridge University Press, Cambridge

Marsilius of Padua (2005) The defender of the peace (trans and ed: Brett A). Cambridge University Press, New York

Marsilius of Padua (2010) The defender of peace. Hackett Publishing Company, Indianapolis

Mencius (1895) The Chinese classics, vol. 2, the works of Mencius (trans: Legge J). Clarendon Press, Oxford

Mencius (340 BC–250 BC) 孟子 - Mengzi. Chinese Text Project. https://ctext.org/mengzi/ens. Accessed 05 Dec 2022. English edition

Miu CQ (1637) The legacy of Congyetang. Shanghai Chinese Classics Publishing House, Shanghai. (缪昌期, 从野堂存稿, 上海古籍出版社, 上海, 1637年)

Nicholas of Cusa (1991) Book II. Cambridge University Press, Cambridge

Nikolaus of Cusa (1968) De concordantia catholica. Meiner Verlag, Hamburg

Ockham (1612) Dialogus. In: Goldast M, Monarchia S (eds) Romani Imperii. Biermanni & confort, Hanovie

Ockham (1914a) An Rex Angliae Pro Succursu Guerrae. In: Scholz R (ed) Unbekannte Kirchenpolitische Streitschriften aus der Zeit Ludwigs des Bayern (1327–1354). Verlag Von Loescher & Co, Rom, pp 432–453

Ockham (1914b) De Imperatorum et Pontificum potestate. In: Scholz R (ed) Unbekannte Kirchenpolitische Streitschriften aus der Zeit Ludwigs des Bayern (1327–1354). Verlag Von Loescher & Co, Rom, pp 453–480

Ockham (1974) Octo Quaestiones. Manchester University Press, Manchester

Ockham (2015) Dialogus. British Academy. http://publications.thebritishacademy.ac.uk/pubs/dialogus/wtc.html. Accessed 31 Dec 2020

Pascal B (1849) Thoughts of Blaise Pasca. Gould, Kendall and Lincoln, Boston

Plato (2012) Republic (trans: Rowe C). Penguin, London

Potthast A (1874) Regesta Pontificum Romanorum, vol 1/2. Rudolphi de Decker, Berlin

Pufendorf S (1994) The political writings of Samuel Pufendorf. Oxford University Press, New York

Pufendorf S (1998) De Jure et Gentium. Akademie Verlag, Berlin

Richter AL (1939) In: Friedberg E (ed) Corpus iuris canonici, vol 2. Tauchnitz, Leipzig

Rousseau JJ (1994) The social contract (trans: Betts C). Oxford University Press, New York

Shen YL (1967) Political documents of the years Xuantong. Taiwan Wen Hai Press Company, Taipei. (沈云龙主编, 宣统政纪, 台湾文海出版社, 台北, 1967年)

Shen Y (2002) Collected works of Luofanlou. Shanghai Chinese Classics Publishing House, Shanghai. (沈垚, 落帆楼文集, 上海古籍出版社, 上海, 2002年)

Siéyès EJ (2003) Sieyès: political writings (trans: Sonencher M). Hackett Publishing Company, Indianapolis

Sophocles (2003) Antigone (trans and eds: Gibbons, Segal). Oxford University Press, New York

Sun ZS (1986) Complete works of Sun Zhongshan, vol 9. Zhonghua Book Company, Beijing. (孙中山, 孙中山全集, 中华书局, 北京, 1986年)

The Codification Committee of the Great Compendium of Chinese Characters (1988) The great Chinese dictionary. Hubei Dictionary Publishing Company and Sichuan Dictionary Publishing Company, Wuhan and Chengdu. (汉语大字典编纂委员会, 汉语大字典, 湖北辞书出版社, 四川辞书出版社, 成都, 1988年)

Weiland L (1896) Constitutiones et acta publica imperatorum et regum inde ab a. MCXCVIII usque ad a. In: MCCLXXII (1198-1272) (ed) Monumenta Germaniae Historica (MGH). Harrassowitz Verlag, Wiesbaden

Wilhelm R (ed) (1994) Li Gi, Das Buch der Riten, Sitten und Bräuche. Eugen Diederichs Verlag, München

Xu S (1979) Shuo Wen Jie Zi. Zhonghua Book Company, Beijing. (许慎, 说文解字, 中华书局, 北京, 1979年)

Xu S (1981) Shuo Wen Jie Zi Zhu. Shanghai Chinese Classics Publishing House, Shanghai. (许慎, 说文解字注, 上海古籍出版社, 上海, 1981年)

Yat-sen S (1942) San Min Chu I. Ministry of Information of the Republic of China, Calcutta

Zhao NX (1985) Collected works of Weibozhai. Zhonghua Book Company, Beijing. (赵南星, 味檗斋文集, 中华书局, 北京, 1985年)

Secondary Literature

Ames RT (2009) Seeking harmony not sameness: comparative philosophy and east-west understanding. Beijing University Press, Beijing. (安乐哲, 和而不同: 中西哲学的会通, 北京大学出版社, 北京, 2009年)

Barker E (1913) The Dominican order and convocation. At the Clarendon, Oxford

Bauer W (1990) Das Antlitz Chinas. Carl Hanser Verlag, Munich

Begère M (1998) Sun Yat-sen. Stanford University Press, Redwood City

Bell AA (2014) Reconciling Confucianism and nationalism. J Chin Philos 41:33–54

Billioud S (2007) Confucianism, "cultural tradition" and official discourses in China at the start of the new century. China Perspectives 3:50–65

Blythe JM (1992) Ideal government and the mixed constitution in the middle ages. Princeton University Press, Princeton

Bourdieu P, Thompson JB (eds) (1991) Language and symbolic power. Polity Press, Cambridge

Breay C (2002) Magna Carta. The British Library, London

Brösch M et al (eds) (2014) Handbuch Nikolaus von Kues: Leben und Werk. WBG, Darmstadt

Brundage JA (2013) Medieval Canon Law. Routledge, New York

Bullinger M (1968) Öffentliches Recht und Privatrech: Studien über Sinn und Funktionen der Unterscheidung. W. Kohlhammer Verlag, Stuttgart

Burns T (2002) Sopholcles' Antigone and the history of the concept of natural law. Political Stud 50(3):545–557

Burton DW (1985) Politics, propaganda and public opinion in the reigns of Henry III and Edward I. Dissertation. University of Oxford, Oxford

Busch H (1949) The Tung-Lin academy and its political and philosophical significance. Monumenta Serica 14:1–163

Butterfield H (1931) The Whig interpretation of history. G. Bell And Sons, London

Cassirer E (1954) An Essay on Man. Doubleday Anchor Books, New York

Chan J (2014) Confucian perfectionism: a political philosophy for modern times. Princeton University Press, Princeton

Chang H (1987) Chinese intellectuals in crisis: search for order and meaning (1890–1911). University of California Press, Berkeley and Los Angeles

Chang YZ, Wang ZY (2019) On the ancient Chinese Gan-Zhi(干支) and decimal system and the period of the twelve-digit system. Central Plains Culture Res 3:15–23. (常玉芝, 王曾瑜, 中国古代的干支、十进位制和十二进位制纪时, 中原文化研究, 2019年第3期, 第15-23页)

Chen Y (2013) Confucianism as religion: controversies and consequences. Brill, Leiden

Chen F (2015a) Sources of two famous quotes. http://www.cssn.cn/wx/wx_bh/201506/t20150605_2023840.shtml Accessed Feb 27 2018 (陈福康, 说两句名言的出处, 中国社会科学网, 访问时间:2018年2月27日)

Chen L (2015b) The Core values of Chinese civilization. SDX Joint Publishing Company, Beijing. (陈来, 中华文明的核心价值, 三联书店, 北京, 2015年)

Chen P et al (2012) A literature review of the research theme the abdicant of the Qing emperor in the late one hundred year. Qing History J 4:104–125. (陈鹏, 韩祥, 张公政, 百年"清帝逊位"问题研究综述), 清史研究, 2012年第4期, 第104-125页

Cheng C-Y (2016) Transforming virtues into rights--the practical ability and potential of human in Confucian ethic. In: Liang T (ed) Virtues and rights, on Confucianism and human rights from cross-cultural perspectives. China Social Sciences Press, Beijing, pp 241–255. (成中英, 将儒家美德转化为权利——儒家伦理观中人之实践能力与潜能研究, 梁涛编, 美德与权利, 中国社会科学出版社, 北京, 2016年)

Cheng P-K et al (eds) (1999) The search for modern China: a documentary collection. W. W. Norton, New York

Clayton LA (2012) Bartolomé de las Casas: A Biography. Cambridge University Press, New York

Congar Y (1980) Quod omnes tangit ab omnibus tractari et approbari debet. In: Heinz R (ed) Die geschichtlichen Grundlagen der modernen Volksvertretung. Wissenschaftliche Buchgesellschaft, Darmstadt, pp 115–182

Dallmayr F (2009) Comparative political theory: what is it good for? In: Shogimen T, Nederman CJ (eds) Western political thought in dialogue with Asia. Lexington Books, Lanham, pp 13–24

Danziger D, Gillingham J (2004) 1215, the year of magna carta. Hodder and Stoughton, London

Ding D (2014) Ding Ding Talking about the Classic and Fashional Traits of Li Ji. http://www.rmzxb.com.cn/c/2014-11-03/401857.shtml. Accessed 26 Feb 2018 (丁鼎, 丁鼎谈《礼记》的"古典"与"时尚", 人民政协网, 访问时间:2018年2月26日)

Ding S (2020) Review and a new interpretation of the issue of "rites do not extend down to the common people; criminal Laws do not extend up to the senior nobles". Jianghan Acad 8(4): 92–101. (丁四新, "礼不下庶人, 刑不上大夫"问题检讨与新论, 江汉学术, 2020年8月第4期, 第92-101页)

Du H (2012) On the tendency towards the public and its social values of the early idea of the public and private. J Liaoning Normal Univ 35:561–565. (杜洪义, 早期公司观念的尚公取向及其社会价值, 辽宁师范大学学报, 2012年第35期, 第561-565页)

Duggan C (2003) Decretals. In: Carson T, Cerrito J (eds) New Catholic encyclopedia, vol 4. Thompson/Gale, Washington, DC, pp 599–601

Elman BA (1989) Imperial politics and Confucian societies in late Imperial China: the Hanlin and Donglin academies. Modern China 15:379–418

Elvin M (1998) Who was responsible for the weather? Moral Meteorol Late Imperial China Osiris 13:213–237

Encyclopædia Britannica (2022) The Britannica Group, Chicago. https://www.britannica.com/. Accessed 05 Dec 2022

Fairbank JK (1967) The Chinese written language. In: Schurmann F, Shell O (eds) Imperial China. Random House, Harmondsworth, pp 60–63

Fairbank JK (1978) The Cambridge history of China. In: Late Ch'ing, 1800–1911, part 1, vol 10. Cambridge University Press, Cambridge

Fairbank JK, Liu K-C (1980) The Cambridge history of China, vol. 11, late Ch'ing 1800–1911, part 2. Cambridge University Press, Cambridge
Fasolt C (1991) Council and hierarchy: the political thought of William Durant the younger. Cambridge University Press, Cambridge
Fasolt C (2014) Past sense: studies in medieval and early modern European history. Brill, Leiden
Feifel E (1982) Geschichte der chinesischen Literatur. Wissenschaftliche Buchgesellschaft, Darmstadt
Feng YL (1948) A short history of Chinese philosophy. The Free Press, New York
Feng YL (1982) A new codification of Chinese philosophy history. People's Publishing House, Beijing. (冯友兰, 中国哲学史新编, 人民出版社, 北京, 1982年)
Feng S (2001) Archeoastronomy in China. Social Sciences Academic Press, Beijing. (冯时, 中国天文考古学, 中国天文考古学, 社会科学文献出版社, 北京, 2001年)
Feng YL (2017) A short history of Chinese history. Beijing Lianhe Publishing House, Beijing. (冯友兰, 中国哲学简史, 北京联合出版公司, 北京, 2017年)
Figgis JN (1999) Political thought from Gerson to Grotius: 1414–1625. Batoche Books, Kitchener
Flaig E (2013) Die Mehrheitsentscheidung: Entstehung und kulturelle Dynamik. Ferdinand Schöningh, Paderborn
Forke A (1964) Geschichte der mittelalterlichen chinesischen Philosophie. De Gruyter, Hamburg
Frank T (ed) (1959) An economic survey of ancient Rome, vol 4. Pageant Books, Paterson
Fukuyama F (2011) The origins of political order. Farrar, Straus and Giroux, New York
Gao QX (2011a) The Imperial edict of Abdicaiton by the Qing emperor in a political and constitutional view. Global Law Rev 5:26–36. (高全喜, 政治宪法学视野中的清帝《逊位诏书》, 环球法律评论, 2011年第5期, 第26-36页)
Gao QX (2011b) The moment for constitutionalism. Guangxi Normal University Press, Guilin. (高全喜, 立宪时刻, 广西师范大学出版社, 桂林, 2011年)
Gewirth A (1951) Marsilius of Padua: the defender of peace, vol. 1: Marsilius of Padua and medieval political philosophy. Columbia University Press, New York
Gierke O (1868) Das deutsche Genossenschaftsrecht. Weidmann, Berlin
Glasser TL, Salmon CT (1995) Public opinion and the communication of consent. The Guilford Press, New York
Glenn HP (2007) Legal tradition of the world. Oxford University Press, Oxford
Godthardt F (2006) The philosopher as political actor – Marsilius of Padua at the court of Ludwig the Bavarian: the sources revised. In: Gerson M-R (ed) The world of Marsilius of Padua. Brepols, Turnhout, pp 29–46
Godthardt F (2011) Marsilius von Padua und der Romzug Ludwigs des Bayern: Politische Theorie und politisches Handeln. V&R Unipress, Göttingen
Godthardt F (2012) The life of Marsilius of Padua. In: Moreno-Riano G, Nederman CJ (eds) A companion to Marsilius of Padua. Brill, Leiden, pp 13–56
Goodsell TL, Whiting JB (2016) An Aristotelian theory of family. J Family Theory Rev 8:484–502
Grondin J (2016) The hermeneutical circle. In: Keane N, Lawn C (eds) The Blackwell companion to hermeneutics. Blackwell, Oxford, pp 299–305
Grotius H (2006) Commentary on the law of prize and booty. Liberty Fund, Indianapolis
Gu XC (1987) The legacy of Jinggao. Shanghai Classic Publishing House, Shanghai. (顾宪成, 泾皋藏稿, 上海古籍出版社, 上海, 1987年)
Gu XC (2002) Wanli Shuchao. Shanghai Classic Publishing House, Shanghai. (顾宪成, 万历疏钞, 上海古籍出版社, 上海, 2002年)
Gunn JAW (1983) Beyond liberty and property. McGill-Queen's University Press, Kingston
Haller J (1903) Papsttum und Kirchenreform. Weidmann, Berlin
Hauck A (1920) Kirchengeschichte Deutschlands. Hinrich, Leipzig
He BD (1996) The culture of Chinese humanism: source, feature and significance. 21 Century 33: 91–101, 34: 88-101(何炳棣, 华夏人本主义文化:渊源、特征及意义, 二十一世纪, 第33期, 第91-101页, 第34期, 第88-101页)

Head JW (2011) Great legal traditions: civil law, common law, and Chinese law in historical and operational perspective. Carolina Academic Press, Durham
Heine SJ et al (1999) Is there a universal need for positive self-regard? Psychol Rev 106:766–794
Hintze O (1931) Weltgeschichtliche Bedingung der Repräsentativverfassung. Hist Z 143:1–47
Hoang P (1910) Concordance des chronologies néoméniques chinoise et européenne. Imprimerie de la mission catholique, Shanghai
Hobson JM (2004) The eastern origins of Western civilisation. Cambridge University Press, Cambridge
Hofmann H (2003) Repräsentation. Duncker & Humblot, Berlin
Hölscher L (1979) Öffentlichkeit und Geheimnis. Klett-Cotta, Stuttgart
Holt JC (1992) The northerners. Clarendon Press, Oxford
Holt JC et al (eds) (2015) Magna Carta. Cambridge University Press, Cambridge
Hsü IC-Y (2000) The rise of modern China. Oxford University Press, Oxford
Hu S (2013) English writings of Hu Shih. Springer, Heidelberg
Hu M (2015) China's transition to modernity: the new classical vision of Dai Zhen. University of Washington Press, Seattle and London
Hu S (2020) An outline of the history of Chinese thought by Hu Shih. Springer, Berlin
Huang PC (1969) Liang Ch'i-ch'ao. In: Opitz PJ (ed) Vom Konfuzianismus zum Kommunismus. List Verlag, Munich, pp 61–105
Huillard-Bréholles J-L-A (1852) Historia diplomatica Friderici secondi, vol 2. Henricus Plon, Paris
Hummel AW et al (eds) (2010) Eminent Chinese of the Ch'ing period. Global Oriental, Folkestone
Huser P (2011) Vernunft and Herrschaft. LIT, Berlin
Jasper D, Fuhrmann H (2001) Papal letters in the early middle ages. CUA Press, Washington, DC
Jenco L (2015) Changing referents: learning across space and time in China and the west. Oxford University Press, New York
Jiang D (2011) Probe of doctrine of "Li" in Chinese traditional legal culture through analysis on the word "Li". Hebei law. Science 29:39–44. (姜栋, 从"礼"字管窥中国传统法文化中的"礼"的起源, 河北法学, 2011年第29期, 第39-44页)
Jiang L (2012) The spatial formation and transformation of Chinese rural clan settlements. Dissertation. Bauhaus-Universität, Weimer
Jin GT, Liu QF (2004) A quantitative study of China's selective absorption of modern Western ideas and the origins of certain key concepts (1840-1915). 21 Century 48:52–66. (金观涛, 刘青峰, 二十一世纪, 2004年第48期, 第52-66页。)
Johnston D (2010) A history of consent in Western thought. In: Miller FG, Wertheimer A (eds) The ethics of consent: theory and practice. Oxford Academic Press, Oxford, pp 25–54
Kandler K-H (1995) Nikolaus Von Kues: Denker zwishen Mittelalter und Neuzeit. Vandenhoeck & Ruprecht, Göttingen
Kempshall MS (1999) The common good in late medieval political thought. Clarendon Press, Oxford
Kim J (2016) Phenomenology of public opinion. In: Jung HY, Embree L (eds) Political phenomenology. Springer, Cham
Kuang YM (1990) A critical biography of Confucius. Nanjing University Press, Nanjing. (匡亚明, 孔子评传, 南京大学出版社, 南京, 1990年)
Kwong LSK (1984) A mosaic of the hundred days: personalities, politics, and ideas of 1898. Harvard University Press, Cambridge
Kyoson T (1927) Contemporary thought of Japan and China. Williams and Norgate, London
Landau P (2013) Europäische Rechtsgeschichte und kanonisches Recht im Mittelalter. Wissenschaftlicher Verlag Bachmann, Badenweiler
Landau P (2015) The origin of the regula iuris, quod omnes tangit in the Anglo-Norman School of Canon law during the twelfth century. Bull Medieval Canon Law 32(1):19–35
Laski H (1936) Political theory in the later middle age. In: Prévité-Orton CW, Brooke ZN (eds) The Cambridge medieval History, vol. 8, the close of middle ages. Cambridge University Press, Cambridge, pp 620–645

Lee S-H (2006) A topography of Confucian discourse. Homa & Sekey Books, Paramus

Lee H-Y (2008) Political representation in the later middle ages: Marsilius in context. Peter Lang Publishing, New York

Legrand P (2010) European legal systems are not converging. In: Merryman JH et al (eds) Comparative law: historical development of the civil law tradition in Europe, Latin America, and East Asia. LexisNexis, New Providence

Levy E (1951) West Roman vulgar law. Am Philos Soc, Philadelphia

Levy MJ (1992) Confucianism and modernization. Society 29:15–17

Li X (2001) The Chinese cultural revolution revisited. China Rev 1(1):137–165

Li M (2015a) Natural society: natural law and the formation of modern moral world. SDX Joint Publishing Company, Beijing. (李猛, 自然社会:自然法与现代道德世界的形成, 三联书店, 北京, 2015年)

Li ZH (2015b) From shaman to ritual, rooting in Ren. SDX Joint Publishing Company, Beijing. (李泽厚, 由巫到礼释礼归仁, 三联书店, 北京, 2015年) English edition

Li L (2016) A warring states period Ganzhi instrument in the National Museum of China. J Natl Museum China 5:137–142. (李零, 中国国家博物馆藏战国错金干支仪, 馆藏文物研究, 2016年第5期, 第137-142页)

Li ZH (2018) The origins of Chinese thought: from shamanism to ritual regulations and humaneness (trans.: Carleo III R.A.). Brill, Leiden

Liang SM (1982) The key to Chinese culture. Le Jin BKS, Taipei. (梁漱溟, 中国文化要义, 里仁书局, 台北, 1982年)

Liang ZP (2014b) The concept of Wei gong. China Law Rev 2:66–86. (梁治平, "为公"的理念, 中国法律评论, 2014年第2期, 第66-86页)

Liang ZP (2016) The concept of Tianxia: from ancient to modern. Tsinghua Univ Law J 10:5–31. (梁治平, "天下"的观念:从古代到现代, 清华法学, 2016年第10期, 第5-31页)

Liang Z (2021) Tianxia and Ideology. https://www.readingthechinadream.com/liang-zhiping-tianxia-and-ideology.html, Accessed 20 Mar 2021

Liebs D (ed) (2007) Lateinische Rechtsregeln und Rechtssprichwörter. C. H. Beck, Munich

Lin A-w (2017) Confucianism and civil society. In: Hon T-K, Stapleton K (eds) Confucianism for the contemporary world. Sunny Press, New York, pp 107–116

Ling B (2013) The legitimate Foundation for the Nation Building. The Jurist 4:159–160. (凌斌, 从清帝逊位诏书解读看国家建立的规范基础, 法学家, 2013年第4期, 第159, 160页)

Liu JB (1903) Xiaoxue Xiushen Jiaokeshu. Wenmin Shuju, Shanghai. (刘剑白, 小学修身教科书, 文明书局, 上海, 1903年)

Liu XS (2001) Natural law outside the Christian world. In: Braybrooke D (ed) Natural law modernized. University of Toronto Press, Toronto, pp 258–294

Liu J (2006) An introduction to Chinese philosophy. Blackwell Publishing, Malden

Liu J, Huang D (2006) The evolution of Tianxia cosmology and 1st philosophical implications. Front Philos China 1(4):517–538

Loewe M, Shaughnessy EL (eds) (1999) The Cambridge history of ancient China: from the origins of civilization to 221 B.C. Cambridge University Press, Cambridge

Ma T (2011) Critical biography of Lü kun. Nanjing University Press, Nanjing. (马涛, 吕坤评传, 南京大学出版社, 南京, 2011年)

Macpherson CB (1962) The political theory of possessive individualism. Oxford University Press, Oxford

Mandrella I (2012) Reformhandeln und spekulatives Denken bei Nicolaus Cusanus: Eine Verhältnisbestimmung. In: Frank T, Winkler N (eds) Renovatio et unitas – Nikolaus von Kues als reformer: Theorie und praxis der reformatio im 15. Jahrhundert. V&R Unipress, Göttingen, pp 37–52

Marongiu A (1980) Das Prinzip der Demokratie und der zustimmung (Quod omnes tangit, ab omnibus approbari debet) im 14.Jahrhundert. In: Rausch H (ed) Die geschichtlichen Grundlagen der modernen Volksvertretung, vol 1. Darmstadt, Wissenschaftliche Buchgesellschaft, pp 183–211

Mathews RH (1931) Mathews' Chinese-English dictionary. Harvard University Press, Cambridge
Mayali L (2015) The legacy of Roman law. In: Johnston D (ed) Cambridge companion to Roman law. Cambridge University Press, Cambridge, pp 374–395
Merryman JH, Pérez-Perdomo R (2007) The civil law tradition. Stanford University Press, Stanford
Miethke J (2008) Politiktheorie im Mittelalter: von Thomas von Aquin bis Wilhelm von Ockham. Mohr Siebeck, Tübingen
Mizoguchi Y (2011) Gong and Si of China. SDX Joint Publishing Company, Beijing. (沟口雄三, 中国的公与私, 三联书店, 北京, 2011年)
Monahan AP (1987) Consent, coercion and limit, the medieval origins of parliamentary democracy. McGill-Queen's University Press, Montreal
Monahan AP (1994) From personal duties towards personal rights. McGill-Queen's University Press, Montreal & Kinston
Moos P (2004) Öffentlich' und 'privat' im Mittelalter: Zu einem Problem historischer Begriffsbildung. Universitätverlag Winter, Heidelberg
Morrall JB (1961) Ockham and ecclesiology. In: Watt JA et al (eds) Medieval studies: presented to Aubrey Gwynn, S. J. The Three Candles, Dublin, pp 481–491
Mote FW (1971) Intellectual foundations of China. Alfred A. Knopf, New York
Mote FW (2009) Intellectual foundations of China. Beijing University Press, Beijing. (牟复礼, 中国思想之渊源, 北京大学出版社, 北京, 2009年)
Mousourakis G (2003) The historical and institutional context of Roman law. Ashgate, Hampshire
Mousourakis G (2012) Fundamentals of Roman private law. Springer, Heidelberg
Mühlemann G (2006) Chinas Experimente mit westlichen Staatsideen. Schulthess, Zürich
Mulgan R (1990) Aristotle and the value of political participation. Polit Theory 18(2):195–215
Müllejans H (1961) Publicus und Privatus im römischen Recht und im älteren kanonishen Recht. Max Hueber, Munich
Murthy V (2011) The political philosophy of Zhang Taiyan. Brill, Leiden
Müßig U (ed) (2016) Reconsidering constitutional formation I National Sovereignty. Springer, Cham
Müßig U (2019) Reason and fairness. Brill, Leiden
Mutschler F-H (2008) The problem of 'Imperial historiography' in Rome. In: Mutschler F-H, Mittag A (eds) Conceiving the empire China and Rome compared. Oxford University Press, New York, pp 119–142
Myers DG, Twenge JM (2017) Social psychology. McGraw-Hill Education, New York
Nagel J (1987) Participation. Prentice-Hall, Englewood Cliffs
Nathan AJ (1985) Chinese democracy. Alfred A. Knopf, New York
National Geographic (2022) National Geographic Society, Washington, DC https://www.nationalgeographic.org/. Accessed 05 Dec 2022
Nationalgeographic (2021) Chinese Religions and Philosophies. https://www.nationalgeographic.org/article/chinese-religions-and-philosophies/. Accessed 11 Apr 2021
Nederman CJ (2009) Varieties of dialogue: dialogical models of intercultural communication in medieval inter-religious writings. In: Takashi S, Nederman CJ (eds) Western political thought in dialogue with Asia. Lexington Books, Lanham, pp 45–64
Needham J (1991) Science and civilisation in China. Cambridge University Press, Cambridge
New World Encyclopedia (2021) Confucianism. https://www.newworldencyclopedia.org/entry/Confucianism. Accessed Apr 9 2021
New World Encyclopedia (2022). https://www.newworldencyclopedia.org/. Accessed 05 Dec 2022
Nylan M (2009) The rhetoric of 'empire' in the classical era in China. In: Mutschler F-H, Mittag A (eds) Conceiving the Empire China and Rome compared. Oxford University Press, New York, pp 39–64
Oakley F (1962) On the road from Constance to 1688: the political thought of John major and George Buchanan. J Br Stud 1:1–31
Oakley F (1965) Almain and major: conciliar theory on the eve of the reformation. Am Hist Rev 70: 673–690

Oakley F (1983) Legitimation by consent: the question of the medieval roots. In: Viator: medieval and renaissance studies, vol 14. University of California Press, Berkeley, pp 303–335
Opitz PJ (1969) Vom Konfuzianismus zum Kommuinismus. Paul List Verlag, Munich
Parish HR et al (1976) The correct birth Dec 05 2022 of Bartolomé de Las Casas. Hisp Am Hist Rev 56:385–403
Pennington K (1970) Bartolome de Las Casas and the tradition of medieval law. Church History 39: 149–161
Pennington K (2018) Bartolomé de Las Casas. In: Domingo R, Martínez-Torrón J (eds) Great Christian jurists in Spanish history. Cambridge University Press, Cambridge, pp 98–114
Peters JD (1995) Historical tensions in the concept of public opinion. In: Glasser TL, Salmon CT (eds) Public opinion and the communication of consent. The Guilford Press, New York, London, pp 3–36
Pi M (2017) The moralization of gong and Si. Modern Philos 7:155–160. (皮迷迷, "公"与"私"的道德化, 现代哲学, 2017年第7期, 第155-160页)
Pitkin HF (1967) The concept of representation. University of California, California
Plessis P (2015) Borkowski's textbook on Roman law. Oxford University Press, Oxford
Poetzelberger B (1993) Tianxia und guojia bei Liang Shuming (1893–1988): Konsens und Konflikt im chinesischen Beitrag yu traditionellen Ordnungsvorstellungen. Dissertation. Universität Bonn, Bonn
Post G (1943a) Plena Potestas and consent in medieval assemblies: a study in Romano-canonical procedure and the rise of representation, 1150–1325. Traditio 1:355–408
Post G (1943b) Roman law Roman law and early representation in Spain and Italy, 1150–1250. Speculum 18:211–232
Post G (1946) A Romanon-canonical maxim, 'Quod Omnes Tangit,' in Bracton. Traditio 4:197–251
Post G (1964) Studies in medieval legal thought: public law and the state, 1100–1322. Princeton University Press, Princeton
Prestwich M (1997) Edward I. Yale University Press, New Haven
Rathmann T (2000) Geschehen und Geschichten des Konstanzer Konzils. Wilhelm Fink Verlag, Munich
Reading the China Dream (2022). https://www.readingthechinadream.com/. Accessed 05 Dec 2022
Reid CJ (1991) The canonistic contribution to the Western rights tradition: an historical inquiry. Boston College Law Rev 33:37–92
Reilly R (2020) America on trial: a defense of the founding. Ignatius Press, San Francisco
Rubinstein N (2004) Studies in Italian history in the middle ages and the renaissance. Ediyioni Di Storia E Letteratura, Roma
Sanetou K (1983) The Chinese studying in Japan. SDX Publishing House, Nanjing. (实藤惠秀, 中国人留学日本, 三联书店, 北京, 1983年)
Saxonhouse AW (1983) Classical Greek conceptions of public and private. In: Benn SI, Gaus GF (eds) Public and private in social life. St. Martin's Press, New York, pp 363–384
Schiffrin HZ (1968) Sun Yat-sen and the origins of the Chinese revolution. University of California Press, Berkeley and Los Angeles
Schiffrin HZ (1980) Sun Yat-sen: reluctant revolutionary. Little, Brown and Company, Boston
Schmidt-Glintzer H (1990) Geschichte der chinesischen Literatur. Scherz, Bern
Scholz R (1903) Die Publizistik zur Zeit Phillipps des Schönen und Bonifaz' VIII. F. Enke, Stuttgart
Schuessler A (1987) A dictionary of early Chinese. University of Hawaii, Honolulu
Schwartz BI (2004) The world of thought in ancient China. People's Publishing House, Nanjing. (史华慈, 古代中国的思想世界, 江苏人民出版社, 南京, 2004年)
Shang B et al (2008) History of Chinese Confucianism development. Lanzhou University Press, Lanzhou. (尚斌, 任鹏, 李明珠, 中国儒学发展史, 兰州大学出版社, 兰州, 2008年)
Shen DD, Wu TJ (2015) Critical biography of Liang Qichao. Baihuazhou Wenyi Press, Nanchang. (沈大德, 吴廷嘉, 梁启超评传, 百花洲文艺出版社, 南昌, 2015年)

Shin TSW (1980) The concept of state (Kuo-chia) and people (min) in the late Ch'ing, 1890–1907: the case of Liang Ch'i-Ch'ao, Tan Ssu-T'ung and Huang Tsun-Hsien. Dissertation. University of California, Berkeley
Shogimen T, Nederman CJ (2009) Western political thought in dialogue with Asia. Lexington Books, Lanham
Sieben HJ (1983) Traktate und Theorien zum Konzil. Knecht, Frankfurt am Mein
Sievers GS-V (1972) Die Reformbewegung von 1898. In: Opitz PJ (ed) Chinas große Wandlung. C H Beck, München, pp 55–81
Sigmund PE (1963) Nicholas of Cusa and medieval political thought. Cambridge University Press, Cambridge
Skinner Q (1978) Foundations of modern political thought, vol.1, the renaissance. Cambridge University Press, Cambridge
Skinner Q (2002) Conquest and consent: Hobbes and the engagement controversy. In: Aylmer GE (ed) Visions of politics. Cambridge University Press, Cambridge, pp 287–307
Song PJ (2019) The discovery of the Imperial edict of Qing emperor' abdication signed by yuan Shikai and its significance for understanding the state system transformation in late Qing and early republican period. Lit History Philos 4:74–93, 166-167 (宋培军, 袁世凯手批清帝辞位诏书的发现及其对清末民初国体因革的认知意义, 文史哲, 2019年第4期, 第74-93, 166-167页)
Speck T (2009) Quod omnes tangit: Rezeption als ekklesiologisches Phänomen bei Matthäus Romanus und Wilhelm von Ockham. Dissertation. Universität Freiburg, Freiburg im Breisgau
Spence JD (2008) Chinas Weg in die Moderne. Carl Hanser Verlag, Munich
Spengler T (1974) Liang Ch'i-ch'ao. In: Opitz PJ (ed) Die Söhne des Drachen. List, Munich, pp 110–127
Stanford Encyclopedia of Philosophy (2022) Metaphysics Research Lab, Stanford. https://plato.stanford.edu/. Accessed 05 Dec 2022
Stasavage D (2016) Representation and consent: why they arose in Europe and not elsewhere. Annu Rev Polit Sci 19:145–162
Stein P (1995) Ulpian and the distinction between ius publicum and Ius privatum. In: Feenstra R et al (eds) Collatio Iuris Romani: études dédiées à Hans Ankum à l'occasion de son 65e anniversaire, vol 2. J. C. Gieben, Amsterdam, pp 499–504
Strauss L (1953) Natural right and history. The University of Chicago Press, Chicago
Stubbs W (1913) Charters and excerpts illustrative of the reign of Edward I. In: Davis H (ed) Select charters and other illustrations of English constitutional history. Clarendon, Oxford, pp 417–506
Sun A (2013) Confucianism as a world religion. Princeton University Press, Princeton
Tan CC (1971) Chinese political thought in the twentieth century. Doubleday & Company, New York
Tan S (2012) Democracy in Confucianism. Philos Compass 7(5):292–303
Teng S-Y, Fairbank JK (1979) China's response to the west: a documentary survey 1839–1923. Harvard University Press, Cambridge
Thøgersen S (2009) Revisiting a dramatic triangle. J Curr Chin Aff 38(4):9–33
Thompson LG (1958) Biographical Sketsch of K'ang Yu-wei. In: Kang YW (ed) Ta Tung Shu. George Allen & Unwin, London, pp 11–25
Tierney B (1966) Medieval canon law and Western constitutionalism. Catholic Hist Rev 52:1–17
Tierney B (1982) Religion, law and the growth of constitutional thought 1150–1650. Cambridge University Press, Cambridge
Tierney B (1983) Tuck on rights: some medieval problems. Hist Polit Thought 4(429):431–444
Tierney B (1995) Freedom and the medieval church. In: Davis RW (ed) The origins of modern freedom in the west. Stanford University Press, Stanford, pp 64–100
Tierney B (1998) Foundations of the conciliar theory. Brill, Leiden
Tierney B, Painter S (1983) Western Europe in the middle ages 300–1475, 4th edn. Alfred A. Knopf, New York

Treadgold DW (1973) The west in Russia and China, vol 2. Cambridge University Press, Cambridge

Tsai JF (1981) The predicament of the comprador ideologists: He Qi (Ho Kai, 1859-1914) and Hu Liyuan (1847-1916). Modern China 7(2):191–225

Tuck R (1979) Natural rights theories: their origin and development. Cambridge University Press, New York

Tuck R (2001) History of political thought. In: Burke P (ed) New perspectives on historical writings. The Pennsylvania State University Press, Pennsylvania, pp 218–232

Tuck R (2007) History. In: Goodin RE et al (eds) Companion to contemporary political philosophy. Blackwell, Malden

Ullmann W (1972) A short history of the papacy in the middle ages. Methuen, London

Viechtbauer H, Wegmann K (1969) Sun Yat-sen. In: Opitz PJ (ed) Vom Konfuzianismus zum Kommunismus. List Verlag, Munich, pp 107–148

Villey M (1946) L'idée de droit subjectif et les systèmes juridiques romains. Revue historique de droit français et étranger 24:201

Villey M (1964) La genese du droit subjectif chez Guillaume d'Occam. Archives de Philosophic du Droit 9:97

Vogel C (2011) Zur Rolle der Beherrschten in der mittelalterlichen Herrschaftslegitimation. Düsseldorf University Press, Düsseldorf

Wang RZ (1983) The reform thinking in late Qing dynasty. Linking Publishing, Taipei. (汪荣祖, 晚清变法思想论丛, 联经出版事业公司, 台北, 1983年)

Wang CN (2003) Reading the inscription from Sun Zhongshan. People's Tribune 1:57–59. (王春南, 读孙中山题词——"天下为公"), 人民论坛, 2003年第1期, 第57-59页)

Wang E (2007) An investigation on the creation of the book of rites. Zhonghua Book Company, Beijing. (王锷, 礼记成书考, 中华书局, 北京, 2007年)

Wang N (2009) Ancient Chinese. Beijing University Press, Beijing. (王宁 主编, 古代汉语, 北京大学出版社, 北京, 2009年)

Wang M (2012) All under heaven (tianxia). J Ethnographic Theory 2(1):337–383

Watner C (2005) Quod Omnes Tangit: consent theory in the radical libertarian tradition in the middle ages. J Libertarian Stud 19:67–85

Weber M (1989) The religion of China: Confucianism and Taoism. Yuan-Liou Publishing, Taipei. (马克斯·韦伯, 中国的宗教:儒教与道教, 远流出版社, 台北, 1989年)

Wei JT, Chen XC (1995) Exploring the civil rights thinking of Sun Zhongshan. Guangxi Normal University Press, Guilin. (韦杰廷, 陈先初, 孙中山民权主义探微, 广西师范大学出版, 桂林, 1995年)

Wells A (2001) The political thought of Sun Yat-sen-development and impact. Palgrave, New York

Whitehead AN (1933) The adventure of ideas. Simon & Schuster, New York

Wilhelm R (1931) Preface. In: Tai TT (ed) Die geistigen Grundlagen des Sun Yat Senismus. Würfel Verlag, Gießen, p 8

Wippel JF (1981) The metaphysical thought of Godfrey of Fontaines: a study in late thirteenth-century philosophy. CUA Press, Washington, DC

Wu K-C (1928) Ancient Chinese political theories. The Commercial Press, Beijing

Wu G (2018) Striving for democracy: Confucian political philosophy in the Ming and Qing dynasties. In: Ames RT, Hershock PD (eds) Confucianisms for a changing world cultural order. University of Hawaii Press, Honolulu, pp 252–262

Wyduckel D (1984) Ius Publicum: Grundlagen und Entwicklung des öffentlichen Rechts und der deutschen Staasrechtwissenschaft. Duncker & Humblot, Berlin

Xiao GQ (1998) The history of Chinese political thought. Liaoning Education Press, Shenyang. (萧公权, 中国政治思想史, 辽宁教育出版社, 沈阳, 1998年)

Xiao WY (2017) The westerners' translation toward Chinese sixty cycle. J Graduates Sun Yat-Sen Univ 38:25–36. (肖文远, 西方人对干支纪年的转译, 中山大学研究生学刊, 2017年第38期, 第25-36页)

Xu XS (1962) The age of legends in ancient Chinese history. Science Press, Beijing. (徐旭生, 中国古史的传说时代, 科学出版社, 北京, 1962年)

Xu SM (2006) Critical biography of Gu Yanwu. Nanjing University Press, Nanjing. (许苏民, 顾炎武评传, 南京大学出版社, 南京, 2006年)

Xu DB (2011) Critical biography of Huang Zongxi. Nanjing University Press, Nanjing. (徐定宝, 黄宗羲评传, 南京大学出版社, 南京, 2011年)

Yang ZG (2000) A research on Chinese rituals. East China Normal University Press, Shanghai. (杨志刚, 中国礼仪制度研究, 华东师范大学出版社, 上海, 2000年)

Yang XY (2005) Research on Zhu Ciqi's scholarstic concepts. Master thesis. East China Normal University, Suzhou. (杨翔宇, 朱次琦学术思想研究, 华东师范大学硕士论文, 2005年)

Yao X (2000) An introduction to Confucianism. Cambridge University Press, Cambridge

Yao D (2010) The wisdom of Reading history. Fudan University Press, Shanghai. (姚大力, 读史的智慧, 复旦大学出版社, 上海, 2010年)

Yao X (2014) An eco-ethical interpretation of Confucian Tianren Heyi. Front Philos China 9(4): 570–585

Zarrow P (2009) Chinese conceptions of the state during the late Qing dynasty (1860–1911). In: Shogimen T, Nederman CJ (eds) Western political thought in dialogue with Asia. Lexington Books, Lanham

Zarrow P (2012) After empire: the conceptual transformation of the Chinese state, 1885–1924. Stanford University Press, Stanford

Zhang LH (2011) Critical biography of He qi and Hu Liyuan. Nanjing University Press, Nanjing. (张礼恒, 何启 胡礼垣评传, 南京大学出版社, 南京, 2011年)

Zhao T (2009) A political world philosophy in terms of all-under-heaven (Tian-xia). Diogenes 221: 5–18

Zhao T (2011) The Tianxai system. China Renmin University Press, Beijing. (赵汀阳, 天下体系, 中国人民大学出版社, 北京, 2011年)

Zhou CZ (2009) Research on the ancient shaman doctor and the 'six poems'. Shanghai Classic Publishing House, Shanghai. (周策纵, 古巫医与"六诗"考, 上海古籍出版社, 上海, 2009年)

Zhou PP (2015) I Jing. Joint Publishing House of Beijing, Beijing. (周鹏鹏 编译, 易经, 北京联合出版公司, 北京, 2015年)

Zhou L, Liu G (2008) Tianxia Wei gong: the life pursuit of Sun Yat-Sen in his theory and practice. Journal of. Lit Hist 6:39–42. (周莉莉, 刘桂兰, 天下为公:孙中山毕生追求的理想和实践, 文史杂志, 2008年第6期, 第39-42页)

Zhu W (2011) The religion thinking of early modern neo-Confucianism. Shanghai Classic Publishing House, Shanghai. (祝薇, 论早期现代新儒家的宗教观, 上海古籍出版社, 上海, 2011年)

Zweigert K, Kötz H (1998) An introduction to comparative law. Oxford University Press, Oxford